a-z of subst

MW00464237

professional keywords

Every field of practice has its own methods, terminology, conceptual debates and landmark publications. The *Professional Keywords* series expertly structures this material into easy-reference A to Z format. Focusing on the ideas and themes that shape the field, and informed by the latest research, these books are designed both to guide the student reader and to refresh practitioners' thinking and understanding.

Available now

Mark Doel and Timothy B. Kelly: *A–Z of Groups & Groupwork*
Jon Glasby and Helen Dickinson: *A–Z of Inter-agency Working*
Richard Hugman: *A–Z of Professional Ethics*
Glenn Laverack: *A–Z of Health Promotion*
Neil McKeganey: *A–Z of Addiction and Substance Misuse*
Steve Nolan and Margaret Holloway: *A–Z of Spirituality*
Marian Roberts: *A–Z of Mediation*

Available soon

Jane Dalrymple: *A–Z of Advocacy*
David Shemmings, Yvonne Shemmings and David Wilkins:
    A–Z of Attachment Theory
Jeffrey Longhofer: *A–Z of Psychodynamic Practice*
David Garnett: *A–Z of Housing*
Fiona Timmins: *A–Z of Reflective Practice*

a-z of
substance misuse & drug addiction

Neil McKeganey

palgrave
macmillan

First published 2014 by
PALGRAVE MACMILLAN

Palgrave Macmillan in the UK is an imprint of Macmillan Publishers Limited, registered in England, company number 785998, of Houndmills, Basingstoke, Hampshire RG21 6XS.

Palgrave Macmillan in the US is a division of St Martin's Press LLC, 175 Fifth Avenue, New York, NY 10010.

Palgrave Macmillan is the global academic imprint of the above companies and has companies and representatives throughout the world.

Palgrave® and Macmillan® are registered trademarks in the United States, the United Kingdom, Europe and other countries

ISBN 978-0-230-31420-7   ISBN 978-1-137-31923-4 (eBook)
DOI 10.1007/978-1-137-31923-4

A catalogue record for this book is available from the British Library.

A catalog record for this book is available from the Library of Congress.

To Marina – When it rained
you made the sun shine

contents

acknowledgements

I am grateful to Catherine Gray at Palgrave Macmillan for raising the possibility of writing an A to Z of substance misuse. I agreed with unbridled enthusiasm though without realizing the journey that I would then embark upon in covering the various topics that needed to be reviewed. Writing any book involves stealing time from other commitments and other people. I am grateful to my current and former colleagues within the Centre for Drug Misuse Research: Marina Barnard, Carole Bain, Chris Russell, Joe McGallagly, Uday Mukherji, Jim McIntosh, and Mick Bloor. I would like to thank Sarah Cunningham-Burley of Edinburgh University for arranging my access to the University Library without which it would not have been possible to compile this A to Z. Finally, I would like to thank my children: Rebecca, Gabriel and Daniella and my grandchildren: Elise and Leo.

how to use this book

In writing this A to Z, I have tried to cover the breadth of territory that the use and abuse of various substances encompasses, with a view to introducing the student or general reader to a range of new concepts and debates. There is something of a silo approach to so much of the work going on in the field of addictions research. The person whose engagement in the drugs field has to do with drug treatment may barely think about the dynamics of drug markets or drugs enforcement. Similarly, the person whose interest lies principally in the field of criminology may pay scant attention to the challenges of addictions treatment. I hope that this book will break down some of these divides and thereby offer a helpful starting-point and guide.

In terms of my selection criteria, I have largely avoided including entries for the multiplicity of drugs that are now available. The production of new substances is occurring at such a pace that any listing would be out of date by the time this book found its way through production. There are also a number of highly regarded public sources of drugs information, some of them online, such as Talk to Frank (http://www.talktofrank.com/). This said, I have included entries for some substances that remain long-standing problems and which I feel warrant discussion as 'professional keywords'.

My aim with this book is to bring a sensitivity to the discussion that is borne of many years working in the field of addictions. The entries that I have included cover a range of terminology and include a variety of drug-related issues, and strategies for dealing with them, whether at a policy or individual treatment level. The entries vary in length - some being limited to a few paragraphs and others more akin to a short essay. In each, I have tried to convey something of the liveliness of the debates that run through our field and the research evidence that supports different knowledge claims. I have included a small number of references to recent work at the end of each entry, which can be followed up by those with an interest in a specific line of argument. I have also sought to show the inter-connectness of many of the terms and concepts in the field by highlighting my chosen 'keywords' in italics in the text, as well as signposting related topics at the start of each entry.

Unavoidably this compilation has a personal element to it, both in the entries I have selected and the materials I have reviewed. However, I have sought to go beyond my own personal views and prejudices in trying to give a flavour of the issues that characterise our field. In compiling this book I was asked to work to a limit or around 70,000 words and at the time I thought that was more than generous. I realise now that I could easily have doubled or trebled that word limit and still there would have been omissions or debates dealt with only superficially. Such is the richness and breadth of this diverse and contested field, which I hope this book will help you to appreciate and explore.

a

addiction

SEE ALSO chronic relapsing condition; gateway thesis; harm reduction; maturing out; prevalence; set and setting; spontaneous remission; stages of change

In the minds of many people, 'addiction' is a term that hardly needs a definition, so obvious is its meaning: too much of anything – too much sex, too much *alcohol*, too many drugs, too much gambling, too much food. Beyond the simple notion that addiction is about too much, there is an array of complex questions that underpin what it means to be addicted. Is addiction a matter of a lifestyle choice? Is it a form of language or a cultural meme that enables individuals to indulge in behaviours that give them some level of pleasure? Is it a clinical condition with a genetic component? Is it a brain disease or an environmentally determined condition? Is it something from which one can be cured or something that you simply have to live with for the rest of your life? These are just some of the questions that surround the notion of addiction.

John Davies has written one of the most challenging texts on the nature of addiction in his book *The Myth of Addiction* (1992). For Davies, the idea that individuals are somehow taken over by the power of the drugs they are consuming is a myth. Instead Davies suggests that individuals learn the language of addiction and use that language to justify behaviour that they have chosen to embark upon and continue to be involved in. Addiction is less a fact of life so much as a language that serves the purpose of portraying individuals as being controlled by external, powerful forces determining their actions and releasing them from the need to take responsibility for the decisions they have taken to engage in personally and socially harmful behaviours.

The notion of addiction as a useful fiction has also been suggested by Theodore Dalrymple who in the course of his work as a *prison* doctor came to question whether the drug users he was seeing were actually dependent on the drugs they were using, or were merely using the language of dependence to persuade him to prescribe the drugs they wanted. Their professed addiction to the substances they desired was little more than a theatrical technique for requesting the drugs they sought (Dalrymple, 2006).

In contrast to the notion of addiction as a language game or a theatrical device, Nora Volkow, Director of the United States National Institute on Drug Abuse, has characterized addiction as a brain disease (Volkow and Li, 2005; Volkow *et al.*, 2003). Using the technology of brain imaging Volkow and her colleagues have shown how distinct areas of the brain are involved in the process of drug use and dependency. They have also shown that the brains of addicted individuals show signs of repair once the individual ceases or reduces his or her drug use. The ingestion of drugs such as opiates and benzodiazepines has been shown to influence the release of dopamine within the brain, stimulating the brain's reward system and encouraging the repeated ingestion of the drugs themselves. Addiction within these terms comes to be seen as a perversion of the brain's own reward system-stimulating behaviour that may be injurious to the individual but which at the same time is pleasurable.

The potential value of understanding the neurological pathways of addiction are incalculable, holding out the prospect of developing entirely new forms of treatments that are targeted at specific areas of the brain. At present many of the current addiction treatments involve lengthy counselling sessions in which the addicts are encouraged to talk about their life and in turn to develop an insight into the possible causes of their addiction. If drug addiction turns out to be a malfunction in the addict's brain, then in time, counselling may come to be seen as a stone-age *treatment* in a world that has been overtaken with the availability of neurological smart drugs.

Whilst neuroscience is exerting a powerful influence over our view of addiction, the very notion that individuals become addicted to particular substances has been subjected to far-reaching criticism by Professor Bruce Alexander. Alexander's most widely known study involved exploring the behaviour of rats self-administering opiate-laced solutions under laboratory conditions. The observation that laboratory-based rats can become so addicted to opiates that they will ignore their need for food and water in preference to consuming opiates is one of the foundation stones underpinning the knowledge of what it means to be addicted. In his classic 'rat park' study, Alexander noticed that the rats involved in these experiments were typically housed in environments that bore no similarity to their normal living conditions. As an alternative Alexander built his 'rat park' in which the laboratory rats were housed in an environment that more closely approximated their normal living conditions. While the rats in the conventional cages acted in the same way as other laboratory rats in continuing to self-administer an opiate based solution in preference to accessing food and water, the 'rat park' rats showed no signs of being addicted to the opiate-laced solutions that they could self-administer. Crucially when Alexander re-housed the conventionally accommodated and now addicted laboratory rats within his 'rat park' cage their dependency diminished. The clear finding from this *research* was that the process of becoming addicted was mediated by the environment in which the rats were living. Addiction, it seemed, was less a matter of the drugs ingested than the living circumstances the rats were exposed to.

Startling as Alexander's findings were the research team struggled to get the top journals to publish the papers based on his work – the scientific establishment it seemed was not quite ready for research that questioned the very fundamentals of addiction science. Alexander and colleagues published a full account of their research in the much less well-known journal *Pharmacology Biochemistry and Behaviour* (Alexander *et al.*, 1981).

In his latest book *The Globalisation of Addiction* (2008), Alexander has explored the notion of addiction as a malady of modern-day living characterized by a dislocation of the spirit that has followed the unparalleled emphasis that developed societies are now giving to the importance of consumption.

KEY TEXTS

- Alexander, B. (2008) *The Globalisation of Addiction: A Study in the Poverty of the Spirit* (Oxford: Oxford University Press)
- Alexander, B. *et al.* (1981) 'Effect of Early and Later Colony Housing on Oral Ingestion of Morphine in Rats', *Pharmacology, Biochemistry and Behaviour*, 15: pp. 571–576

- Dalrymple, T. (2006) *Romancing the Opiates: Pharmacological Lies and the Addiction Bureaucracy* (New York: Encounter Books)
- Davies, J.B. (1992) *The Myth of Addiction* (Switzerland: Harwood Academic Publishers)
- Leshner, A. (1997) 'Addiction Is a Brain Disease, and It Matters', *Science*, 278 (5335): pp. 45–47
- Volkow, N. and Li, T. (2005) 'The Neuroscience of Addiction', *Nature Neuroscience*, 8: pp. 1429–1430

alcohol

SEE ALSO **brief interventions; chronic relapsing conditions; motivational interviewing; project match; relapse; twelve-step programmes; UKATT**

Alcohol has been described as the world's favourite drug (22003) and the drug associated with the greatest level of harm (Nutt *et al.*, 2010). Alcohol, in varying amounts, is toxic to every system within the human body. Within the United Kingdom alcohol is thought to be associated with between 18,000 and 30,000 deaths per year (Sheron *et al.*, 2011), within the United States around 79,000 deaths a year and within Russia around 48,000 deaths a year (Pridemore and Kim, 2006).

The most recent statistics on alcohol consumption in the United Kingdom show that 17% of men and 10% of women drank alcohol on five or more days in a week, whilst 9% of men and 5% of women drank alcohol on every day of the week. Twenty-six per cent of men reported drinking more than 21 units of alcohol in a typical week compared to 17% of women who reported drinking more than 14 units. Between 2010 and 2011 there were 813,600 hospital admissions in England where the primary diagnosis was a disease attributed to the consumption of alcohol (National Statistics, 2012).

The *treatment* for alcoholism ranges from short-term detoxification, *residential rehabilitation, brief interventions*, prescription medication including the drug 'disulfiram' that causes an adverse reaction where the individual resumes drinking. By far the largest evaluation of alcohol treatment within the United Kingdom was the *UKATT* trial, which randomly allocated a large sample of problem drinkers to receive either social behaviour network therapy or motivational enhancement therapy. Social behaviour network therapy was developed by the *research* team and comprised an approach aimed at encouraging the development of a supportive social and *family* network around the problem drinker. The results of the UKATT evaluation were that both treatments were equally effective and equally cost effective in reducing an individual's alcohol consumption (Godfrey *et al.*, 2005; Orford *et al.*, 2005).

Along with the UKATT evaluation showing the value of treatment provided for alcohol problems, a wide range of studies have also shown that brief interventions can have a positive impact on reducing individuals' alcohol consumption. On the basis of an extensive review of the *evidence* Professor Nick Heather, one of the world's leading researchers on brief interventions, concluded that:

> The weight of accumulated evidence supports the offer of briefer forms of moderation-orientated treatments with clients who have comparatively less severe alcohol problems and levels of dependence. Brief treatment of this kind may be especially suited to problem drinkers who refer themselves for help rather than those who have been coerced or persuaded by others to attend a treatment service. (Heather, 2004, p. 126)

One of the most controversial areas to do with alcohol policy in recent years has been the debate as to whether the imposition of a minimum price of alcohol would be the single most effective means for reducing the overall level of alcohol consumption in society. This approach has been called for by a wide variety of experts and commentators but has been resisted by the alcohol trade and various government on the basis that the imposition of such a 'tax' would effectively penalize all consumers of alcohol – both those who drink responsibly and those who drink excessively causing themselves and others extensive harm. In the absence of imposition of a minimum alcohol price however the price of alcohol relative to income has steadily reduced over the years with some retail outlets in the United Kingdom and elsewhere now selling alcohol for less than the price of bottled water. Whatever the actual effect of the imposition of a minimum unit price for alcohol it is hard not to accept that the low overall price of the drug has been a key factor in promoting the widespread consumption of it by young people and other population groups within the United Kingdom and elsewhere.

KEY TEXTS

- Babor, T. *et al.* (2010) *Alcohol: No Ordinary Commodity* (Oxford: Oxford University Press)
- Edwards, G. (1997) 'Alcohol Policy and the Public Good', *Addiction*, 92 (3s1) March: pp. 73–80
- Edwards, G. (2002) *Alcohol: The Worlds Favorite Drug* (New York: St Martins Press)
- Rehn, N., Room, R. and Edwards, G. (2001) *Alcohol in the European Region – Consumption Harm and Policies* (World Health Organization Regional Office for Europe)

b

brief interventions

SEE ALSO addiction; chronic relapsing condition; motivational interviewing; UKATT

If there is an element of magic within the substance abuse field it must surely have to do with the success of brief interventions in treating individuals with long-standing drug and *alcohol* dependence. Most people, if asked how difficult it is to stop or reduce an addictive behaviour, would say that it is extremely difficult. Indeed the very notion of *addiction* and dependency rests on some notion of individuals being compelled to continue with a behaviour that is causing them serious harm, and which they would cease to engage in, if they could. Simply stopping the behaviour on little more than a whim seems hardly possible and seems to fly in the face of the very notion of being addicted in the first place. However, in the case of brief interventions what appears to happen is that individuals are able to make significant changes in the nature and extent of their drug or alcohol consumption on the basis of the most fleeting of contact with a health professional. The contact in question may be no more than a few minutes discussion either face to face or over the telephone, via a letter sent to an individual from a health professional or a passing contact with a health professional that provides an opportunity of raising the question in the individual's mind as to whether they should change their behaviour and, reduce their drug and/or alcohol use. Professor Nick Heather, one of the world's leading researchers into the effectiveness of brief interventions, has stated that:

> Brief interventions are not merely a passing fancy in the alcohol problems field but a crucial and permanent addition to the range of strategies used to combat alcohol related harm. (Heather, 2004, p. 117)

Within the United Kingdom, the National Institute for Health and Clinical Excellence has provided guidance on the use of brief interventions in relation to alcohol (NICE, 2010), *tobacco* (NICE, 2006), and other drugs (NCCMH, 2007). The guidance recommends that brief interventions should consist of talking with the drug user in two sessions of between 10 and 45 minutes duration about their drug use, the possibility of *treatment* and encouraging the individual to focus on the prospect of changing their behaviour. Brief interventions are simple, quick and able to be delivered by a wide range of staff on the basis of relatively modest training. It is recognized that brief interventions differ markedly between those that can be described as involving the provision of simple brief advice and those that amount to a form of extended brief intervention or brief treatment (Heather, 2004).

The *evidence* on the impact of brief interventions within the alcohol field is substantial although important areas of uncertainty remain. For example, *research* is inconclusive as to what level of alcohol or drug problems are most effectively dealt with by brief interventions. Similarly, the evidence in relation to the most effective settings to provide brief interventions is very much evolving. In their review of brief intervention studies used in relation to heavy alcohol users treated in general hospital wards McQueen and colleagues noted that:

> The main results of this review indicate that the benefits of delivering brief interventions to heavy alcohol users in general hospitals are inconclusive. (McQueen *et al.*, 2009, p. 16)

Similarly on the basis of an extensive review of the evidence Heather concluded that:

> The weight of accumulated evidence supports the offer of briefer forms of moderation-orientated treatments with clients who have comparatively less severe alcohol problems and levels of dependence. Brief treatment of this kind may be especially suited to problem drinkers who refer themselves for help rather than those who have been coerced or persuaded by others to attend a treatment service. (Heather, 2004, p. 126)

McCambridge and Jenkins (2008) undertook a systematic review and meta-analysis of 41 studies reporting the results of brief interventions designed to reduce alcohol consumption. In this case the researchers were interested in whether brief interventions targeted at one drug (alcohol) might have a positive effect in reducing levels of consumption of another drug (tobacco). The reviewed studies did not show any significant difference in the level of smoking reduction between the brief intervention-treated group and the controls, leading the researcher to conclude that the brief interventions targeted at one behaviour did not have secondary effects on other behaviours.

KEY TEXTS

- Aveyard, P. *et al.* (2012) 'Brief Opportunistic Smoking Cessation Interventions: A Systematic Review and Meta-Analysis to Compare Advice to Quit and Offer of Assistance', *Addiction*, 107 (6): pp. 1066–1073
- Heather, N. and Stockwell, T. (2004) *The Essential Handbook of Treatment and Prevention of Alcohol Problems* (England: John Wiley and Sons)
- Kaner, E. *et al.* (2009) 'The Effectiveness of Brief Alcohol Interventions in Primary Care Settings: A Systematic Review', *Drug and Alcohol Review*, 28 (3): pp. 301–323

c

cannabis

SEE ALSO classification of drugs; decriminalization; dual diagnosis; gateway thesis; harm reduction

Cannabis is by a substantial margin the world's favourite illegal drug. The United Nations Office on Drugs and *Crime* has estimated that in 2009 the drug had been used at least once in the previous year by between 125 and 203 million people – which represents between 2.8% and 4.5% of the world's population. Within the United States it is estimated that around 10.7% of the adult population have used cannabis in the last year and that around 2.4 million people started using illegal drugs with cannabis. Within Europe the annual *prevalence* of cannabis use is thought to be around 5.2%–5.3% of the adult population.

The health risks associated with cannabis consumption are multiple and disputed. It has been suggested that there is a link between cannabis and a range of physical illnesses including the development of respiratory cancers and weakened immune system. Most attention, however, has focused upon the link between cannabis consumption and mental health problems. In a systematic review of the mental health harms of cannabis, Moore and colleagues concluded that:

> We found a consistent increase in incidence of psychotic outcomes in people who had used cannabis … The pooled analysis revealed an increase in risk of psychosis of about 40% in participants who had ever used cannabis … A dose response effect was observed in all studies that examined the relation to increasing cannabis exposure. (Moore *et al.*, 2007, p. 325)

The authors of this report urged governments to develop a public *education* campaign informing people of the dangers of cannabis consumption. In 2009 Di Forti and colleagues reported that amongst those who had developed a psychotic illness there was an increased likelihood that the individual had used cannabis with a higher potency, for longer, and with greater frequency. In 2008 the UK Advisory Council on the Misuse of Drugs reviewed the *evidence* on cannabis mental health harms and concluded that:

> The ... evidence supports a causal association between the use of cannabis, in adolescence, and the later development of schizophrenia. (ACMD, 2008, p. 18)

Despite the growing awareness of the health harms associated with cannabis, judgements of just how harmful cannabis is has been a matter of deep and contested debate. In 2009 the United Kingdom's leading drug advisor, Professor David Nutt, was sacked by the then Home Secretary for repeatedly asserting that cannabis was less harmful than a range of other drugs including *alcohol* and *tobacco*, and for suggesting that consuming ecstasy was less harmful than engaging in the leisure pursuit of riding horses (Nutt, 2009).

KEY TEXTS
- Advisory Council on the Misuse of Drugs (2002) *The Classification of Cannabis under the Misuse of Drugs Act 1971* (London: Home Office)
- Advisory Council on the Misuse of Drugs (2007) *Further Consideration of the Classification of Cannabis under the Misuse of Drugs Act 1971* (London: Home Office)
- Arseneault, L. *et al.* (2002) 'Cannabis Use in Adolescence and Risk for Adult Psychosis: Longitudinal Prospective Study', *British Medical Journal*, 325: p. 1212
- Casadio, P. *et al.* (2011) 'Cannabis Use in Young People: The Risk for Schizophrenia', *Neuroscience and Biobehavioral Reviews*, 35 (8): pp. 1779–1787
- Hall, W. and Solowij, N. (1998) 'Adverse Effects of Cannabis', *Lancet*, 352 (9140) 14 November: pp. 1611–1616

celebrity drug use

SEE ALSO **addiction; cocaine; identity; overdose; stigma**

The notion that drug and *alcohol* use on the part of celebrities can result in increased number of young people also using illegal drugs and drinking to excess is a view that has gained considerable currency in recent years as the cult of celebrity has expanded. In its 2007 annual report the International Narcotics Control Board sounded a note of concern as to the impact of celebrity drug use on young people:

> Celebrity drug offenders can profoundly influence public attitudes, values and behaviour towards drug abuse, particularly among young people who have not yet taken a firm and fully informed position on drug issues. (INCB, 2007, p. 49)

The claim that celebrity substance use can exert a powerful influence on young people is plausible. It may be that young people are inclined to mimic the actions of well-known public figures whose drug and alcohol use has come to public attention. Similarly, it may be that celebrity substance use could play an important role in creating a climate of acceptability around the use of illegal drugs and excessive alcohol. There may be a perception that drug and alcohol use on the part of celebrities is a marker of their creative talents such that other people may seek to lay claim to their own creative talents by engaging in similar forms of excessive drug and alcohol use.

Media coverage of celebrities using illegal drugs, or drinking to excess, may also exert a powerful influence in creating the view that it is possible to both enjoy great wealth and success at the same time as having a drug or alcohol problem. The view that one can be successful, and a drug user, can convey the impression that one's excessive drug or alcohol use does not result necessarily in adverse consequences. On the other side of the coin one would also have to acknowledge the long list of celebrities whose drug or alcohol use has had a dramatically negative impact on their lives: Jimmy Hendrix, Jim Morrison, Michael Jackson, Amy Winehouse, Diego Maradona to name but a few. The experience of these celebrities could hardly be said to provide a powerful advert in favour of the benefits of the drug and alcohol dependent lifestyle.

Assertions that celebrity drug use may have a profound impact on young people's drug and alcohol choices is not the same thing as proving that such influence does occur in reality. Equally, it should not be assumed that the nature of any influence that celebrities may exert would only be in a single direction, that is promoting drug use. It is entirely possible that witness to the adverse effects of drug and alcohol use on the lives of celebrities, young people may be less likely to use drink and drugs to excess.

Shaw and colleagues (2010) looked at young people's reactions to stories in the media regarding the drink and drug use of the singer Amy Winehouse. Interestingly, the reactions of the young people were by no means predictable and centred around a number of distinct themes. One theme concerned the notion of Amy Winehouse as a troubled genius with her drug use being seen as an indication of her abilities and the tortuous process of their expression. However, some of the young people were of the view that the details of the singer's drug and alcohol use were part of an image created by the singer herself to present a particular marketable image. The second theme which emerged from the focus groups concerned a sense of people having lost patience with the singer as the stories of her drink and drug excess surfaced repeatedly in the media. The third theme concerned an ambivalence between whether the media were simply reporting the behaviour of drink and drug fuelled excess or whether they were effectively glamorizing the behaviours in their reporting. Some of the young people commenting negatively on the way in which the status of being a celebrity had somehow resulted in the individual's drug use being socially accepted in a way in which other people's drug use would not be accepted.

On the basis of this *research* it is by no means clear that young people are influenced in a single direction by stories in the media of celebrity drink and drug excess. Other commentators have been more critical in their assessment of the evidential basis for the claim that celebrities are influencing young people's drug and alcohol use. Harry Shapiro, from the drug information charity Drugscope, speaking at the UK Home Affairs Select Committee commented specifically on the claim that young people were being influenced by reports of celebrity's cocaine use:

That is a massive red herring, to be perfectly honest. I think it is completely ludicrous to start blaming celebrities whose alleged use of dodgy, fuzzy photos of doing whatever are only made public because the tabloid press are prepared to put them on the front page and pay huge amounts of money for doing so. (Shapiro, 2011, p. 83)

Despite Shapiro's confident assertion to the contrary the mere fact that the advertising industry makes such widespread and expensive use of celebrities in marketing various products (e.g. using the actor George Clooney to market a particular brand of coffee) suggests a perception on the part of the advertising industry and their clients that well-known names and faces do exert an influence on young people's choices.

KEY TEXTS

- Bellis, M. *et al.* (2012) 'Dying to Be Famous: Retrospective Cohort Study of Rock and Pop Star Mortality and Its Association with Adverse Childhood Experiences', *British Medical Journal*, open access, doi: 10.1136/bmjopen-2012–002089
- Oksanen, A. (2012) 'To Hell and Back: Excessive Drug Use Addiction and the Process of Recovery in Mainsram Rock Autobiographies', *Substance Use and Misuse*, 47 (2): pp 143–154
- Shaw, R., Whitehead, C. and Giles, D. (2010) 'Crack Down on the Celebrity Junkies': Does Media Coverage of Celebrity Drug Use Pose a Risk to Young People?' *Health, Risk and Society*, 12 (6): pp. 575–589

chronic relapsing condition

SEE ALSO **addiction; brief interventions; motivational interviewing; recovery; relapse; spontaneous remission; stages of change**

The view that drug dependency is a chronic relapsing condition has been enormously influential within recent debates in the addictions. Associated with some of the most influential thinkers within the *addiction* field (Professors Tom McLellan, Charles O'Brien, Herbert Kleber) the notion here is that drug dependency shares many of the same characteristics as other chronic relapsing conditions (hypertension, type 1 diabetes) and should be seen, and treated, as a chronic rather than an acute condition (McLellan *et al.*, 2000).

The argument here is that there is no reliable cure for drug dependency although *research* has shown the benefits of engaging dependent drug users and alcoholics in *treatment*. As with other chronic conditions, research has shown that drug and *alcohol* dependency may have a significant genetic component, that drug and alcohol intake can have a persisting effect on the brain, that individual's often drop out of treatment prematurely or fail to comply with treatment regimens, and that where treatment is provided without time limit there are distinct advantages to the individual. According to McLellan and colleagues, treating drug dependency as an acute condition would be akin to limiting a patient's access to hypertension medication for a limited period. Whilst nobody would suggest limiting a diabetic's access to insulin after a given period of time there is often an expectation in the case of drug dependency that an individual's addiction will abate with the right treatment and sufficient will-power exerted by the individual to cease his or her drug use.

The perception of drug or alcohol dependency as a chronic relapsing condition is based almost entirely upon drawing a parallel between drug and alcohol dependency and various other chronic conditions. The parallel being drawn here is by no means totally persuasive. In the case of diabetes, for example, we do not have treatments that could enable the individual to live a full life without recourse to their insulin medication. If such treatments were available there would be few individuals who would choose to continue to use their daily insulin injection. In the case of drug and alcohol dependency there is *evidence* of individuals being able to cease their drug and alcohol intake for the remainder of their life either with or without the assistance of drug treatment services. *Recovery* is regarded as an achievable goal in the case of drug and alcohol dependency and for this reason it is by no means universally accepted that drug and alcohol dependency is a chronic relapsing condition even if it is accepted that it is a condition from which recovery is difficult and something that may take many years to come about.

The implications of viewing drug or alcohol dependency as a chronic relapsing condition are far-reaching. For example, the concept gives rise to the prospect of lifelong treatment. In the case of substitute *prescribing*, the notion that the condition being treated is chronic, and subject to repeated *relapse*, suggests that the individual may remain on substitute medication for the remainder of his or her life with little prospect of ever coming off the medication. The perception of lifelong treatment runs counter to the notion that drug treatment services ought to be working towards enabling addicts to overcome their dependency and become drug or alcohol free. Viewing oneself as suffering from a chronic relapsing condition can be seen to sit somewhat uncomfortably with the notion of recovery and the cessation of treatment.

KEY TEXTS

- Cunningham, J. and McCambridge, J. (2012) 'Is Alcohol Dependence Best Viewed as a Chronic Relapsing Disorder?' *Addiction*, 107 (1): pp. 6–12
- McLellan, T. *et al.* (2000) 'Drug Dependence, a Chronic Medical Illness: Implications for Treatment Insurance and Outcome Evaluation', *Journal of American Medical Association*, 248 (13): pp. 1689–1695
- O'Brien, C. and McLellan, A. (1996) 'Myths about the Treatment of Addiction', *Lancet*, 347: pp. 237–240

classification of drugs

SEE ALSO **cannabis; decriminalization; harm reduction; politics**

The classification of different drugs in terms of their relative harm is a common element in many countries' drug laws and drug strategies. Within the United Kingdom, the Misuse of Drugs Act (1971) allocates various substances into one of three classes reflecting what is seen to be the harmfulness of the substance involved and identifying the level of criminal penalty associated with the drug. Class A within the UK Misuse of Drugs Act includes a wide range of opioid/opiate drugs such as *Methadone*, Morphine, Dipipanone; stimulant drugs such as Cocaine, Methamphetamine; Ecstasy, and various drugs such as LSD, Magic Mushrooms. Class B includes such substances as *Cannabis*, Amphetamines, Codeine. Class C includes a wide range of Benzodiazepine drugs such as Diazepam, Midazolam, Triazolam, a range of sedative drugs such as Ketamine, Gamma Butyrolactone and various stimulant drugs such as Khat. Within the United Kingdom, possession of a Class A drug can lead to an individual being given a *prison* sentence of up to seven years with or without an unlimited fine. Possession offences of Class B drugs can involve a prison sentence of up to five years with a possible unlimited fine. Class C possession offences can attract a maximum two-year prison sentence and an unlimited fine. In cases where possession of an illegal drug is seen to be indicative of the individual's involvement in drug supply the penalties increase substantially to a maximum of a life sentence.

Within the United States, substances are divided into five schedules ranging from schedule one drugs that have the highest likelihood of abuse and the lowest level of medical use (e.g. marijuana, ecstasy, *heroin*), through to the schedule five drugs which have the highest medical use but the lowest likelihood of abuse (e.g. no more than 200 milligrams of codeine). Within the Netherlands, drugs are divided into two classes: those that present an unacceptable health risk (heroin, cocaine) and those that present a very low level of risk (cannabis). In Sweden, drugs are divided into five Lists ranging from List one which includes drugs such as heroin, cannabis and MDMA through to List five, which includes narcotic drugs that are currently outside of the system of international regulation.

Within the United Kingdom the classification of different drugs into one or other class has been a source of near constant dispute in recent years covering such issues as the placement of cannabis, the lack of scientific underpinning to the classification system, and the failure to include *alcohol* and *tobacco* within the classificatory system. In relation to cannabis, successive Home Secretaries have requested the UK Advisory Council on the Misuse of Drugs to review the *evidence* on the harms associated with the drug and advise on the appropriate classification. Spectacularly though the government has rejected the advice of its own advisory council on more than a single occasion in deciding to shift cannabis from Class C back to Class B.

In relation to the lack of scientific underpinning to the classificatory system researchers have pointed out that the system:

> Evolved in an unsystematic way from somewhat arbitrary foundations with seemingly little scientific basis. (Nutt *et al.*, 2007, p. 1047)

There have been discussions as to the wisdom of excluding two of the most harmful drugs (alcohol and tobacco) from the classificatory system. Within the last few years researchers have sought to produce a more empirically based classification system focusing on the level of harm associated with different drugs. Professor David Nutt and colleagues have produced a ranking of different substances based on the assessments of a wide range of addictions experts. The classification system that Nutt and colleagues produced placed alcohol at the very top as the most harmful substance, followed by heroin and crack cocaine, down to magic mushrooms that were classified as the least harmful substance. Oddly, given the level of mortality involved tobacco was placed as the sixth most harmful of the 20 drugs reviewed (Nutt *et al.*, 2010).

KEY TEXTS

- Caulkins, J., Reuter, P. and Coulson, C. (2011) 'Basing Drug Scheduling Decisions on Scientific Ranking of Harmfulness False Promise from False Premises', *Addiction*, 106 (11): pp. 1886–1890
- Nutt, D. (2012) *Drugs without the Hot Air: Minimising the Harms of Legal and Illegal Drugs* (England: UIT Cambridge)
- Nutt, D., King, L. and Phillips, L. (2010) 'Drug Harms in the UK: A Multi-Criteria Decision Analysis', *Lancet*, 376: pp. 1558–1565

community sentences

SEE ALSO decriminalization; prison; stigma

The use of community sentences as an alternative to *prison* originated within the United States in 1996 as a result of concern at overcrowding within US prisons. In the following years community sentencing has been developed in countries across the globe. The notion of serving a criminal justice sentence within the community has frequently generated considerable controversy as to the appropriate balance between punishment and *rehabilitation* in sentencing decisions.

It is widely recognized within many countries that the high rate of reoffending by released prisoners is a clear indication of the failure on the part of prison services to evoke a sustained *recovery* of offenders, and that in many instances a community sentence may be more appropriate. It has also been recognized in the case of certain classes of offenders, including those whose offending is connected to their drug dependence, that prison may not be an effective way of changing individual's behaviour. Equally, there is a widespread perception that in the case of serious crimes, including those involving violence, that community sentencing may not be an appropriate response as a result of the perception of the punishment being a 'soft option'.

Community sentences comprise a range of elements that are by no means devoid of a significant element of punishment and inconvenience to the individuals involved. For example, the sentence can involve the use of extended curfew periods during which individuals may be required to remain in their home or to refrain from visiting certain areas of their local community. Curfews may be supported with the use of satellite-tracking equipment that provides 24-hour monitoring of offenders. Community sentences can also involve the use of fines, confiscation orders relating to properties or possessions that are seen to have been acquired as a result of criminal acts, the use of restorative justice meetings between offenders and their victims, the use of drug and *alcohol testing*, and some level of voluntary work through which offenders are required to contribute to improving the local community (e.g. graffiti removal).

Despite the fact that community sentences can include a significant element of punishment, politicians within many countries have often been critical of what they see as the inadequate punishment element associated with such sentences. Within the United Kingdom, for example, the coalition government is currently undertaking a consultation exercise as to the various ways in which community sentencing can be toughened up. Quoted in the *Guardian*, for example, the minister responsible for criminal justice announced that the government was 'putting punishment back into community sentencing' (Jowitt, 2012). In similar terms a consultation document from the UK government on the future of community sentences has also stressed the importance of strengthening the punishment element of community sentences:

> Ensuring sentences in the community are properly punitive is
> the counterpart of our efforts to ensure that prison sentences are
> properly reformative. (HM Government, 2012, p. 2)

The experience of community sentences, where they have been evaluated, is mixed. One of the most positive recent examples of the use of community sentence is the evaluation of the Project HOPE initiative within Hawaii. The Hawaii Opportunity Probation with *Enforcement* (HOPE) is a community based probation programme for methamphetamine user/offenders that requires drug users to remain drug free during the period they are engaged with the programme or face a custodial sentence where there are indications that their drug use is persisting. HOPE involves the close monitoring of offenders, utilizing regular drug testing and delivering swift, certain and proportionate sanctions (e.g. a few days in prison) where individuals violate the conditions of their parole:

> Under HOPE every positive drug test and every missed probation appointment is met with a sanction. Parsimonious use of punishment enhances the legitimacy of the sanction package and reduces the potential negative impacts of tougher sentences, such as long prison stays. (Harken and Kleiman, 2009, p. 9)

The evaluation of project HOPE by Harken and Kleiman identified a marked reduction in positive drug tests on the part of those participating within the programme compared to a comparison group. Positive drug tests on HOPE participants reduced from 53% to 4% over a 12-month period compared to the 22% to 19% amongst the comparison group. HOPE also had a positive effect in reducing the number of missed appointments, revoked probation orders, and in the number of days spent in prison (Harken and Kleiman, 2009).

In contrast to the positive experience of the HOPE programme, *research* undertaken on community sentences in Canada documented a much less positive set of outcomes. Initially enthusiastically endorsed by sentencers, the use of community punishments in Canada came to be seen in more negative terms. According to Cole and Green (2012) the failure of community sentences within Canada was a result of insufficient attention being given to educating people about the nature of the sentences involved, coupled with a failure to provide adequate resources to support the level of intensive monitoring and supervision that was required to ensure effective implementation of the sentences. As a result of these shortcomings the conservative government within Canada sought to restrict the use of what had come to be seen as a failing option in preference to the use of custodial sentences.

Despite the mixed evaluation and political sensitivity around community sentencing it is hard to see how, given the level of prison overcrowding in many countries, community sentencing will not continue to be used.

KEY TEXTS

- HM Government (2012) *Punishment and Reform: Effective Community Sentences* (London: HMSO)

- Kleiman, M. (2009) *When Brute Force Fails How to Have Less Crime and Less Punishment* (Princeton: Princeton University Press)
- Malloch, M. and McIvor, G. (2011) 'Women and Community Sentences', *Criminology and Criminal Justice*, 11 (4): pp. 325–344
- Roberts, J. and Hough, M. (2011) 'Custody or Community? Exploring the Boundaries of Public Punitiveness in England and Wales', *Criminology and Criminal Justice*, 11 (2): pp. 181–197

contingency management

SEE ALSO **addiction; chronic relapsing condition; community sentences; recovery; relapse**

Contingency management refers to the use of various incentives to encourage behaviour change on the part of those with a drug or *alcohol* problem. The changes in behaviour encouraged may include abstinence from drugs, reduction in drug misuse, attending for *hepatitis C* tests (Petry, 2006). The incentives used can include vouchers with a monetary value (exchangeable for goods such as food), cash rewards (of low monetary value), prizes (including cash and goods) and clinic privileges (such as non-supervised consumption). All the incentives have been shown to be effective in changing behaviour although the UK National Institute for Health and Clinical Excellence recommends that vouchers and clinic privileges are likely to be more easily implemented within National Health Service facilities (NICE, 2007, p. 31).

Prendergast *et al.* undertook a meta-analysis of almost 50 studies evaluating the impact of contingency management in substance abuse *treatment*. On the basis of this analysis the authors reported that:

The findings from this meta-analysis … indicate that CM (contingency management) is able to establish and maintain abstinence for many clients during treatment, thereby permitting clients to engage more productively in treatment services that promote the broader psychosocial aspects of *recovery*. From this perspective, CM may be viewed as an adjunct to standard treatment enhancing its effectiveness. (Prendergast *et al.*, 2006, p. 1556; emphasis added)

Kellogg and Tatarsky have suggested that given the modest outcomes associated with conventional drug and alcohol treatment contingency management should become a core element of treatment:

> Contingency management, particularly the use of positive reinforcement systems, has proven to be one of the most powerful psychosocial mechanisms for behaviour change available. Forty years of *research* have shown that when using reinforcements of significant magnitude clinicians can dramatically improve retention, decrease substance use and increase group attendance. (Kellogg and Tatarsky, 2012; emphasis added)

The practice of rewarding patients/clients in this way became controversial within the United Kingdom when it was acknowledged in a BBC news interview between the head of the National Treatment Agency (Paul Hayes) and the BBC Home Affairs editor (Mark Easton) that some patients in contact with drug treatment services in England were being rewarded with additional dosages of the *heroin* substitute *methadone* (BBC, 2007). Initially disavowing any knowledge that such a practice was widespread, the Head of the National Treatment Agency subsequently conceded that a published report from the NTA itself had drawn attention to the widespread practice. In a following interview the minister with responsibility for drug treatment in England commented in the strongest possible terms that in her view it would be unethical to use medication in this way (BBC, 2007).

Whilst there seems little objection to the general principle of rewarding individuals for positive changes in their behaviour, the practice of using medication as an inducement is hugely controversial – raising the prospect that the individual's drug dependency is being used as a tool in the treatment process. Controversial as the practice undoubtedly is, the furore around contingency management highlights the ethical dilemma of determining how far treatment services should go in seeking to change individuals' behaviour and motivation. If it were found that providing drug users with additional doses of the drug methadone was successful in encouraging individuals to make positive changes in their lives, the question would then follow as to whether the practice should be facilitated or forbidden. In simple terms the dilemma here is one of whether the ends (of fostering positive changes in individual's drug and alcohol use) justifies the means (of using medication as a tool of manipulation).

There is a further worry about using medication as a tool of contingency management, which is whether treatment services are in danger of fostering a culture of dependency on the part of clients. Whilst there may be clear indications that small improvements in behaviour can be encouraged through contingency management there is a worry that the practice may result in the individual becoming increasingly dependent on the very medication (methadone) that is being used to treat his or her heroin dependency. Clearly, the worry here is that drug treatment services might succeed in weaning individuals off heroin only to find that they have cemented the individual's dependency on prescribed medication in the process. Few people would regard such a development as a positive outcome of drug treatment.

KEY TEXTS
- National Institute for Health and Clinical Excellence (2007) 'Drug Misuse Psychosocial Interventions', *NICE Clinical Guidelines* 51
- Petry, N. *et al.* (2012) 'A Randomized Trial Adapting Contingency Management Target Based on Initial Abstinence Status of Cocaine Dependent Patients', *Journal of Consulting and Clinical Psychology*, 80 (2): pp. 276–285
- Prendergast, M. *et al.* (2006) 'Contingency Management for Treatment of Substance Use Disorders: A Meta-Analysis', *Addiction*, 101 (11): pp. 1546–1560
- Stitzer, M. and Petry, N. (2006) 'Contingency Management for the Treatment of Substance Abuse', *Annual Review of Clinical Psychology*, 2: pp. 411–434

contraception

SEE ALSO **parental drug use**

The issue of contraception in relation to drug users is an extremely sensitive topic. The sensitivity largely has to do with what is seen as the negative impact of dependent drug use on parenting capacity. *Research* has shown that the children of dependent drug users experience a wide range of negative consequences as a result of their parent's drug dependency. The 2008 UK Drug Strategy Drugs Protecting Families and Communities notes, for example, that:

> Drug misuse can prevent parents from providing their children with the care and support they need and greatly increases the likelihood that their children will grow up to develop drug problems themselves. (Home Office, 2008)

Research has shown that the children of dependent drug users often have a lower birth weight than that of their non drug-using peers (low birth weight is a measure of a range of developmental difficulties that the child will experience as they grow). Such children are also at an increased risk of experiencing parental neglect, poor diet, early exposure to drug use and drug related paraphernalia, and they are likely to perform less well in school and to have difficult peer relationships. The children of dependent drug users are at increased risk of using illegal drugs themselves at a young age and of forming associations with peers who have a similar range of behavioural problems. On the basis of their qualitative interviews with the children of drug dependent parents Kroll and Taylor noted that:

> The young people's data reflect the long shadow cast by the emotional and physical impact of parental drug misuse and its consequences for felt security, sense of safety and day-to-day life. The majority (of young people) were in no doubt that using drugs and caring for children did not mix and had come to believe that drugs came first and were more important than they were. (Kroll and Taylor, 2008, p. 2)

Research has also shown that where one or both parents have a serious drug problem there is a much greater risk of *family* breakdown. In undertaking its Hidden Harm investigation, the UK Advisory Council on the Misuse of Drugs looked at from the national drug monitoring system on 77,928 drug dependent parents. The Council found that 54% of the parents were no longer looking after their dependent children (ACMD, 2003). In Scotland it has been estimated that only 37% of drug dependent mothers, and 13% of drug dependent fathers, were actually living with their dependent children (ACMD, 2003).

According to the National Center on *Addiction* and Substance Abuse the children of drug dependent parents are at increased risk of experiencing various forms of child abuse:

> Parents with substance abuse problems are approximately three times likelier to report abuse towards their children and four times likelier to report neglect than parents without substance abuse problems. (National Center on Addiction and Substance Abuse, 2005, p. 12)

As a result of these findings there have been discussions about the most appropriate forms of contraception that individuals with a drug dependency problem should be encouraged to use. These discussions are very much premised on the idea that in many instances drug-using females and drug-using males become parents not as a result of an active decision to start a family but as a consequence of the level of chaos that may be a characteristic feature of their lives and their inconsistent use of contraception. There have been discussions as to whether female drug users should be encouraged to use long-acting contraception (depo-provera injection), whether they should be paid to use contraception and indeed even whether such women should be paid to be sterilized. One of the most controversial projects working in this area is the US-based 'Project *Prevention*' that offers to pay drug dependent females to be sterilized. Clearly, any project offering drug-using women a financial reward for agreeing to be sterilized is highly controversial, raising as it does fundamental questions as to whether the human rights of such women are being violated. Equally there are concerns that such projects tend to target the contraceptive choices of female rather than male drug users and that they are rooted in an assumption that individuals with a drug problem will invariably be poor parents.

Within the context of the concern that drug dependent adults (both male and female) may not be making the most appropriate choices with regard to contraception, drug *treatment* services within the United Kingdom have been encouraged to ensure that staff discuss issues to do with family planning with their drug-using clients and encourage the individuals involved to make use of appropriate contraception in order to reduce the likelihood of unwanted pregnancies.

Finally, within the context of concerns over the need to reduce the risk of *HIV* transmission, both female and male drug users (particularly those who are *injecting* drugs and working within the sex industry) have been encouraged to use barrier means of contraception. Whilst research has shown that the use of barrier contraception on the part of those working within the sex industry tends to be relatively high, nevertheless, levels of condom use within long-term stable relationships involving dependent drug users may be relatively low as a result of the understandable need on the part of the individuals involved to distinguish between their personal and their work-related relationships.

KEY TEXTS

- DiClemente, R. and Young, A. (2012) 'Incentiving Drug Using Women's Long Term Contraceptive Use: Some Answers More Questions', *Addiction*, 107 (6): pp. 1042–1043
- Heil, S. and Higgins, S. (2012) 'The Scientific and Ethical Rationale for Using Incentives to Promote Contraceptive Use among Drug Abusing Women', *Addiction*, 107 (6): pp. 1044–1046
- Kellog, S. and Tatarsky, A. (2012) 'Reinvisioning Addictions Treatment', *Alcoholism Treatment Quarterly*, 30 (1): pp. 109–128
- Lucke, J. and Hall, W. (2012) 'Under What Circumstances Is It Ethical to Offer Incentives to Encourage Drug Using Women to Use Long Acting Forms of Contraception?' *Addiction*, 107 (6): pp. 1036–1041
- Morgan, M. (2004) 'The Payment of Drug Addicts to Increase Their Sterilisation Rate Is Morally Unjustified and Not Simply a Fine Balance', *Journal* of *Obstetrics and Gynaecology*, 24: pp. 119–123
- Project Prevention (2011), available at http://www.projectprevention.org

corruption

SEE ALSO **crime; enforcement; police**

The link between drugs and corruption has one single and abiding cause – the enormous sums of money involved in the trade in illegal drugs. As a result of the drugs trade being illegal it is necessary for those involved to resort to corrupt practices and corrupt relationships to protect their business interests. Such corruption operates at every level of the drugs trade from the street level where there may be a need to pay *police* officers and others to enable such transactions to proceed unimpeded, through to the need to pay border-protection officials to enable safe passage of drugs across national borders. Corruption also extends to the laundering of drug money through lax banking systems, and the possible corruption of political figures to protect the huge financial assets of those who sit at the very top of the drug-dealing networks.

The United Nations Office on Drugs and *Crime* has repeatedly drawn attention to the national and international threats associated with the corruption linked to the trade in illegal drugs. Within some countries, such as Mexico, the corruption of law *enforcement* services has led to the increased use of the military to provide a drugs enforcement role tackling the heavily armed drug gangs (Padgett, 2012). However, it would be a mistake to assume that corruption is solely to be found within the developing countries. Within the United States and the United Kingdom, the major HSBC Bank was fined a record $1.9 billion to settle a money-laundering case brought against the bank by the US government (Treanor, 2012). Similarly, a report for the UK Government's Foresight Programme, anticipating the impact of the drugs problem over the next 20 years, drew attention to the potential for the drugs trade to threaten the democratic process by seeking to gain influence over political parties through the mechanism of political donations (McKeganey *et al.*, 2005).

KEY TEXTS
- BBC (2011) 'Mexico Drugs War: Corruption Grows on US Border', available at www.bbc.co.uk/news/world-latin-america-13723991
- Garrido, R. (1997) 'Corruption Drug Trafficking and the Armed Forces', Transnational Institute, available at www.tni.org/article/corruption-drug-traficking-and-armed-forces
- Morris, S. (2013) 'Drug Trafficking Corruption and Violence in Mexico: Mapping the Linkages', *Trends in Organised Crime*, doi 10.1007/s12117–013–9191–7

crime

SEE ALSO **corruption; enforcement; police**

The link between drugs and crime is in one sense obvious – since many of the drugs involved are illegal then possession or trade in those substances will inevitably involve a criminal offence. The extent of the link between drug use and crime has been shown in the various studies that have involved the regular drug *testing* of arrestees. These programmes, which originated within the United States, have now been extended to cities throughout the world, provide a robust measure of the proportion of arrestees who have recently used a variety of legal and illegal substances. The 2011 Arrestee Drug Abuse Monitoring programme carried out in ten sites across the United States involved interviewing 5051 arrestees over a 14-day period, 4,412 of whom provided urine samples for drug testing. Over 60% of arrestees in all ten sites tested positive for at least one drug, and in five sites the proportion of arrestees testing positive was greater than 70%. Marijuana use was widespread with at least 45% of arrestees across nine of the ten sites testing positive for the drug; in six of the ten sites at least 20% of arrestees tested positive for cocaine, rising to as high as 33% in Atlanta. In Sacramento 43% of arrestees tested positive for methamphetamine, and 8% of arrestees tested positive for opiates in Minneapolis (ONDCP, 2012).

In 2002 the results of an international arrestee drug abuse monitoring programme was published with countries as diverse as South Africa, Scotland, England, the Netherlands, Australia, Chile, and Malaysia reporting the results of having tested samples of arrestees. In Western Australia 22% of males and 47% of females tested positive for opiates, in Scotland 31% of arrestees tested positive for opiates, in the Netherlands 17% of arrestees tested positive for opiates (US Dept of Justice, 2002).

On the basis of these data there is little doubt as to the close relationship between drug use and criminality, however from that point on the link between these two becomes far from clear. Perhaps the most vigorous debate around the relationship between drugs and crime has to do with the direction of causality – is it the drug use that is generating the crime or the crime that is generating the drug use? Confusingly there is a plethora of *research* in support of either theory. There is ample *evidence* of drug users committing crimes to pay for the drugs they are dependent upon, and there is evidence of drug users committing crimes prior to their becoming drug users. The reality is almost certainly that both of these propositions are accurate with some drug users having a propensity to commit crimes in advance of their drug use, and others committing crimes in order to pay for the drugs they have become dependent upon.

Perhaps the greatest challenge which the link between drugs and crime poses has to do with the policies and interventions that might weaken the link between drugs and crime. On the one hand there are those who advocate that drug users committing crimes should not receive custodial sentences but should be encouraged or required instead to undergo drug *treatment*. Whilst such a proposal can be seen to make sense in circumstances where an individual's criminality is directly linked to their drug dependency, in reality it may be difficult to determine how much the individuals' criminality is actually determined by their drug use, and how much represents their personal choice. In addition the proposal to treat drug related criminality different to non drug related criminality (to provide treatment for the former and custodial sentences for the latter) could create a two-tier criminal justice system in which the same criminal act could receive very different sentences depending upon whether the individual could show that he or she was drug dependent. There could also be a danger such a system might actually encourage individuals to use drugs as a way of avoiding a custodial sentence for their criminality.

In addition to the uncertainty as to how to tackle drug related criminality there are also arguments that drug use itself should not be regarded as a crime at all. This argument is often favoured by those who also support some form of drugs decriminalization.

KEY TEXTS
- Bean, P. (2008) *Drugs and Crime* (Cullompton, UK: Willan Publishing)
- Hammersley, R. (2008) *Drugs and Crime* (Cambridge: Polity Press)
- Stevens, A. (2011) *Drugs Crime and Public Health: The Political Economy of Drug Policy* (London: Routledge)

d

death

SEE ALSO **harm reduction; HIV; methadone; prison; recovery**

Problematic drug users (those who may be *injecting* and those using *heroin* or cocaine) are at increased risk of dying as a result of their drug use. Studies that have tracked samples of dependent or problematic drug users over a number of years have been able to calculate drug users' risk of dying and to quantify the size of the increased risk of death experienced by dependent drug users as well as identifying some of the factors that are associated with their risk of dying. On the basis of this *research* we know, for example, that people who inject heroin are some 14 times more likely to die than their non-heroin injecting peers (National Treatment Agency, 2004).

In relation to the factors that have been shown to be associated with drug users' risk of dying, these have been shown to include marked fluctuations in the purity of the drugs being used, reduced tolerance to substances, injecting drugs rather than smoking or snorting, using multiple drugs especially those that have a shared depressive effect on individuals' cardio-vascular system, beginning and ceasing opiate substitution *treatment*. Drug users released from *prison* have been shown to be at particularly high risk of dying as a result of their reduced tolerance associated with their limited access to illegal drugs during the period of their incarceration. Leach and Oliver reported that drug users recently released from prison were 40 times more likely to die than similar individuals from the general population (Leach and Oliver, 2011, p. 292). Similarly, Farrell and Marsden analysed recorded deaths amongst recently released prisoners in England and Wales between 1998 and 2000. These researchers found that in the first year following prison release there were 342 male deaths and 100 female deaths – in comparison within the general population over a similar time period there would have been 45.8 male deaths and 8.3 female deaths (Farrell and Marsden, 2008, p. 251). From the United States, Vlahov and colleagues looked at the risk of death amongst those who had recently began injecting drugs (within the last five years) and found that even amongst these individuals their risk of dying was substantially greater than the general population (Vlahov *et al.*, 2008).

In the light of the data showing that drug users are at a much increased risk of death than their non-drug-using peers there have been a wide range of programmes designed to try to reduce drug related mortality. These include providing drug users with the *overdose* reversal drug *naloxone* on their release from prison, training drug users and their families to administer naloxone in the event that they become aware of an individual experiencing a possibly fatal drug overdose, providing counselling to those drug users who are thought to be at heightened risk of overdose and encouraging injecting drug users to switch to non-injecting forms of drug use (snorting or smoking their drugs).

Cornish and colleagues have looked specifically at the impact of opiate substitution treatment on drug users' risk of dying and found that those drug users receiving opiate substitution treatment were substantially less likely to die than their peers not in contact with such treatment services. In addition the researchers found, however, that at the start of opiate substitution treatment drug users' risk of death increased two- to three-fold whilst on the cessation of such treatment their risk of death increased some eight- to nine-fold (Cornish *et al.*, 2010).

KEY TEXTS

- Advisory Council on the Misuse of Drugs (2000) *Reducing Drug Related Deaths* (London: Stationery Office)
- Mathers, B. *et al.* (2013) 'Mortality among People Who Inject Drugs: A Systematic Review and Meta-analysis', *Bulletin of the World Health Organisation*, 91: pp. 102–123
- National Records of Scotland (2012) *Drug Related Deaths in Scotland in 2011* (National Statistics for Scotland)
- National Treatment Agency (2004) Reducing Drug Related Deaths – Guidance for Drug Treatment Providers, http://www.emcdda.europa.eu/attachements.cfm/att_134818_EN_UK%20-%20Reducing%20drug-

related%20deaths%20-%20guidance%20for%20drug-treatment%20
providers.pdf

decriminalization

SEE ALSO cannabis; classification of drugs; harm reduction;
prescribing; zero tolerance

The policy of drugs decriminalization is distinct from the policy of
drugs legalization in that the latter policy involves the withdrawal
of any legal/criminal penalty associated with the use and or the
production of certain substances. The policy of decriminalization
refers to the situation in which legal penalties may remain with
regard to the production and trafficking of certain substances but
there is an acceptance that there will be no recourse to the criminal
law in relation to the use of particular drugs. There have been a
number of recent high profile calls for the United Kingdom and
other countries to adopt the policy of drugs decriminalization. These
calls have come mostly from a range of organizations including
the Global Commission on Drugs Policy which produced a report
in 2011 representing the views of a number of influential figures
(amongst whom were included Sir Richard Branson, founder and
chief executive of the Virgin Group; Kofi Annan, former secretary
general of the UN; Ruth Dreifuss, former president of Switzerland;
Paul Volcker, former chairman of the United States Federal
Reserve Bank; George Schultz, former US secretary of state; George
Papandreou, former prime minister of Greece.

The call for drugs decriminalization is often made on the basis of
a range of arguments. It is pointed out, for example, that utilizing
the criminal law results in a large number of individuals receiving a
criminal record for having used substances that in many instances
are less harmful than the current legal drugs of *alcohol* and *tobacco*;
that maintaining legal penalties creates a lucrative black market in
drug supply fuelling the financial coffers of organized criminals;
that the current criminal penalties associated with certain drugs
have singularly failed to stem the flow of those substances; that as
a result of the criminal penalties drug users are stigmatized and
marginalized and that the government misses out on the collection
of substantial tax revenue that could be obtained from the regulated
supply of currently illegal drugs.

The country most often cited as a model for the policy of drugs decriminalization is Portugal, which passed domestic *legislation* in 2002 ruling out the use of criminal penalties for the use of previously illegal drugs. Importantly, Portugal retained the use of criminal sanctions in relation to the production and trafficking in illegal drugs.

Glen Greenwald, a freelance writer and constitutional lawyer, produced an effusive endorsement of the Portuguese policy for the US-based left-leaning Cato Institute, stating that:

> The data shows that, judged by virtually every metric, the Portuguese decriminalization framework has been a resounding success. Within this success lie self-evident lessons that should guide drug policy debates around the world. (Greenwald, 2009, p. 1)

Academics Caitlin Hughes and Alex Stevens from the University of Kent have been more cautious in their assessment of the impact of drugs decriminalization in Portugal:

> By comparing the trends in Portugal and the neighbouring Spain and Italy we can say that whilst some trends clearly reflect regional shifts (e.g. the increase in use amongst adults) and/or the expansion of services throughout Portugal, some effects do appear to be specific to Portugal... The problem is that it is impossible to state that any of these changes were the direct result of the decriminalization policy. (Hughes and Stevens, 2010, p. 1017)

Aside from the uncertainty as to the impact of drugs decriminalization in Portugal there are a number of arguments that have been presented in opposition to such a policy being adopted elsewhere. Journalist Peter Hitchens has suggested that the United Kingdom has already effectively decriminalized illegal drug use given that only a very small fraction of those who come into contact with the *police* are fined or imprisoned as a result of their drug use – the greatest proportion being dealt with on the basis of a non-custodial sentence (Hitchens, 2012). For the year ending March 2012 there were a total of 229,103 recorded drug offences in England and Wales, only 4.2% (9460) of which resulted in a custodial sentence (Criminal Justice Quarterly Update, 2012).

Opponents of decriminalization point out that the number of people using drugs could increase substantially in the event that the policy were implemented. The *evidence* that Portugal appears not to have witnessed a marked increase in the *prevalence* of illegal drug use following decriminalization is not regarded by the critics of this policy as a strong argument against the possibility of such an occurrence taking place in other countries. It is pointed out that the policy of drugs decriminalization would be a policy from which it would be difficult to pull back from once implemented; that the so-called tax revenue resulting from decriminalization might be a good deal less than is often claimed; that there is no evidence that the criminal gangs currently involved in drug production and supply would simply cease to operate under a decriminalized regime and finally that the claim that existing drug laws have failed is hard to sustain given the prevalence of illegal drug use is only a fraction of the legal drugs.

KEY TEXTS
- Bean, P. (2010) *Legalising Drugs: Debates and Dilemmas* (Bristol: Policy Press)
- Hitchens, P. (2012) *The War We Never Fought: The British Establishments Surrender to Drugs* (London: Bloomsbury)
- McKeganey, N. (2011) *Controversies in Drugs Policy and Practice* (Basingstoke: Palgrave Macmillan)
- Pryce, S. (2012) *Fixing Drugs: The Politics of Drugs Prohibition* (Basingstoke: Palgrave Macmillan)

doctors

SEE ALSO **harm reduction; methadone; prescribing; treatment**

It is perhaps inevitable that doctors should have such a key role in shaping drug policy and in delivering drug *treatment* services within countries. Within the United Kingdom, medical practitioners have had a unique and long-standing role in determining drugs policies as a result of holding key governmental advisory positions, chairing key committees and submitting influential *evidence* in various enquiries over the years. The medical model which sees drug use as largely a medical condition has been the predominant paradigm through which the United Kingdom and many other societies have sought to understand the phenomenon of individuals using a variety of mild altering substances and experiencing a range of difficulties associated with such use. It is important to stress that whilst persuasive, the medical model is by no means the only paradigm for viewing drug use and drug users. Within the San Patrignano therapeutic community drug use and drug *addiction* are seen first as educational problems, remediable not through the process of *prescribing* but through the drug user learning new skills (including work-related skills) and developing a clear sense of their own personal and social worth.

Nevertheless the medical model has predominated in many countries providing a readily accessible notion of individual addiction and a range of treatments that are deemed to be appropriate in enabling the individual to recover from his or her dependence. Whilst medical practitioners have had a key role to play in shaping drug policy, and the provision of drug treatment services, it is by no means the case that there is universal agreement amongst medical practitioners as to the most effective treatments for drug dependence. Indeed some of the most heated debates within the world of drugs policy are to do with disagreements between doctors as to what their role should be in treating individuals suffering from a drug dependency. Whilst some doctors are passionate supporters of the value of prescribing *heroin* to opiate addicts, other doctors regard such a practice as little more than further encouragement to the drug user to continue to use the drugs that he or she has become dependent upon. There are similar disputes around the prescribing of the opiate substitute drug *methadone*, which although widely prescribed to dependent opiate addicts in the United Kingdom and elsewhere is still seen by many medical practitioners as amounting to little more than one more drug which the addict can become dependent upon. These are just two of the most hotly contested disputes within the world of addictions medicine.

Other disputes amongst medical practitioners have to do with whether it is the role of the doctor to encourage the individual drug user to cease his or her drug use or whether the primary goal of treatment should be to try to reduce the harm associated with the individuals' continuing drug use. The dispute here centres around the dangers associated with dependent drug users being encouraged to cease their drug consumption thereby reducing their tolerance for the drugs they were using. Whilst on the face of it such reduced tolerance may not be seen as a bad thing, one of the consequences

35

of this is an increased risk of *overdose* where the individual resumes his or her previous level of drug use. Initiatives aimed at detoxing drug users carry a very real risk of increasing the individuals' risk of dying in the event that they resume their previous pattern of drug use. As a result there are some doctors who would argue that the risks of detoxification are too high, and that it is preferable to provide substitute opiate medication to the individual for as long as he or she wishes and until the individual decides that they wish to reduce their drug use.

Along with the disputes that have arisen between doctors there has also been a recognition that as a result of their capacity to prescribe medication doctors can actually cause a drug use epidemic. Within the United Kingdom, it is widely recognized that private medical physicians providing drug users with access to prescribed opiates actually created the epidemic of heroin use that took off in the 1960s in London (Spear and Mott, 2002).

Finally, it is important to acknowledge that as a result of their unique access to drugs doctors are at increased risk of developing drug problems themselves. Whilst there is very little data available on the extent of such drug use by physicians it has been suggested that as many as 15% of doctors may develop a substance dependency problem at some point in their lives, with the greatest frequency involving those working in anaesthesiology and emergency room medicine (Lutsky *et al.*, 1994). *Research* has shown that with appropriate treatment physicians who have developed a substance abuse problem have a very high likelihood of *recovery* (McLellan *et al.*, 2008).

KEY TEXTS

- Mars, S. (2012) *The Politics of Addiction: Medical Conflict and Drug Dependence in England since 1960* (Basingstoke: Palgrave Macmillan)
- McLellan, T. *et al.* (2008) 'Five Year Outcomes in a Cohort Study of Physicians Treated for Substance Use Disorders in the United States', *British Medical Journal*, 337: p. a2038
- Strang, J. and Gossop, M. (1994) *Heroin Addiction and Drug Policy: The British System* (Oxford: Oxford University Press)

driving and drugs

SEE ALSO **cannabis; normalization; stigma**

Within the last few years, increasing attention has focused on the phenomenon of drugged driving. Surveys from multiple countries have identified the proportion of both recreational and problematic drug users who drive after having recently ingested both legal and illegal drugs (Bates and Blakely, 1999). In Scotland researchers surveyed 547 drivers and found that 15% of 17 to 39 year olds had smoked *cannabis* in the preceding 12 hours (Neale *et al.*, 2000). Similar *research* involving roadside surveys of drivers found that 11.8% tested positive for illicit drugs in Canada (Dussault *et al.*, 2002), 15% tested positive in the United States (Lacey *et al.*, 2007). In Australia, a survey carried out by Davey and colleagues found that 13% of females and 20% of males reported having driven under the influence of drugs in the last 12 months (Davey *et al.*, 2005).

Understanding the impact of drugged driving and, in particular, establishing whether specific substances consumed by drivers increase their risk of an accident has largely consisted of monitoring drugged drivers' motor skills using driving simulators. Whilst these studies have shown the adverse effects of different drugs on individual's driving skills, it is by no means straightforward to translate the results of these studies into the real world to assess the degree to which drug use increases driver's risks of collision.

In Spain, Del Rio and colleagues reported the results of having analysed the blood of 5745 drivers killed in road accidents between 1991 and 2000. In this study illicit drugs were identified in 8.8% of samples whilst *alcohol* was identified in 43.8% of samples (Del Rio *et al.*, 2002). Drummer and colleagues undertook a similar analysis, focusing on drivers killed in road accidents in Australia; the researchers on this study found that 13.5% of fatally injured drivers had signs of cannabis consumption and 4.9% had *evidence* of opiate consumption (Drummer *et al.*, 2003).

Asbridge and colleagues undertook a systematic review and meta-analysis looking at real world collisions, comparing those instances where drivers had consumed cannabis with control accidents where no cannabis had been consumed by the driver:

After a systematic review of the literature, this meta analysis of studies examining acute cannabis consumption and motor vehicle collisions ... found a near doubling of risk of a driver being involved in a motor vehicle collision resulting in serious injury or *death*. (Asbridge *et al.*, 2012; emphasis added)

On the basis of these studies there is little doubt that drug and alcohol use presents a serious problem in relation to driving. Roadside alcohol *testing* has been a major aid in tackling drink-related driving. However the development of comparable equipment in relation to illegal drug use has proven to be challenging. Part of the difficulty has to do with the need to develop technology that can rapidly identify what drugs a driver has consumed. That challenge is becoming ever greater as the range of drugs is expanding. In the case of the legal high drugs, for example, there is presently no possibility of developing testing equipment that can cope with the proliferation in the substances that are now being consumed.

In addition, in contrast to alcohol where we have a measure of blood alcohol concentration above which it is illegal to drive (0.08 in the UK) there is no equivalent level at which illegal drugs are judged to have an adverse impact on driving capacity. There are political sensitivities here since it would be difficult for a government to publish a safe level of cannabis use, for example, in the case of drivers whilst at the same time maintaining that the possession of the drug itself is a criminal offence.

In the absence of effective drugalyser equipment similar to the breathalyser for alcohol, *police* officers have to rely on the use of what are called field sobriety tests (walking a straight line, standing on one leg) to determine whether a motorist is impaired and whether they should arrest the individual and require a blood test which would then be carried out at the police station. These field sobriety tests are a poor substitute for effective drugalyser equipment and as a result many drivers feel that there is a relative low risk of their being detected where they are driving under the influence of illegal drugs.

KEY TEXTS

- Asbridge, M., Hayden, J. and Cartwright, J. (2012) 'Acute Cannabis Consumption and Motor Vehicle Collision Risk: Systematic Review of Observational Studies and Meta-Analysis', *British Medical Journal*, 344: p. e536
- Elvik, R. (2012) 'Risk of Road Accident Associated with the Use of Drugs: A Systematic Review and Meta-Analysis of Evidence from Epidemiological Studies', *Accident Analysis and Prevention*, available

online, 9 July 2012, pii: S0001-4575(12)00241-2, doi: 10.1016/j. aap.2012.06.017.

- Neale, J. *et al.* (2000) *Recreational Drug Use and Driving: A Qualitative Study* (Scottish Executive Central Research Unit)
- Silverstone, T. (2012) 'Drugs and Driving British', *Journal of Clinical Pharmacology*, 1 (6) December: pp. 451–454

dual diagnosis

SEE ALSO **brief interventions; chronic relapsing condition; recovery; stages of change**

Dual diagnosis refers to the situation in which individuals may be suffering from both drug or *alcohol* dependency and significant mental health problems. *Research* carried out in a wide range of countries has shown that a significant proportion of those with drug or alcohol dependency problems are also likely to be experiencing a mental health problem; and similarly that a significant proportion of those who are in contact with mental health services are likely to have a substance dependency problem. Kavanagh and colleagues (2004) reported that 42.1% of people with schizophrenia in Australia had a lifetime *prevalence* of substance misuse or dependence. Similarly, Weaver *et al.* (2003) have reported that 44% of people in contact with community mental health teams within the United Kingdom were experiencing problems with their alcohol consumption and 31% reported problem drug use. Lyne and colleagues, in Ireland, reported that amongst 465 patients in contact with a national alcohol addition *treatment* unit over a quarter of contacts overall and more than a third of the female contacts had experienced a depressive episode (Lyne *et al.*, 2011).

There is also clear *evidence* that the use of certain drugs can exacerbate the onset of mental health problems, even where those drugs are being used by individuals to self-medicate problems they are aware of (Patton *et al.*, 2002; Lynskey *et al.*, 2004; Hall and Degenhardt, 2009). It has been shown that where individuals are suffering from both mental health problems and substance dependency problems that their *recovery* may be impeded and their contact with services less effective than it might otherwise have been. Research has also shown that negative feelings on the part of mental health agency staff towards those with a dependency problem, and negative feelings on the part of drug and treatment agency staff towards those with a mental health problem, can severely exacerbate individuals' difficulties. There is the danger too of individuals failing to have their more complex needs met as a result of the silo focus of many drug and alcohol dependency services and mental health services (National Collaborating Centre for Mental health, 2011).

The UK National Institute for Health and Clinical Excellence sought to offer guidance to services working with individuals with both mental health problems and dependency issues. The guidance stresses the importance of listening to individuals and providing them with the opportunity to express their needs, of ensuring good communication between individuals and clinic staff and of the benefits of combining both mental health agency staff and drug treatment agency staff in processes of joint review and intervention. To an extent it is unrealistic to expect agency workers to be expert in both areas (mental health and substance dependency) and as a result there is a clear need for joint working and joint training across agencies. Health care workers within mental health agencies are encouraged to ask clients about any concurrent drug and alcohol use whilst agency workers in drug and alcohol treatment agencies are encouraged to assess clients in terms of any current or past mental health problems. The NICE report recommends that:

> Healthcare professionals in all settings ... should routinely ask adults and young people with known or suspected psychosis about their use of alcohol and or prescribed and non prescribed (including illicit) drugs. (NICE, 2011, p. 17)

> Adults and young people with psychosis and coexisting substance misuse, attending substance misuse services, should be offered a comprehensive multidisciplinary mental health assessment in addition to an assessment of their substance use. (NICE, 2011, p. 23)

NICE also recommend that staff working in mental health and drug treatment services can rapidly organize referrals between services where this is needed for individuals with dual diagnoses. It is recognized that coexisting mental health and substance dependency problems can undermine the effectiveness of different treatments.

For example, within the substance dependency field there is a widespread use of group counselling. However, we know much less about the suitability of group counselling for individuals with a psychotic illness and a substance dependency problem. It is possible that some individuals may be harmed by the kinds of counselling support that would otherwise be routinely provided to individuals with drug and alcohol dependency problem (National Collaborating Centre for Mental Health, 2011). Saleh and Crome (2011) have underlined the importance of strengthening the evidence base in relation to co-occurring psychosis and substance misuse problems recommending the importance of ensuring that individuals with mental health problems are not excluded from substance abuse treatment effectiveness trials.

KEY TEXTS

- Colpaert, C. and Vanderplaschen, W. (2012) 'Prevalence and Determinants of Personality Disorders in a Clinical Sample of Alcohol-, Drug-, and Dual-Dependent Patients', *Substance Use and Misuse*, 47 (6): pp. 649–661
- National Institute for Health and Clinical Excellence (2011) 'Psychosis with Coexisting Substance Misuse: Assessment and Management in Adults and Young People', *NICE Clinical Guidelines 120*. Developed by the National Collaborating Centre for Mental Health
- Staiger, P. *et al.* (2011) 'Improving Services for Individuals with a Dual Diagnosis: A Qualitative Study Reporting the Views of Service Users', *Addiction Research and Theory*, 19 (1): pp. 47–55

e

education

SEE ALSO harm reduction; prevention; testing

Education has had a particular role to play in the area of substance misuse and is viewed by many as a key element of drugs *prevention*. The premise here is that by providing young people with appropriate education it will be possible to protect them from developing problematic use or indeed in some cases any use of the substances involved.

Whilst there is wide acceptance of the necessity of providing school based education on substance use and misuse there is very little agreement as to the most appropriate forms of education to provide. One of the most hotly disputed topics within the world of drugs education has to do with whether young people should be provided with a very strong steer towards avoiding drug use (through, for example, providing graphic information on the harms of drugs misuse) or whether they should be provided instead with information about different substances with the emphasis being to encourage young people to decide for themselves whether to use the drugs involved. The dispute here is very much between those who emphasize 'prevention' and those who emphasize '*harm reduction*' and is akin to the dispute within the world of drugs *treatment* between harm reduction and drug user abstinence.

One of the most well-known approaches to drugs prevention education in schools is the Drug Abuse Resistance Education (DARE) programme in which law *enforcement* officers go into schools to outline to the young people the various dangers of becoming involved in drugs and gangs. The DARE programme was widely developed within the United States. Where evaluations have been undertaken the results of the DARE programmes have not been particularly positive. There has been some suggestion that young people participating within the DARE programme may be more rather than less likely to use certain drugs (Rosenbaum, 1998), whilst other *research* has questioned whether there is a long-term benefit associated with the DARE programme (Sherman *et al.*, 1998). In 2001, the US Surgeon General listed the DARE programme as one of the ineffective primary prevention programmes.

Other education-based interventions that have been widely used within schools in the United States and the United Kingdom include the 'Life Skills' approach developed by Gilbert Botvin and various colleagues. In this approach the aim is not to frighten young people away from using *tobacco, alcohol* or illegal drugs. Rather it is to boost their knowledge of the actual levels at which these drugs are being used (to counter the impression that everybody is using these drugs), to provide young people with the skills to avoid using these drugs given that there will be many situations in which they are likely to be offered a variety of substances, and to provide young people with a range of wider social or life skills that can assist them in the formation of relationships and their engagement in positive activities. The life skills approach has been widely evaluated with very positive results in relation to a variety of forms of drugs misuse including smoking, drinking and the use of illegal drugs – principally marijuana (Botvin and Griffin, 2004; Botvin and Kantor, 2000; Botvin *et al.*, 2000). Early evaluations of the life skills approach showed that young people who had participated within one of Botvin's programmes were much less likely than their peers to smoke, and further that the positive effect associated with the programme seemed to be maintained over many months (Botvin *et al.*, 1980; Botvin *et al.*, 1983; Botvin *et al.*, 1989; Botvin *et al.*, 1995a,b).

Whilst there have been numerous positive evaluations of the life skills approach to drug prevention education, the field of drug prevention education itself is littered with studies that have failed to document a positive effect for educational programmes. Within the United Kingdom the largest evaluation of drug prevention education was the Blueprint Programme developed in the mid-2000s and targeted on 11–13 year olds. The programme focused on a wide range of participating schools and sought to integrate drug prevention initiatives within the school with similar initiatives in the wider community. Although there were high expectations that the Blueprint evaluation would guide the provision of drug prevention education in the years to come, in fact the research was assessed as largely having failed to provide such guidance as a result of shortcomings in the sample sizes for the numbers of children and numbers of schools participating in the research (Goldacre, 2009).

KEY TEXTS
- Donohew, L., Sypher, H. and Bukoski, W. (1991) *Persuasive Communication and Drug Abuse Prevention* (London: Routledge)
- European Monitoring Centre for Drugs and Drug Addiction (2006) *Prevention of Substance Use* (Lisbon: EMCDDA)
- Faggiano, F. *et al.* (2005) 'Schoolbased Prevention for Illicit Drug Use', *Cochrane Database of Systematic Reviews*, 2: CD003020
- Hawkins, J. and Catalano, R. (2002) 'Promoting Science Based Prevention in Communities', *Addictive Behaviors*, 27: pp. 951–976

employment

SEE ALSO identity; recovery; stigma; treatment

It has been estimated that as many as 80% of problem drug users are not in employment (Jones *et al.*, 2007) and that the lack of employment in this group increases the severity of the individual's drug use and reduces the likelihood of their *recovery*. The reasons for the lack of employment amongst problematic drug users are multiple and are proving difficult to remedy. These reasons include the low level of *education* and skills amongst problematic drug users, the likely past involvement of problematic drug users in criminal activities, the negative attitudes of employers towards those using illegal drugs, the high level of mental health problems amongst problematic drug users and the fact that the drug-using lifestyle itself may mean that relatively little of the drug users' time is available for work. There is also the very strong likelihood that individuals with a long history of problematic drug use may have very low expectations of ever being able to secure mean-ingful employment and, over the years of their drug use, may have developed a lifestyle that itself is hardly conducive to successfully meeting the demands of employers (e.g. many problematic drug users may spend a significant proportion of the night looking to secure drugs and then spend a proportion of the daytime asleep or experiencing the effects of drug usage). Klee and colleagues undertook qualitative *research* with 70 problem drug users who were seeking employment. According to Klee *et al.*:

> Stereotypes of drug users in society are a major barrier to them returning to working life. In general, they are seen as deviant, dishonest, unreliable manipulative individuals prone to poor health and self-neglect. (Klee *et al.*, 2002, p. 4)

In similar interviews with local employers, Klee and colleagues found that many of those interviewed viewed the employment of drug users as posing a risk to the reputation of their company; there was a feeling that drug users were unreliable, untrustworthy and prone to absenteeism. More positively a web-based survey of 52 employers found that whilst 26% of those surveyed said that they would not employ an ex-drug user, 48% indicated that this would really depend on the nature of the individual's drug problem (Spencer *et al.*, 2008).

With the development of a recovery focus in drug *treatment* policy there has been a concern to reduce the levels of unemployment and benefit payments paid to problematic drug users. There have been repeated discussions, for example, as to whether drug users who refuse to engage with drug treatment services should have their state benefits cut (Watt, 2012). Whilst it is understandable within an environment of financial austerity that there may be a wish to reduce the proportion of problematic drug users who are unemployed, and claiming state benefits, there can be little doubt as to the magnitude of the challenge that any government is going to face in enabling problematic drug users to secure long-term employment. For example, whilst there has been an understandable commitment on the part of the UK government to increase the numbers of problematic drug users in treatment, in fact the very nature of that treatment may militate against the individual securing employment. The requirement for problematic drug users to attend a pharmacy on a daily basis to consume their medication under some level of supervision can make it very difficult for the individual to take on the responsibilities that may be part of most jobs.

KEY TEXTS

- Bauld, L. *et al.* (2010) 'Problem Drug Users Experience of Employment and the Benefit System', Department of Work and Pensions Research Report No 640
- Henkel, D. (2011) 'Unemployment and Substance Use: A Review of the Literature', *Current Drug Abuse Reviews*, 4 (1): pp. 4–27
- McIntosh, J., Bloor, M. and Roberson, M. (2008) 'Drug Treatment and the Achievement of Paid Employment', *Addiction Research and Theory*, 16 (1): pp. 37–45
- UKDPC (2008) *Working towards Recovery: Getting Problem Drug Users into Jobs* (London: UKDPC)

enforcement

SEE ALSO **harm reduction; international treaties; zero tolerance**

Drugs enforcement is a key part of every country's approach to tackling the problem of illegal drugs, including those that have adopted policies of decriminalization or legalization of drugs for personal use. In the Netherlands, for example, the government allocates 75% of its drugs budget to enforcement-related activities compared to 49% in the United Kingdom (Gyngell, 2009). Within Portugal, which decriminalized the possession of drugs for personal use in 2001, there were nevertheless 4260 arrests for drug trafficking offences in 2009, an increase of nearly 15% on the previous year (EU *Crime* Stats).

The activities that fall under the heading of enforcement are extraordinarily broad ranging from the use the satellite monitoring of poppy fields in Afghanistan and coca production in Columbia, aerial spraying of chemical agents to reduce crop production, the use of undercover drug enforcement agents to collect human intelligence on the operation of the major drug production and drug trafficking organizations, border inspection of vehicles and containers, the use of naval and coast guard facilities to interdict ships carrying drugs, and the more familiar street level 'buy and bust' and 'test purchase' *police* operations in which an attempt is made to disrupt local drug supply networks. Whilst the range of activities incorporable under the heading of drugs enforcement is bewilderingly large the effectiveness of much of this activity is by no means well established. Caulkins and Reuter, for example, looked at the impact of drugs enforcement activities within the United States on the price at which certain drugs were being sold on the streets – ordinarily one would assume that effective enforcement that resulted in reducing the availability of illegal drugs would have the effect of pushing up drug prices according to the simple laws of supply and demand. In fact, Caulkins and Reuter found a very different relationship between drugs enforcement and the price at which illegal drugs were being sold within the United States:

> Over the last 30 years the most striking observation about drug markets is that the number of persons serving time in *prison* for drug offenses in the United States has risen steadily and substantially, while the prices of cocaine and *heroin*, adjusted for purity, have declined. The price decline was sharp during the 1980s and has been gradual since then. (Caulkins and Reuter, 2010, p. 7; emphasis added)

On the basis of Caulkins and Reuter's analysis, tough enforcement within the United States does not appear to have had the impact of reducing the availability of illegal drugs – at least using price as a proxy measure of availability. This is not to say that the enforcement approach itself is without impact since it is not possible to know what level drug prices might have fallen to over the last 30 years in the absence of robust enforcement.

But why might enforcement have less of an impact than one might have assumed given the level of investment in enforcement activities and the incarceration of large number of individuals for drugs offences and the seizure of what on the face of it appear to be large quantities of illegal drugs by enforcement agencies. In assessing the impact of drugs enforcement, however, it is important to look beyond the surface appearance of some of the statistics involved. In Scotland, for example, researchers were able to calculate the quantity of seized heroin as a fraction of the quantity of consumed heroin over a six-year period from 2000 to 2006. This *research* showed that in only two of the six years studied was the quantity of seized heroin greater than 1% of the quantity of consumed heroin (McKeganey *et al.*, 2009). Large as heroin seizures may appear when they are reported in the *media* by agencies that have a vested interest in trumpeting the success of robust enforcement, in fact the quantities seized may represent only the tiniest fraction of the

47

quantity of illegal drugs being consumed. On this basis then it is hardly surprising if the seizure of less than 1% of heroin is failing to have an impact on the price at which the other 99% of the product is being sold.

In recent years, however, there has been a concerted move away from viewing the quantity of illegal drugs seized as the most appropriate measure for assessing the impact of drugs enforcement. Within the United Kingdom, for example, there has been a concerted lobby to use the notion of *harm reduction* and specifically the goal of reducing the harm of local drug markets as a much better measure of the impact of drugs enforcement activities. The use of the term 'harm reduction' in relation to drugs enforcement is no less controversial than the use of the term in relation to drug treatment (see harm reduction).

Although the idea of reducing drug related harm has been applied most fully in relation to health interventions the ideas of harm reduction have also been increasingly influential within the drug enforcement arena. Some commentators have suggested that certain forms of robust drug policing amount to a health hazard in themselves. In Australia, Maher and Dixon (1999) have looked at how the policing of local drug markets can have an adverse impact on the health of drug users through impeding their access to health services, increasing the likelihood that they will share *injecting* equipment, and increasing the likelihood that drug users will inject in unhygienic environments. Fitzgerald has gone even further in describing some forms of drug policing as amounting to a 'public health menace' (Fitzgerald, 2005).

In 2009, the United Kingdom Drug Policy Commission produced a report that aimed to flesh out what a harm reduction approach to drug enforcement might look like. The UKDPC suggested that since drug markets differ in the amount of harm that they can be seen to be causing local communities, ranging from relatively low levels of harm to relatively high levels of harm, the police might be encouraged to focus first on the high harm causing drug markets. As the UKDPC have pointed, developing a more harm reduction approach to drug policing could see the police shifting their focus from reducing the quantity of drugs being sold on the streets to reducing the level of violence or the visibility of a particular drug market. This could involve trying to encourage dealers who are engaged in an 'open drug market' within a residential area to move to a more secluded, less residential area, where the drug marketing activities were less visible to residents.

Contentious or not, it is clear that harm reduction ideas are having a powerful impact on perceptions of policing including amongst the police themselves. A UK government report on tackling serious organized *crime*, for example, included the statement that:

Harm reduction, rather than quantities of drugs seized or individuals convicted, is a more useful way of prioritising activities to improve the lives of citizens in the UK. (Home Office, 2009, p. 24)

As part of the UKDPC project looking at harm reduction policing, the researchers sent questionnaires to 427 individuals who were involved in one way or another with enforcement. Individuals were asked to identify the primary aim of drug enforcement; interestingly the largest proportion of respondents (39%) identified reducing drug related harm as the primary aim while the second largest group (28%) identified 'enforcing the law' and 'delivering justice'. Less that a quarter (22%) of those questioned cited reducing drug availability as being the primary aim of drug law enforcement. Over half of those questioned (64%) said that it was possible to reduce the harms caused by drug markets without reducing the amount of drugs sold, and 80% of respondents said that in their view enforcement agencies could help shape drug markets through their activities (UKDPC, 2009, pp. 95/96).

On the basis of these figures one would have to assume that harm reduction ideas are having a significant impact on drugs enforcement approaches – at least within the United Kingdom. Perhaps the greatest challenge that enforcement is likely to face in the coming years, however, is the one of combining the commitment to reduce the availability of illegal drugs on the streets along with the commitment to reduce the harm associated with drug misuse. According to Wilson and Stevens it is perhaps appropriate to expect only a modest impact of drugs enforcement approaches on the drugs trade itself:

Experience has shown that it is extremely difficult for law enforcement agencies to achieve a significant and sustained impact on the overall scale of illicit drug markets. However, there is clear *evidence* that some enforcement activities can impact on the structure and methods of operation of trafficking organizations at all levels – from production to retail distribution. This review of studies examining the behaviour of drug dealers shows that they do (sometimes unconsciously) adjust their operations in response to law enforcement strategies and actions, but to a large degree continue to pursue the same principles as any legitimate commodity business – setting of margins, and management of risk. Much greater analysis and understanding of market behaviour is needed if the international law enforcement community is to increase its effectiveness in reducing the harms associated with the illegal market in controlled drugs – an important conceptual step would be for strategists to focus more on the harms associated with drug markets (for example, violence and intimidation, or the *corruption* of public officials), rather than just the overall scale of those markets. (Wilson and Stevens, 2010, p. 10; emphasis added)

KEY TEXTS
- Caulkins, J. and Reuter, P. (2010) 'How Drug Enforcement Affects Price', available at https://docs.google.com/a/drugmisuseresearch.org/
- Fitzgerald, J. (2009) 'Policing As a Public Health Menace in the Policy Struggles Over Public Injecting', *International Journal of Drug Policy*, 20: pp. 261–269
- McKeganey, N. *et al.* (2009) 'Heroin Seizures and Heroin Use in Scotland', *Journal of Substance Use*, 14 (3): pp. 252–260
- United Kingdom Drug Policy Commission (2009) *Refocusing Drug Related Enforcement to Address Harms* (London: UKDPC)
- Wilson, L. and Stevens, A. (2010) 'Understanding Drug Markets and How to Influence Them Report 14'. Beckley Foundation

European Monitoring Centre for Drugs and Drug Addiction

SEE ALSO harm reduction; international treaties; politics; research

Based in Lisbon since it opened in 1995, the Centre currently has an annual budget of some 15.5 million euros. The idea behind the setting up of the centre was the need for accurate and up-to-date information on the evolving drug problem throughout Europe and the importance of ensuring the availability of independent scientific analysis and commentary on the nature of that problem. Information collection, collation and exchange are very much at the heart of what the EMCDDA is all about. The Centre manages an international network of focal points located within individual countries, each charged with the responsibility of distilling key information on the nature of the drug problem and passing this information to the EMCDDA for it to form part of the 'state of the drug problem in Europe' report that the EMCDDA produces on an annual basis. The Centre has been active in encouraging the development of an early warning system to identify the appearance of new drugs of abuse throughout Europe, collating information on effective means for drugs preventions, identifying best practice in the areas of drug *prevention* drug *enforcement* and drugs *treatment.*

In focusing on information collation and exchange and encouraging the development of high-quality scientific *research*, the Centre has sought to avoid becoming involved in policy disputes between nations and experts as to how the drugs problem may be best tackled. The Centre has no published views on such topics as decriminalization or legalization of illegal drugs. Nevertheless, the Centre has supported the contribution of *harm reduction* ideas and principles and has produced a number of documents that have advocated the development and extension of harm reduction ideas and practices throughout the drugs field (EMCDDA, 2011). A recent EMCDDA review, for example, has called for further application of the ideas and practices of harm reduction throughout Europe:

> The relative success of harm reduction strategies adopted in many European countries over the past two decades, and the *evidence* gathered in their support, provides a framework for the development, expansion and evaluation of harm reduction across multiple forms of substance use. (EMCDDA, 2011, p. 27; emphasis added)

Harm reduction, however, is a deeply political notion, linked in the minds of many of its supporters (and critics) to the goal of drugs legalization and decriminalization. Many harm reduction supporters would argue that the current restrictive drug laws cause more harm to drug users than the substances they are seeking to prevent access to, and that as a result a key part of the harm reduction agenda must be to weaken and liberalize current restrictive drug laws. Whilst commenting favourably upon harm reduction within the drugs field, the monitoring centre has been keen to avoid becoming embroiled within these political discussions and has stressed instead the public health orientation which it sees as is predominant throughout Europe and which provides a much less contentious basis for the continued development of harm reduction interventions throughout the continent.

The Centre has remained largely free from criticism which, given the highly disputatious nature of the drugs issue, is no mean feat in itself. However, within a much tighter financial environment, there will inevitably be a growing demand for it to provide evidence of its worth and effectiveness. This will not be an easy task for the Centre given that its key aim is to ensure the flow of high-quality information and analysis about the evolving drug problem in Europe. Whilst it is relatively easy to assess its success in disseminating accurate and up-to-date information about Europe's drug problem, it will be much harder to show that the information made available has resulted in improvements in how the various European countries are responding to their shared drug problem.

KEY TEXTS
- EMCDDA (2011) *Harm Reduction: Evidence, Impacts and Challenges* (European Monitoring Centre for Drugs and Drug Addiction)
- Griffiths, P. *et al.* (2012) 'Addiction Research Centres and the Nurturing of Creativity. Monitoring the European Drug Situation: The Ongoing Challenge for the European Monitoring Centre for Drugs and Drug Addiction (EMCDDA)', *Addiction*, 107 (2) February: pp. 254–258

evidence

SEE ALSO **classification of drugs; politics; strategies, drugs**

We live in an age where evidence is deemed to be the desirable touchstone for all public policy decisions. In relation to drug use and drug users the claim is often made that policy and interventions should be based on the best available evidence rather than on polit-ical or personal preference, *morality*, funding or historical accident (we do what we do now because we have always done it that way in the past). In fact the drugs field is littered with examples where decisions have been taken, where services have been set up or shut down, where drug users have been channelled in one direc-tion rather than another on the flimsiest possible evidence base. When one looks at the funding for *research* this should surprise nobody, but the fact that it may be surprising to many is due to the fact that the rhetoric of evidence based decision-making has stretched so far beyond what actually happens in reality. In 2000 the Royal College of Physicians published the results of the report 'Drugs Dilemmas and Choices' enquiry within which it noted that less than a quarter of 1% of the money spent in the United Kingdom on tackling drugs misuse was allocated to research (RCP, 2000). Whilst that figure is now somewhat out of date and research funding in the addictions has increased in the inter-vening years it must also be noted that the drug problem itself has increased in scale as has the level of funding for drugs *treatment* and drug *enforcement* – in reality then it is highly likely that the 0.25% figure remains as an accurate assessment of the level of funding for research in the addictions. What this means in effect is that 99.75% of the money spent tackling the problem of illegal drug use in the United Kingdom is being directed on the basis of evidence obtained by the remaining 0.25%. Hardly a ringing endorsement as to the centrality of evidence in UK drug policy and drug interventions.

Perhaps the area that has attracted the greatest political and public interest to do with drugs and drug users over recent years has been the classification of *cannabis* where successive UK Home Secretaries have asked the UK Advisory Council on the Misuse of Drugs to review the drug and provide advice as to its appropriate classification within the UK Misuse of Drugs Act. Despite repeated advice from the Council that the drug should be included within the lowest level of harm within the Misuse of Drugs Act (Class C), as a result of political decision-making the drug remains within Class B within the Misuse of Drugs Act attracting a higher penalty for use and trafficking in the drug. The lack of evidence or the repudia-tion of evidence in forming political judgements as to how we are tackling the drugs problem goes much deeper than the classification of a single substance. Professor David Nutt and colleagues, for example, have described the entire system of classifying drugs in terms of their level of harm and which underpins the UK drug laws as having

> evolved in an unsystematic way from somewhat arbitrary foundations with seemingly little scientific basis. (Nutt *et al.*, 2007, p. 1047)

Similarly, the most recent shift in UK drug treatment policy that is now giving unprecedented emphasis to the importance of ensuring that services are working towards *recovery* has not evolved out of a clear evidence base favouring recovery – rather it was ushered in on the basis of a change in government and the development of a new drug strategy. Whilst there are now studies underway assessing the degree to which services are realizing the new recovery agenda, what we have here is a classic example of the evidence following rather than preceding the policy development.

It is questionable, however, whether evidence could ever form the basis for all or even most of the decisions in the public policy arena – even despite the rhetoric to the contrary. The reasons for this are multiple and long standing. Research, for example, can take many years to complete yielding what one might regard as ambiguous recommendations for policy interventions. By contrast politicians will be judged on their capacity to respond to problems in the 'here and now'. Equally it is by no means the case, that even where studies have been carried out, that the findings from those studies are consistent and lead to a single policy option being identified. More probably studies vary substantially in the interpretations of the data and the recommendations that are held to flow from the analyses undertaken. Equally, it might be accepted that politicians have to weigh more than the evidence base in reaching the public policy decisions they are taking. In deciding whether, and for how long to fund a national *methadone* programme, politicians are required to look beyond the evidence as to the effectiveness of this particular treatment to consider the range of other possible uses to which the money could be spent (e.g. funding hospitals, schools, pensions) and in this sense need to pay attention to a wider range of issues than those solely having to do with the evidence base around a particular treatment. Jeremy Sare writing in the influential *British Medical Journal* has offered a provocative characterization of the gulf between *politics* and evidence when it comes to public policy:

> A scientist will usually only present a new finding once it has been carefully researched, tested, and peer reviewed, whereas politicians can happily advocate any crackpot theory based on little more than anecdotal experience, personal prejudice, and questionable *media* reports. A scientist's professional reputation can rely on the integrity of the data but a politician just needs enough plausible deniability. (Sare, 2012; emphasis added)

Susanne MacGregor, however, has offered a contrasting view of the gulf that can be seen to exist between politicians and the evidence base:

> Politicians stress that politics has more to it than just academic evidence: elected politicians have to be able to play the political game and should also pay heed to manifesto commitments which indicate a framework of beliefs. And often the public want government to be seen to act. Politicians stress the interplay between values and evidence: they accept that evidence matters but they say it is their role to link evidence to a narrative, an argument and vision. The specific contribution of the politician is to use intuition and exercise judgment. Facts do not lead to self-evident conclusions – information is interpreted by politicians through the frame of their value-set and on the basis of other information they have acquired in their lives. (MacGregor, 2013, p. 6)

The gap between evidence and public policy in relation to drugs misuse will unquestionably continue such that the key question is not so much when will the two domains meet but rather how much value should we place as a society on the contribution of science in forming public policy. In other words the rhetoric of evidence based policy may need to be set aside to form a more enlightened view of the role of science in public policy.

KEY TEXTS

- MacGregor, S. (2013) 'Barriers to the Influence of Evidence on Policy: Are Politicians the Problem? Drugs Education Prevention and Policy', doi 10.3109/09687637.2012.754403
- Sare, J. (2013) 'Drug Driving Limits', *British Medical Journal*, 18 March
- UKDPC (2012) *A Fresh Approach to Drugs: The Final Report of the UK Drugs Policy Commission* (London: UKDPC)

f

family

SEE ALSO contraception; parental drug use

The impact of drug misuse upon families can be profound, long-standing and enduring. It has been estimated that within the United Kingdom there may be as many as 756,000 children aged under one living with a parent with a drug or *alcohol* problem (Manning *et al.*, 2009). Although most of the attention in terms of *research* and service interventions has been targeted on the individual with the drug problem, in fact the impact of the individual's drug problem very often ripple throughout the wider family affecting siblings, parents and grandparents (Barnard, 2007). Where the drug user within the family is a parent then research has shown that young children and infants are at risk of a wide range of adverse outcomes including developmental delays, poorer educational outcomes, neglect, early onset of drug use, exposure to drug related paraphernalia, poor diet, reduced access to appropriate health and medical services. Within such circumstances, it is by no means uncommon for grandparents to take on the parenting role of the children involved resulting in considerable strain on the grandparents' own emotional and economic resources. Where the drug user within the family is a child, parents can experience substantial relationship strain both with regard to the young person as well as between each other as feelings of guilt, reproach, regret, suspicion, anger, and anxiety can overcome the adult relationship. Where there are non-drug-using siblings within the family, those children can suffer too as disproportionate attention and family resources are targeted on the drug-using sibling and they by contrast are left somewhat un-noticed.

Although there has been a marked increase in the policy priority that is being given to meeting the needs of children within drug-using households, there is little doubt that for the most part the families involved here remain in substantial and enduring need.

In the case of children living with one or both parents who have a dependency problem, research has shown that the adverse impact of their early childhood experience can persist well beyond their own childhood and into adulthood (Kroll and Taylor, 2008; Bancroft *et al.*, 2004). In interviews with the adult survivors of early childhood exposure to parental drug and alcohol problems it was evident that many of the lives of those involved continued to bear the imprint of their disordered childhood, with many finding it difficult to form and maintain long-term relationships as a result of their lack of self-confidence and fearful of relying on other people (Bancroft *et al.*, 2004). In interviews with grandparents caring for the children whose own parents had a drug dependency problem, it was evident that many of those involved were poorly equipped to meet the needs of the children they were caring for. Grandparents would describe trying to provide a normal family circumstance for children who were often continuing to be traumatized by the loss of their parents (Barnard, 2003, 2007). Often the grandparents were fearful of what would happen to the children when they were no longer able to look after them.

Whilst there has been a plethora of services developed to meet the needs of families affected by parental drug and alcohol problems it is by no means clear that any services, no matter how well resourced, can truly meet the needs of young people who have been exposed to the chaos resulting from their parent's dependency problems. Catalano and colleagues reported on the results of an intensive programme to support families where one or both parents had a dependency problem. Assessing the families at 12-months following the provision of the intervention, the researchers found that whilst there was some *evidence* of a reduction in *parental drug use* and an improvement in household routines there appeared to be little positive impact on the children, with the older children in particular more resistant to the attempts to improve household routines (Catalano *et al.*, 1999). Another intensive family support interventions (Parents UNDER Pressure) was evaluated by Sharon Dawe who similarly found that whilst it was possible to stimulate some improvements in parents behaviour, nevertheless a third of parents continued to pose a risk of child neglect and child abuse even after the intervention had been delivered (Dawe *et al.*, 2003).

KEY TEXTS

- Barnard, M. (2006) *Drug Addiction and Families* (London: Jessica Kingsley Publishers)
- Harwin, J. *et al.* (2011) *The Family Drug and Alcohol Court (FDAC) Evaluation Project* (London: Brunel University)
- McKeganey, N., Barnard, M. and McIntosh, J. (2002) 'Paying the Price for Their Parents' Addiction: Meeting the Needs of the Children of Drug-Using Parents', *Drugs: Education Prevention and Policy*, 9 (3): pp. 233–246
- Silva, S. *et al.* (2013) 'Balancing Motherhood and Drug Addiction: The Transition to Parenthood of Addicted Mothers', *Journal of Health Psychology*, 18 (3): pp. 359–367

g

gateway thesis

SEE ALSO chronic relapsing condition; learning to become a marijuana user; stages of change

The gateway thesis is associated most closely with the work of the US addictions researcher Professor Denise Kandel. Originally expounded by Kandel in 1975, the thesis proposed a sequence of stages in the development of drug-using behaviours of young people. Stage one involved the use of beer or wine, stage two involved use of *tobacco* and spirits, stage three referred to the use marijuana, and stage four related to the use of harder illegal drugs (Kandel, 1975). According to Kandel, and various co-workers, the developmental sequence in young peoples' drug use comprised a simple Guttman-scale in which individuals using the substances in any one stage will also tend to have used the substances in the lower stage but not those included in the higher stage. Characterized in this way young peoples' use of the legal substances were seen as a precursor to their use of illegal substances not in the sense of the use of the illegal drugs being determined by the use of the legal drugs, but in the sense that those who have used the illegal drugs will almost certainly have had prior use of the legal drugs. Similarly, the majority of those who have used the harder illegal drugs will also tend to have used marijuana at an earlier point in their life.

It is important to note that the sequencing Kandel identified was based on empirical observation rather than theoretical inference. In a follow-up survey of US adolescents, 27% of the high school students who had smoked and drank *alcohol* progressed to marijuana when they were followed up five months later, whereas only 2% of those who had not used any of the legal substances used marijuana by the time of the five-month follow-up interview (Kandel, 1980).

As well as noting the existence of this developmental sequence in young peoples' drug use, Kandel also identified the existence of particular psychosocial variables that influenced the onset and progression between drug-using stages. Four variables appeared to be key in explaining individuals' progression along the drug-using continuum. These were parental influence, peer influence, adolescent involvement in minor acts of deviancy, and adolescent beliefs:

> Adolescent beliefs and values favourable to the use of marihuana and association with marihuana using peers are the strongest predictors of initiation into marihuana. Poor relations with parents, feelings of depression and exposure to drug using peers are most important for predicting initiation into illicit drugs other than marihuana. (Kandel, 1980, p. 124)

Stated in this way it may seem surprising that Kandel's characterization of a gateway effect has generated the controversy, which it has over the years. However, the very notion of that the use of certain substances may increase the likelihood of individual's using other substances is still being hotly disputed today, nearly 40 years after the thesis was originally proposed. Moore and colleagues, for example, undertook *research* on young peoples' patterns of drug use in the north of England in 2011 and found that many of their respondents were using a version of the gateway thesis in describing the development of the drug-using behaviours amongst their friends (Moore *et al.*, 2011).

At the heart of the controversy is the question of whether the movement between drug use stages is one of causality or association. There is little doubt that *cannabis* use is associated with the use of harder drugs, as evidenced by the fact that there are few individuals who have used *heroin* or cocaine who have not previously used cannabis. The fact that there is an association between cannabis and heroin or cocaine is not the same as identifying a causal relation between the different drugs. In weighing the *evidence* of a possible causal effect between the use of cannabis and the later use of other harder illegal drugs it is important to acknowledge, as Kandel does, that even if there were a causal relationship this does not mean that the use of harder drugs (heroin or cocaine) is an inevitable outcome of the prior use of cannabis (Kandel, 2003). Causality is not the same thing as inevitability and it is entirely possible that a relationship of causality may exist between the use of cannabis and the use of other harder drugs without all of the individuals who have used cannabis progressing to the use of heroin or cocaine.

Some of the strongest evidence of a relationship between use of cannabis and later use of other illegal drugs has come from research involving same sex twins who were discordant in terms of whether or not they had used cannabis (Lynskey et al., 2003). The aim of one such study was to assess whether the association between cannabis use and the use of other drugs remained when genetic factors and environmental factors were controlled. According to Lynskey et al.,

> The results of our co-twin analyses indicated that early initiation of cannabis use was associated with significantly increased risk for other drug use and dependence and were consistent with early cannabis use having a causal role as a risk factor for other drug use and for any drug abuse or dependence. (Lynskey et al., 2003, p. 431)

The researchers on this study acknowledge that even in the face of the evidence for some sort of causal relationship between early use of cannabis, and later use of other drugs, the mechanism through which that causal influence is exerted is by no means clear. They point to three possible mechanisms: (1) the inclination to move from cannabis use to the use of other drugs may occur because the individual feels a need/desire to repeat and extend what he or she sees as having been the pleasurable experience of his or her cannabis use, (2) individuals may perceive the use of other drugs to be less risky as a result of the fact that their prior use of cannabis has not resulted in any particularly adverse outcome, (3) as a result of the individual having had access to cannabis his or her access to other drugs may also become possible. As the authors of this study point out, regardless of what factors are actually influencing the progression from cannabis use to the use of other drugs 'it is apparent that young people who initiate cannabis use at an early age are at heightened risk for progressing to other drug use and drug dependence' (Lynskey et al., 2003).

KEY TEXTS

- Kandel, D. (1975) 'Stages in Adolescent Involvement in Drug Use', *Science*, 190: pp. 912–914
- Kandel, D. (1980) 'Developmental Stages in Adolescent Drug Involvement' in D. Lettieri, M. Sayers, H. Pearson (eds), *Theories on Drug Abuse: Selected Contemporary Perspective* (NIDA Research Monograph 30)
- Kandel, D. (2003) 'Does Marijuana Use Cause the Use of Other Drugs', *Journal of the American Medical Association*, 289 (4): pp. 482–483
- Lynskey, M. *et al.* (2003) 'Escalation of Drug Use in Early Onset Cannabis Users vs Co-Twin Controls', *Journal of the American Medical Association*, 289: pp. 427–433

h

harm reduction

SEE ALSO addiction; EMCDDA; international treaties; recovery; stigma; strategies; zero tolerance

The notion of reducing drug related harm has been the single most influential idea impacting upon the substance misuse field over the last 30 or so years. It is an idea that virtually overnight reshaped the thinking, practice, policies, and funding directed at tackling the use of illegal drugs. What started out as little more than an assertion from the UK Advisory Council on the Misuse of Drugs that 'the spread of *HIV* is a greater danger to individual and public health than drug misuse' became a drug policy mantra and, in a remarkably short time, a global social movement.

The fear, prevalent in the mid-1980s and early 1990s, was that the United Kingdom was on the verge of an epidemic of HIV. That anxiety was fuelled by the results of *research* from Edinburgh, Scotland which revealed that a staggering 50% of *injecting* drug users in contact with an Edinburgh general practitioner were HIV positive (Robertson *et al.*, 1986). Although subsequent research on a wider sample of Edinburgh injectors identified a lower level of infection than Robertson's own research, the findings from these studies sent a shock wave round the world – if half of the injecting drug users in a developed Western city could be HIV positive then there was no way of knowing just how far the virus could spread beyond any specific high risk group (Davies *et al.*, 1995). Within the context of that fear, considerable resources were directed at reducing drug injectors' risks of acquiring and spreading HIV infection. The following are some of the new services which were developed.

- **Advice on safer injecting practices:** Services were developed that involved providing drug injectors with advice on how to inject more safely, how to avoid sharing injecting equipment and how to sterilize injecting equipment. Within the United States, bleach distribution programmes were developed to enable injecting drug users to sterilize their injecting equipment in an attempt to reduce their chances of becoming HIV positive. Those programmes were especially important given the fact that needle and syringe exchange programmes were (and remain) illegal within the United States (Abdul-Quader *et al.*, 2003).

- **Needle and syringe exchange:** The most obvious innovation in the wake of the fears over the spread of HIV infection amongst injecting drug users was the development of needle and syringe exchange clinics. These clinics operated from a variety of locations enabled injecting drug users to exchange their previously used injecting equipment for new equipment, and in doing so, to reduce their chances of acquiring infection (Stimson *et al.*, 1988).

- *Methadone prescribing:* One of the challenges that health services faced in the early days of the HIV epidemic was one attracting more drug users into *treatment* and retaining contact with them. In the period before the HIV epidemic drug services were focused mainly on treating individuals for their drug *addiction*. Many of the services available at that time were relatively hard to access with drug users often being required to demonstrate their commitment to 'coming off' drugs as a prelude to being provided with access to services. Within the context of the fears around HIV infection, much greater emphasis came to be placed on ensuring that as many drug users as possible could contact services, irrespective of their level of motivation. Prescribing substitute opiate drugs such methadone became one of the main ways of attracting drug users into services and encouraging drug users to remain in contact with those services.

- *Safe injecting centres:* One of the most controversial harm reduction services are the safe injecting centres where individuals can inject black market drugs under some level of medical supervision (Hedrich, 2004). Such centres are operating in a variety of European locations including Germany, Switzerland, the Netherlands, as well as in Australia and Canada. Within Canada, the safe injecting centre in Vancouver (Insite) has been running continuously since 2003 though it has been the subject

65

of heated debate and recurring threats of closure (Clement, 2008; Mangham, 2007). Within Australia, the Kings Cross safe injecting centre opened in 2001 and has similarly excited heated debate. The advocates of safe injecting centres have argued that the initiative has saved the lives of many addicts who might otherwise have overdosed or acquired some life-threatening infection. By contrast, the critics of safe injecting centres have suggested that they are in effect facilitating the use of illegal drugs (Mangham, 2007).

- *Heroin* **prescribing:** Whilst the provision of safe injecting centres has been seen as a step too far in the development of harm reduction services in many countries (including the UK) there has been a growing acceptance of the merits of prescribing heroin to drug users who are dependent upon the drug and who have failed to benefit from the wide range of drug treatment services that have otherwise been provided to them. Where research has been undertaken on the prescribing of heroin to dependent drug users there are indications of a positive effect in facilitating individuals' reduced criminality and reduced illegal drug use (Strang *et al.*, 2010). Nevertheless, doubts remain in the mind of many people as to whether providing heroin addicts with access to heroin on prescription actually amounts to treatment in the normal sense of the word (McKeganey, 2008).

Although harm reduction has had a profound influence on drug policy and provision over the last 30 years there is a distinct sense within the United Kingdom that its influence is beginning to reduce. The current UK drug strategy, for example, outlines in an introductory comment from the Home Secretary, the shift from harm reduction to drug user *recovery*:

A fundamental difference between this strategy and those that have gone before is that instead of focusing primarily on reducing the harms caused by drug misuse, our approach will be to go much further and offer every support for people to choose recovery as an achievable way out of dependency. (HM Government, 2010, p. 2)

The challenge facing harm reduction in the future may well be in terms of identifying common ground with the recovery oriented treatment services and diluting its commitment to drug law reform.

KEY TEXTS

- Caulkins, J. and Reuter, P. (2006) 'Setting Goals for Drug Policy Harm or Use Reduction?' *Addiction*, 92: pp. 1143–1150
- EMCDDA (2011) *Harm Reduction: Evidence, Impacts and Challenges* (European Monitoring Centre for Drugs and Drug Addiction)
- Hunt, N. (2004) 'Public Health or Human Rights: Which Comes First?' *International Journal of Drug Policy*, 15: pp. 231–237
- Inciardi, J. (2000) *Harm Reduction National and International Perspectives* (Thousand Oaks, CA: Sage Publications)
- McKeganey, N. (2011) *Controversies in Drugs Policy and Practice* (Basingstoke: Palgrave Macmillan)

hepatitis C

SEE ALSO **harm reduction; HIV; injecting**

Hepatitis C virus (HCV) is very much the poor relation of *HIV*, attracting only a fraction of the *media* headlines, political interest, and funding that HIV has garnered. Whereas HIV threatened to spread to the wider non drug *injecting* population through sexual risk behaviour between male clients of injecting, drug-using female sex workers, Hepatitis C has largely remained confined to specific risk groups, most notably injecting drug users. Like HIV, Hepatitis C is a blood borne infectious disease that has spread widely amongst injecting drug users as a result of their sharing injecting equipment. The *European Monitoring Centre for Drugs and Drug Addiction* in its 2011 annual report has summarized the data on the *prevalence* of Hepatitis C amongst injecting drug users throughout Europe:

> Viral hepatitis in particular, an infection caused by the hepatitis C virus, is highly prevalent in injecting drug users across Europe. HCV antibody levels among national samples of injecting drug users in 2008–09 varied from 22% to 83%, with eight out of the 12 countries reporting findings in excess of 40%. (EMCDDA, 2011, p. 84)

Within some countries outside of Europe the reported levels of hepatitis C infection amongst injecting drug users is even higher than that reported by the EMCDDA. Within St Petersburg, Russia 95% of injecting drug users are thought to be positive for the Hepatitis C virus (Painstill *et al.*, 2009).

The disease causes major problems to the liver and whilst individuals with the disease can remain without symptoms for many years there is significant risk of developing serious health complications associated with the infection including liver failure and liver cancer. Optimal *treatment* for Hepatitis C infection involves a combination of the drugs pegylated interferon alpha and ribavirin over a period of 24–48 weeks. Despite the availability of treatment for Hepatitis C infection that can have a positive effect on the likelihood and extent of disease progression there have been concerns that individuals who continue to inject drugs are not being given access to optimal treatment as a result of a perception that these individuals are unlikely to complete the full course of treatment, or that they are less deserving than others as a result of being seen to have acquired their infection through voluntarily engaging in risk behaviour. Edlin has been very critical of the denial of treatment to injecting drug users as a result of societal and medical antipathy towards this group:

> Like the proverbial elephant in the living room it is impossible not to notice the enormous need for HCV *prevention* and treatment for IDU's, and yet there seems to have been a tacit and perhaps unconscious agreement in the conference room that their needs would not be spoken of. As a consequence, recommended measures skirted the margins of the HCV problem rather than addressing its core, and those most severely affected by the HCV epidemic received no help. (Edlin, 2004, p. 85; emphasis added)

Whilst there has been a determined attempt at a policy and guidelines level to open up optimal HCV treatment to injecting drug users within many countries this does not mean that those who have acquired infection as a result of injecting drug use have ready access to treatment. Mehta and colleagues (2008), for example, undertook a survey of Hepatitis C positive injecting drug users in Baltimore, a city where HCV is virtually ubiquitous amongst injecting drug users – 79% of the 418 respondents included within their survey had never even engaged in a discussion regarding HCV treatment with a medical practitioner, however 78% of the sample said that they were interested in treatment and only 21% of their respondents said they were not interested in HCV treatment. On the basis of these results injecting drug users may well be experiencing continuing difficulty in accessing optimal treatment for their infection thereby indicating the likelihood of widespread unmet need on the part of the large numbers of injecting drug users who are Hepatitis C positive.

The extent of Hepatitis C exposure amongst injecting drug users in many countries also presents a massive challenge in terms of prevention. Clearly in a situation where around 40% or more of local injecting drug users are HCV positive the risks of transmission in the face of even relatively low levels of equipment sharing is very high indeed. Within the United Kingdom, the Health Protection Agency has reported that 47% of current and former injectors in England and Wales are Hepatitis C positive and that amongst those who first injected within the last three years 23% are Hepatitis C positive (Health Protection Agency, 2011). The fact that approaching a quarter of individuals who began injecting within the last three years have already acquired Hepatitis C infection is illustrative of the risks associated with any needle and syringe sharing in a situation where HCV is widespread. However, despite the risks associated with such sharing there is very little indication that the current methods of preventing the spread of blood borne viruses amongst injecting drug users within the United Kingdom (needle and syringe exchange, counselling) are anywhere near as effective as they would need to be to stem the rate of further spread of HCV amongst injecting drug users. Recent research reported by the Health Protection Agency, for example, has shown that 21% of current injectors within England, Wales and Northern Ireland have passed on or received used injecting equipment in the last month whilst amongst those aged under 24 the figure is even higher at 30% (Health Protection Agency, 2011). Given the high level of Hepatitis C infection amongst injecting drug users within the United Kingdom, the finding that around one-fifth of injectors passed on or received used injecting equipment in the last month is an indication that services are failing to foster the degree of risk behaviour change amongst injecting drug users that would be necessary to reduce the further spread of infection amongst injecting drug users.

KEY TEXTS

- Edlin, B. (2004) 'Hepatitis C Prevention and Treatment for Substance Users in the United States Acknowledging the Elephant in the Living Room', *International Journal of Drug Policy*, 15: pp. 81–89
- Health Protection Agency (2011) 'Shooting Up: Infections among People Who Inject Drugs in the UK 2010 – An Update', November 2011, London
- Mehta, S. *et al.* (2008) 'Limited Uptake of Hepatitis C Treatment among Injection Drug Users', *Journal of Community Health*, 33: pp. 126–133
- Paintsil, E. *et al.* (2009) 'Hepatitis C Virus Infection among Drug Injectors in St Petersburg, Russia: Social and Molecular Epidemiology of an Endemic Infection', *Addiction*, 104 (11): pp. 1881–1890

heroin

SEE ALSO **addiction; classification of drugs; injecting; overdose; recovery; stigma**

According to the United Nations Office of Drugs and *Crime* there are thought to be between 12 and 21 million people who have used opiates at least once in the last year (2009) with vast majority of those using heroin. It has been estimated that the global consumption of heroin in 2009 was in the region of 375 metric tonnes (UNODC, 2011). Within Europe, heroin *prevalence* is around 0.6% rising to between 0.9% and 1% in the case of the United Kingdom, where it is thought there may be something in the region of 350,000 users. Within the United States, it has been estimated that the prevalence of non-medical opiate use in the general population is around 0.5%, however it has been estimated that in 2009 around 1.9 million Americans were diagnosed as dependent upon prescription opiates. The value of the global opiate market has been estimated by the United Nations as being around $68 billion in 2009. Within Western Europe the heroin market is thought to be worth around $13 billion and in the United Kingdom around $3 billion.

The health effects of heroin and other opiates are far-reaching with the drug associated with most of the addict deaths in the United

Kingdom. Opiates in general (including heroin) depress respiratory function, and in extreme forms can result in *death*. However, many of the health effects associated with heroin are actually the result of either the way in which the drug is used (injection), impurities that are associated with its production or distribution and storage (such as was the case in relation to anthrax), and the other drugs that users often combine with heroin. Where drug users combine heroin, *alcohol* and other depressant drugs (benzodiazepines) there is an increased risk of death as a result of the cumulative depressant effect of the substances involved.

Other health related effects associated with heroin includes irregular menstrual cycle, constipation, poor dental health, malnutrition. Opiates are associated with a high risk of dependency and with the user experiencing a range of withdrawal effects when use of the drug is reduced or ceased (stomach cramps, sweating, disturbed sleep, tremor and diarrhoea). Although the effects of heroin withdrawal have been described by some commentators as being very unpleasant, others have characterized the experience as little more troubling than that of a heavy cold or flu (Dalrymple, 2006)

In the case of heroin users who use their drugs by injection there is a risk of acquiring serious blood borne infections including *HIV*, Hepatitis B/C. Individuals who inject their drugs are also at risk of developing a range of injection site problems (abscesses) and serious vascular and heart problems. Within the United Kingdom, in 2010, 1.1% of current or former injectors are thought to be HIV positive. In relation to *Hepatitis C*, 93% of known Hepatitis C cases are thought to be acquired the infection as a result of their *injecting* drug use. The equivalent figure in relation to Hepatitis B is thought to be around 38% (Health Protection Agency, 2011).

One of the most controversial areas of *research* that has been undertaken in recent years has involved exploring whether some individuals can use heroin over an extended period of time without experiencing any of the adverse effects often associated with the drug. In 2005, Scottish *addiction* researchers David Shewan and Phil Dalgarno conducted one of the first UK studies of 'controlled non-problematic heroin use' when they interviewed 126 long-term heroin users who had not been in contact with drug *treatment* services. Research in this area was further developed by a team of researchers in London led by Hamish Warburton who carried out an Internet survey of 123 heroin users and interviewed 51 individuals who in their view had used heroin without any serious adverse effects (Warburton *et al.*, 2005). The drug users in this study described how they applied certain rules to their drug use which covered the frequency and amount of heroin they chose to use, the maintenance of other aspects of their daily life (*employment*, relationships) which created a barrier impeding the development of more serious drug problem, and maintaining a strong personal sense of their *identity* as being different from the identity of an addict.

In a follow-up to this study the researchers sought to explore whether the individuals included in their earlier work had gone on to develop a pattern of more chaotic drug use. The research team were able to interview two-thirds of those who had been included in the earlier study and found that most of their interviewees had actually reduced rather than increased their drug use. On the basis of their research, the study team suggested that:

> There are sub-groups of heroin users who are either non dependent or dependent but stable and controlled in their use of the drug. The study has also demonstrated how heroin users will abstain from using for lengthy periods of time without recourse to treatment services. (McSweeney and Turnbull, 2007, p. ix)

What this research was unable to elucidate was the question of how widespread controlled heroin use actually is, for example is the sub-group of controlled users tiny or does it reflect quite a large proportion of those who are using heroin at any one time. The results of the research provided a powerful corrective to the view that any and all heroin use is inevitably a staging post on the road to chaotic uncontrolled use.

KEY TEXTS

- Dalrymple, T. (2006) *Romancing Opiates: Pharmacological Lies and the Addiction Bureaucracy* (New York: Encounter Books)
- McSweeney, T. and Turnbull, P. (2007) *Exploring User Perceptions of Occasional and Controlled Heroin Use: A Follow up Study* (York: Joseph Rowntree Foundation)
- Shewan, D. and Dalgarno, P. (2005) 'Evidence for Controlled Heroin Use? Low Levels of Negative Health and Social Outcomes among

Non-Treatment Heroin Users in Glasgow (Scotland)', *British Journal of Health Psychology*, 10 (1) February: pp. 33–48
• Warburton, H., Turnbull, P. and Hough, M. (2005) *Occasional and Controlled Heroin Use Not a Problem?* (York: Joseph Rowntree Foundation)

HIV

SEE ALSO **harm reduction; hepatitis C; injecting; prevention; stigma**

In 1988 the Advisory Council on the Misuse of Drugs boldly asserted that 'the spread of HIV is a greater danger to individual and public health than drug misuse' and in doing so they changed virtually overnight the entire terrain of drug services and drugs policy in the United Kingdom and many other countries (ACMD, 1988). The origin of that concern lay in part in the *evidence* of the growing levels of HIV infection amongst *injecting* drug users in New York in the mid- to late 1980s (Des Jarlais *et al.*, 1989), however, concern in the United Kingdom moved to an entirely different level with the publication of *research* which had involved *testing* stored blood samples from injecting drug users in contact with an Edinburgh General Practice (Robertson *et al.*, 1986). This research showed that around half of all of the drug users tested were positive for the virus known to cause AIDS. Although subsequent research based on a wider sample of injecting drug users reported a lower level of HIV infection than the Robertson study had done (revising the estimate down to near 30%) the findings from both studies were shattering giving rise to the very real prospect that the United Kingdom could be overtaken by an epidemic of injecting drug use related HIV infection.

Although it could hardly be said that the conservative party in government at that time had been positively inclined towards injecting drug users, the fear regarding HIV was so great that it was accepted that a public health approach needed to be given priority over the criminal justice response to drugs misuse. As a result innovative services were developed with the aim of ensuring that injecting drug users had much easier access than had previously been the case to sterile injecting equipment. In addition, substitute *prescribing* programmes and outreach programmes aimed at counselling drug users on safer injecting techniques were rapidly developed. All of these services had the common aim of trying to reduce injecting drug users' HIV related risk behaviour.

It was recognized at this time too that many female injecting drug users were supporting their drug habit through working within the sex industry. In the light of that knowledge research programmes were rapidly set up within many countries with the aim of establishing the extent of HIV infection amongst female and male sex workers, what proportion of sex workers were injecting drugs and whether condom use was widespread or a rarity in commercial sexual encounters between prostitutes and their clients. In addition to the research studies that were rapidly set up, street based sexual health clinics were also developed in major urban centres aiming to ensure that women working within the sex industry were being counselled on the risks of HIV and provided with condoms and, if they needed it, sterile injecting equipment. Women were also being advised to consistently use condoms as their only way of both protecting their own health and reducing the health risk associated with their work.

Research carried out within the United Kingdom has consistently shown only very low levels of HIV infection amongst women working within the sex industry coupled with widespread condom use. Research in other countries, however, has documented significantly higher levels of infection amongst working women and lower levels of condom use. Research undertaken by Sarkar and colleagues, on brothel based sex workers in Kolkata, India, identified that 27.7% of the sex workers aged between 16 and 20 were HIV positive with the figure reducing to 8.4% for those aged over 20. The overall *prevalence* of HIV amongst the sex workers in this study was 9.6% (Sarkar *et al.*, 2005). In this study all of the women, when asked about condom use, reported consistently using condoms with their clients although on closer questioning 44% of the women indicated that they had not used a condom with their most recent client. Strathdee and colleagues in the United States surveyed prostitute women in the Mexican border region and found that many women reported earning more money for unprotected sex than for protected sex – indicating that there was a powerful economic inducement coming from clients for unprotected sex (Strathdee *et al.*, 2011). In one of the most innovative studies carried out, Egger and colleagues provided condoms to sex workers in various motels in Nicaragua as they arrived with their commercial sex partners. Once the women had exited the motel rooms the researchers sought to retrieve the condoms to assess the proportion of provided condoms that had actually been used. Of the 3106 condoms provided the researchers were able to retrieve 48% that had clearly been used. Interestingly the study found that the provision of health *education* material within the motel rooms actually reduced rather than enhanced the likelihood of condoms being used (Egger *et al.*, 2000).

Although in the 1980s and 1990s HIV was often regarded as a diagnosis of *death* by injecting drug users and others, in the intervening years with developments in combination drug therapies, HIV has come to be seen more along the lines of a chronic illness. Nevertheless one should not doubt the huge impact a diagnosis of HIV infection has on all those to whom it is provided and the very real risk in the case of injecting drug users, in particular, that their sense of fear and despondency on being provided with a diagnosis may increase their injecting risk behaviour. In addition, of course, it is important to ensure that injecting drug users are not excluded from optimal *treatment* on the basis of prejudicial attitudes towards their life style and risk behaviour.

KEY TEXTS

- Egger, M. *et al.* (2000) 'Promotion of Condom Use in a High-Risk Setting in Nicaragua: A Randomised Controlled Trial', *Lancet*, 355 (9221): pp. 2101–2105
- Robertson, R. (1986) *Heroin, AIDS and Society* (London: Hodder and Stoughton)
- Stimson, G. (1989) 'AIDS and HIV and the Challenge for British Drug Services', *Addiction*, 85 (3): pp. 329–339

i

identity

SEE ALSO **learning to become a marijuana user; recovery; stigma; treatment**

In the minds of many people *addiction* and drug dependence has simply to do with the persistence of behaviours beyond the point where those behaviours have ceased to provide pleasure and which actually cause considerable pain to the individual and those close to him or her. It is in these terms that we typically think of the addict as being no longer in control of his or her behaviour since if they were in control they would surely stop such a self-harming behaviour. But addition and drug dependence is about a great deal more than any one individual's excessive appetite. Addiction is also a social role with certain expectations as to how the individual will act. It is also about a sense of self – an identity and perhaps it is for this reason that every alcoholics anonymous meeting over the world involves individuals introducing themselves by acknowledging that they are an alcoholic. The first step on the road to *recovery* is for the individuals to acknowledge that they are indeed addicted.

The notion of somehow having moved from someone who uses certain drugs to someone whose life is controlled by their drug use is a shift not only in the physical pattern of drugs consumption but in the individual's sense of self-identity. It is in this sense that identity is such a powerful part of the drug user's sense of self. For the sociologist Anthony Giddens, one of the key components of identity is the narrative explanation that people offer as to who they are:

> The existential question of self-identity is bound up with the fragile nature of the biography which the individual supplies about herself. A person's identity is not to be found in behaviour, nor – important though this is – in the reactions of

others, but in the capacity to keep a particular narrative going. (Giddens, 1991, p. 54)

Similarly, Riessman has described the contribution of these narratives in the formation of identity:

Narratives allow us to create who we are and to construct definitions of our situations in everyday life ... a near universal form of order for our worlds, narratives allows us to make connections and thus meaning by linking past and present, self and society. (Riessman, 1994, p. 114)

The narratives that construct the identity of the addict may emphasize the fact that the individual no longer has the capacity to exercise his or her free will and is now driven by the drugs they have become dependent upon.

Just as the identity of the addict is key in the evolving sense of self on the part of the drug user the notion is also key in the journey to recovery:

Recovering from addiction is a highly complex and problematic process involving multiple personal and contextual factors. Although it is recognized that social support, self-efficacy, motivation, and the physical environment in which recovering addicts find themselves are all important dimensions that are involved in recovery, a fundamental task is the construction of a self-identity that does not incorporate the characteristic of 'substance abuser'. (Mackintosh and Knight, 2012, p. 1094)

McIntosh and McKeganey (2000) have described how the individuals they interviewed who had managed to overcome their addiction had done that in part through the process of creating a new non-addict identity for themselves. The process of creating such a new identity could involve the individual moving away from the area where they were known to have a drug problem, forming new social relationships with people whose own lives were not defined by their drug use, engaging in new behaviours and building a social world for themselves that was not constructed around the drugs that had formerly been such a central feature of their world. Recovery in this sense could be seen to involve the individual creating a new identity in and through the narratives of recovery.

KEY TEXTS

- Bailey, L. (2005) 'Control and Desire: The Issue of Identity in Popular Discourse of addiction', *Addiction Research and Theory*, 13 (6): pp. 535–543
- Mackintosh, V. and Knight, T. (2012) 'The Notion of Self in the Journey Back from Addiction', *Qualitative Health Research*, 22 (8): pp. 1094–1101
- McIntosh, J. and McKeganey, N. (2000) 'Addicts Narrative of Recovery from Drug Use: Constructing a Non-Addict Identity', *Social Science and Medicine*, 50: pp. 1501–1510
- Reith, G. and Dobbie, F. (2012) 'Lost in the Game: Narratives of Addiction and Identity in Recovery from problem Gambling', *Addiction Research and Theory*, 20 (6): pp. 511–521

injecting

SEE ALSO **harm reduction; hepatitis C; HIV; safe injecting centres; stigma**

Injecting is by far the riskiest means of drug consumption; administering the drug under the skin (skin popping), into the muscle, or directly into the blood stream. The health risks associated with injecting are multiple, serious, and in some cases fatal. There are risks of injection site abscesses – where the injection site itself becomes infected as a result of either the adulterants within the drugs being injected or the non-sterile needle being inserted. Where the drug user has crushed the drug being injected in order to get it into a soluble form for injection, there is the risk that non-soluble material coating the drug can cause an infection in the areas surrounding the injection site. Where the drug has been injected into the individual's vein, there is the risk of serious blockage and infection throughout the individuals venous system. Serious infections can be engendered in the heart as well as throughout the individual's body.

In addition to the health risks associated with injecting there are also significant risks, which arise from bacterial agents that may be present within the drugs being injected. The most dramatic illustration of those risks was the anthrax outbreak that occurred within Scotland in 2009 and which resulted in the deaths of 13 injecting drug users. Along with the risks associated with the practice of injection there is also the risk of drug *overdose*. Whilst it might be thought that the practice of administering a drug via a syringe might provide the drug user with the opportunity of directly measuring the amount of the drug he or she is administering (thereby reducing the risk of overdose), in fact the very practice of administering a drug of unknown purity directly into the blood stream carries an unknowable risk of overdose.

By far the most well-known risk associated with injecting is the risk of acquiring and spreading a blood borne infection – with the two most common being *Hepatitis C* and *HIV*. Hepatitis C is widespread amongst injecting drug users in many countries with levels in some areas (e.g. Luxembourg) in excess of 90%. In Denmark it is estimated that 52.5% of injectors are Hepatitis C positive, in Greece the figure is thought to be between 43% and 64% (EMCDDA, 2011, Statistical Bulletin).

Within the United Kingdom, it is thought that less than 1% of injecting drug users are HIV positive (Health Protection Agency, 2011). By contrast within Spain, the *European Monitoring Centre for Drugs and Drug Addiction* has reported that 32.5% of injecting drug users are HIV positive (EMCDDA, 2011, Statistical Bulletin).

In response to the risks of blood-to-blood transmission of serious infections many countries have developed needle and syringe exchange services that seek to reduce the likelihood of drug injectors sharing non-sterile injecting equipment. Some countries have developed *safe injecting centres* where drug users inject black market purchased drugs under some level of medical supervision. In addition to these services there are also outreach workers in many countries seeking to contact drug injectors on the streets in high drug use areas to advise them on safer injecting practices including, in some cases, distributing dilute bleach samples that can be used to reduce the risk of contamination of injecting equipment. These interventions, though numerous and well organized, have had only limited impact on reducing levels of equipment sharing amongst injecting drug users. Within the United Kingdom, for example, despite the provision of many of these services it is still the case that around, a fifth of injectors have recently shared non-sterile injecting equipment (Health Protection Agency, 2011).

In the light of the known risks associated with injecting there is a strong case for actively discouraging injecting and promoting non-injecting forms of drug consumption.

KEY TEXTS

- Mathers, B. *et al.* (2008) 'Global Epidemiology of Injecting Drug Use and HIV among People Who Inject Drugs: A Systematic Review', Published Online, 24 September, doi: 10.1016/S0140–6736(08)61311–2
- Rhodes, T. (2009) 'Risk Environments and Drug Harms: A Social Science for Harm Reduction Approach', *International*, 20 (3) May: pp. 193–201
- Rhodes, T. *et al.* (2006) 'Public Injecting and the Need for "Safer Environment Interventions" in the Reduction of Drug-Related Harm', *Addiction*, 101 (10) October: pp. 1384–1393

international treaties

SEE ALSO decriminalization; harm reduction; politics; strategies

At first glance it may not be at all obvious why drug use should be a matter of international treaties and regulation at all since the use of the various substances involved takes place within countries by individuals on their own or in social groups rather than between nation states. However, whilst it is certainly the case that drug use occurs within countries, drug trafficking clearly takes place between countries and therein lies the reasoning behind the development of coordinated international action to tackle the drugs problem. That international action really began with the 1909 International Opium Commission in Shanghai and has been formulated into international law with the Single Convention on Narcotic Drugs in 1961, the Psychotropics Convention in 1971, and the Convention against Illicit Traffic in Narcotic Drugs and Psychotropic Substances in 1988.

The concern behind the development of international cooperation and drug treaties was the widespread use of opium in China, which had been deliberately stimulated by a number of influential European economies as a solution to the burgeoning trade imbalance between Europe and China in the 1800s. At that time there was a massive growth in Chinese exports to Europe but relatively modest exportation of goods from Europe to China. As a result there was a major flow of gold and silver reserves from Europe to China. To redress that imbalance, the United Kingdom and the Netherlands set about stimulating a thriving opium market within China which they could meet by exporting opium from their colonies. The trade in opium was so successful that at its height around 10% of the Chinese population were thought to be addicted to opium. Inevitably that level of *addiction* produced massive political tensions within China and between China and Europe leading, in due course, to the two Opium Wars fought between China and Britain as the latter sought to protect its right to export opium to China. In the face of determined lobbying and mounting political pressure the International Opium Commission was convened in Shanghai with support from US President Roosevelt. Although the meeting did not produce any binding international laws there was a voluntary commitment on the part of participating countries to differentiate between the licit production and trade in opium for medical purposes, and the use and trade of the drug for illicit purposes.

The Single Convention on Narcotic Drugs, signed into international law in New York, 1961, bound the 73 countries attending the meeting, to impose criminal penalties for the cultivation, production, manufacture, extraction, preparation, possession, offering, purchase, sale, delivery, brokerage, dispatch, transport importation and exportation of the substances covered by the convention. Those substances included opium, coca, *cannabis, heroin,* and cocaine as well as a range of other drugs and drug products. The convention also required participating countries to indicate what level of the listed drugs they required for their own legitimate medical need and to abolish, over a 25-year period, the trade and misuse of these products. The Single Convention also set up the International Narcotics Control Board, which remains in existence today charged with the responsibility of assessing and monitoring international compliance with the various international treaties and conventions.

The Convention on Psychotropic Substances came about as a result of the massive growth in drug abuse in the 1960s involving such substances as LSD amphetamines and barbiturates. Although the Psychotropic Substances Convention sought to tackle the growth in the misuse of these drugs, in much the same way as the Single Convention had sought to tackle the trade in narcotic drugs, one of the tensions in the international regulation of illicit substances was the need on the part of producer countries to protect their economic interest in the production and marketing of the drugs that were being used for legitimate purposes. One of the difficulties the international regulatory regime sought to address was that of balancing the rights of producer countries whilst curbing the misuse of the same substances where they were being abused. In an attempt to meet that balance the Convention gave a greater role to the World Health Organization, which, it felt, was well placed to assess countries' needs for legitimate pain medication.

Finally, in terms of the international conventions there is the Convention against Illicit Traffic in Narcotic Drugs and Psychoactive Substances signed into international law in 1988. The key aim of this convention was to 'harmonize national drug-related criminal laws and *enforcement* actions around the world and to decrease illicit drug trafficking through the use of the criminalization and punishment' (Sinha, 2001; emphasis added).

The objections to the international drug conventions and treaties have largely come from those favouring some form of decriminalization or legalisation of illegal drugs and who perceive the treaties as an impediment to such a development. Martin Jelsma, a leading advocate of drugs decriminalization, from the Dutch-based Transnational Institute, has argued that whilst the conventions may have been originally driven in by the 'laudable aim to protect the welfare of mankind' over time 'the control system (has) degenerated into a war on drug users' (Jelsma, 2011, p. 16). Peter Cohen, a Dutch-based academic who, like Jelsma, favours the decriminalization of illegal drugs has sought to characterize the international drug conventions as being the core texts of a prohibitionist church, 'The international drug treaties are among the holiest texts of the Drug Prohibition Church' (Cohen, 2003, p. 215).

The Global Commission on Drugs has similarly railed against what it sees as the prohibitionist policies underlining the international drug conventions and has called for countries to be freed from the constraints of the international conventions and allowed to develop their own drug policies. Other critics have complained that the International Drug Conventions place too much emphasis on curbing drug production and trade and in doing so have restricted many countries access to legitimate painkilling medication (Nickerson and Attaran, 2012).

The criticism that the drug conventions have limited the capacity of signatory countries to develop more liberal drug policies, including approaches towards drugs decriminalization and legalisation, are undoubtedly correct since it is the very clear aim of the treaties themselves to seek to tackle the proliferation in illegal drugs use. As a result the treaties do not favour the development of policies and interventions that may be seen as encouraging or facilitating the use of illegal drugs. The International Narcotics Control Board has, for example, criticized the development of *safe injecting centres* believing these to conflict with the various international treaties that so many countries have signed up to (Travis, 2013; INCB, 2013). However, the critical views expressed by the INCB do not appear to have impeded the development of safe injecting centres needle and syringe exchange services, many of those services have proliferated within countries that are signatories to the international drug conventions (Germany, Switzerland, Netherlands, Canada). Where other countries have refused to countenance the development of similar services (such as the US) it could be argued that this is more to do with national drug policies than any influence attributed to the international treaties.

There is no doubt that the international drug conventions are an imperfect and partial solution to the fact that drug use and abuse are occurring both within and between countries. It is difficult to see how, in the absence of a shared international approach, it would be possible to make significant progress in tackling drug production and consumption across countries. Moreover whilst it is unquestionable that one can list the various shortcomings of the international treaties, it is important to recognize that any international legislative system has to find some way of accommodating to the particularities of individual nation states to manage their own internal affairs as they see fit.

KEY TEXTS

- Bayer, I. and Ghodse, H. (1999) 'Evolution of International Drug Control 1945–1995', *Bulletin on Narcotics*, LI (1 and 2): pp. 1–17
- Jelsma, M. (2003) 'Drugs in the UN System: The Unwritten History of the 1998 United Nations General Assembly Special Session on Drugs', *International Journal of Drug Policy*, 14: pp. 181–195
- Room, R. and Reuter, P. (2012) 'How Well Do International Drug Conventions Protect Public Health', *Lancet*, 379: pp. 84–89
- United Nations Office on Drugs and Crime (2008) *A Century of International Drug Control* (UNODC)

1

learning to become a marijuana user

SEE ALSO cannabis; chronic relapsing condition; harm reduction; maturing out; stages of change

Howard Becker is one of the founding fathers of drug use *research* and the author of one of the most widely cited publications in the addictions pantheon. 'Becoming a Marijuana User' published in 1953 was the first detailed ethnographic account of the journey to becoming a marijuana user. Becker's research which involved qualitative interviews with 50 marijuana users broke new ground in elucidating the contribution of biography to understanding the social construction of individual's drug use. Much of the drugs research being undertaken at the time of Becker's own work sought to identify the psychological traits common to those using illegal drugs. For Becker the flaws of that research were evident in the fact that none of the psychological traits identified were ever present in all individuals who were using illegal drugs, nor could it be said that the same traits and behaviours associated with individual's drug use were invariant over time. In the face of those flaws Becker focused on the developmental aspects of the individual's drug-using experience. Part of the process of becoming a marijuana user, according to Becker, involved learning with other marijuana users how to smoke the drug:

> Take in a lot of air, you know, and...I don't know how to describe it, you don't smoke it like a cigarette, you draw in a lot of air and get it deep down in your system and then keep it there. Keep it there as long as you can. (Becker, 1953, p. 237)

The first step in becoming a marijuana user, according to Becker, was to acquire the knowledge of how to smoke. Knowing how to smoke the drug, however, was not enough in itself. Rather the individual also had to recognize the experience of 'getting high'.

This involved two elements: first the effects associated with getting high must be present and second, the individual has to recognize them as the experience of being high. It is not enough simply for the experiences associated with use of the drug to be present. The naïve user has to learn how to recognize the state of 'being high'. Finally Becker identified a third stage which involved coming to see the experience of being high as pleasurable and as something the individual would want to repeat. This third stage, no less crucial than the previous two, requires the individual to push through his or her initial reaction to smoking the drug which may be far from pleasurable. Since marijuana smoking most often occurs within social settings, experienced users often educate the naïve user how to regulate their intake so as to avoid or minimize the unpleasant reactions that might otherwise accompany excessive use.

Although there is much within Becker's account that seems entirely straightforward to us now, at the time his description was produced it represented a radical departure from previous approaches to understanding individuals' drug use. Here, for the first time, was an account that explained individual's drug use in social rather than psychological terms.

As profound a change as Becker was proposing, his analysis has had surprisingly little impact on drug policies and drugs interventions in the subsequent years. Persuaded, as we now are, of the journey from being a naïve user to becoming a fully-fledged user we have yet to determine how that knowledge can be used to positive effect in terms of drug *treatment* or drug *prevention*. The lack of impact in these areas may be because Becker himself had little interest in the way in which 'the establishment' could regulate and respond to individuals' behaviour. His was an ethnography of America's drug use culture, rather than an examination of how that culture could be controlled or regulated by others. Becker's allegiance in the paper 'Becoming a Marijuana User' was very much with the individual drug user rather than the institutions of social control.

In a later paper Becker posed the question, which he felt social scientists should address, 'Who's Side Are We On?' (Becker, 1967). For Becker, social research involved a choice as to where ones allegiance lay, that is with the powerful or the powerless. His own analysis of the journey to becoming a marijuana user showed that in his work he was more aligned with the interests of the drug user rather than the organs of state control.

KEY TEXTS

- Järvinen, M. and Ravn, S. (2011) 'From Recreational to Regular Drug Use: Qualitative Interviews with Young Clubbers', *Sociology of Health and Illness*, 33 (4) May: pp. 554–569
- Kaye, K. (2012) 'De-Medicalizing Addiction: Toward Biocultural Understandings', *Advances in Medical Sociology*, ISSN: 1057–6290
- Østergaard, J. (2009) 'Learning to become an Alcohol User: Adolescents Taking Risks and Parents Living with Uncertainty', *Addiction Research and Theory*, 17 (1): pp. 30–53

legal highs

SEE ALSO **classification of drugs; enforcement; international treaties; prevention**

Legal highs are to the world of illicit drugs what digital transmission has been to analogue television. Just as digital broadcasting has led to the proliferation of hundreds of channels, the world of legal high drugs has opened up a seemingly limitless reservoir of new drugs with names that convey nothing of what the drugs themselves contain (Ivory Wave, Spice, Annihilation, BenzoFury, Bubbles, Meow-Meow). Through the use of these names what is being marketed here is not so much a chemical substance but a lifestyle experience.

The UK Advisory Council on the Misuse of Drugs has defined legal highs in the following terms:

> Psychoactive drugs which are not prohibited by the United Nations Single convention on Narcotic Drugs or by the Misuse of Drugs Act 1971, and which people in the UK are seeking for intoxicant use. (ACMD, 2011, p. 10)

According to the ACMD legal high drugs can be characterized in the following four ways: (1) they are substances whose name often convey very little about their chemical constituents; (2) they are designed to produce similar reactions to illegal drugs but are sufficiently different in their chemical composition to make the drugs legal; (3) they are related to medicines; and (4) they may be based upon herbal or fungal material.

Although the information on the extent to which legal high drugs are being consumed is by no means extensive there are indications that many of these drugs have rapidly attained a level of consumption that in time could eclipse many of the more traditional substances. The 2011 British *Crime* Survey, for example, shows that Mephedrone was the third most widely used drug amongst 16 to 24 year olds, and that 4.4% of respondents overall had used the drug (BCS, 2011). On the basis of surveys carried out in the north of England, Measham and colleagues provided an illustration of the penetration of the legal high drugs into the night-time economy with 11% of young people in their sample reporting having used Mephedrone in the last year, 16% reporting having used Bubble, 6% having used legal herbal high drugs, and 18% having used Ecstasy in the last year (Measham *et al.*, 2011).

In a similar survey carried out with 308 respondents attending two gay friendly dance clubs in South London in 2010, Measham and colleagues were able to collect data on the extent of the sample's drug use. Despite their expectation of higher than average levels of reported drug use, the researchers were still surprised by what they found: 69% of clubbers had used Ecstasy in the last year, 54% had used Mephedrone, 34% had used GHB and 16% had used NRG-1; 73% of the clubbers had used cocaine in the last year, and 77% had used *cannabis* (Measham *et al.* 2011b).

Although there is relatively little information on the source of the legal high drugs it has been widely reported that many of the substances are being produced in laboratories within China, marketed through the internet and advertised as plant food, bath salts, fish food, room odorizers. The growth of legal highs is seen to present a number of serious risks. First, there is the health risks of young people consuming substances about which very little is known of their chemical constituents. In the absence of more detailed knowledge, on the part of consumers, as to exactly what is in the drugs they are consuming there is a risk that young people will consume these substances at a dosage level that is highly dangerous. Data are already available on a number of deaths associated with certain of the legal high drugs. The Advisory Council on the Misuse of Drugs report on the legal high drugs contains data on 42 deaths associated with the drug Mephedrone.

Along with the data on deaths there are also indications of acute drug toxicity associated with legal high substances, particularly where individuals are combining multiple substances. Gee and colleagues (2010) have reported on two cases of multi-organ failure associated with the use of the drug BZP combined with Ecstasy in New Zealand. Similarly, Balmelli and colleagues have reported on the dangers of BZP combined with Ecstasy (Balmelli *et al.*, 2001). Regan and colleagues undertook a retrospective review of admissions to one of the main emergency hospitals in Aberdeen Scotland between 1 December 2009 and 16 April 2010 and identified 89 subjects who were admitted as a result of acute toxicity associated with their use of Mephedrone (Regan *et al.*, 2011).

There are discussions underway within the United Kingdom, and in other countries, as to whether the legal high drugs should be the subject of temporary bans in advance of the availability of detailed and accurate information on what the drugs themselves contain and how harmful they are. Such temporary bans would enable governments to place restrictions upon the sale of legal highs almost immediately on becoming aware of their existence with the bans being lifted once there is clear *evidence* on the nature of the substances involved. Part of the fear around the policy of instituting temporary bans is the possibility that in advance of such a ban being applied users might stock up on specific legal high products.

Despite such fears there are indications that making the legal high drugs illegal does result in a reduction in the extent of their use. A survey of the use of the legal high Mephedrone undertaken by Mixmag reported data on levels of use prior to and following on from the UK government ban. In the period before the ban was announced 34% of respondents reported having used the drug in the previous month, with that figure reducing to 25% in the period following the ban (Mixmag, 2011).

KEY TEXTS

- Advisory Council on the Misuse of Drugs (2011) *Consideration of the Novel Psychoactive Substances* (Legal Highs)
- European Monitoring Centre for Drugs and Drug Addiction (2011) 'New Drugs and Emerging Trends', Annual Report for 2011 (EMCDDA)

- Measham, F., Moore, K. and Ostergaard, J. (2011) 'Mephedrone Bubble and Unidentified White Powders: The Contested Identifies of Synthetic "Legal Highs"', *Drugs and Alcohol Today*, 11 (3): pp. 137–147
- Measham, F. *et al.* (2011) 'The Rise in Legal Highs: Prevalence and Patterns in the Use of Illegal Drugs and First and Second-Generation Legal Highs in South London Gay Dance Clubs', *Journal of Substance Use*, 16 (4): pp. 263–272

legislation

SEE ALSO **decriminalization; international treaties; politics; zero tolerance**

Legislation refers to the accumulation of laws that govern the production, sale, transportation and consumption of legal and illegal drugs. Within the United Kingdom, for example, the key legislation governing illegal drugs is the 1971 Misuse of Drugs Act which identifies a wide range of substances covered by the act and which sets out the various penalties that are associated with the use and trafficking in the drugs listed. All governments enact legislation covering various substances proscribing some and accepting others. The reasons why some substances are regarded as legal (*alcohol* and *tobacco*) and others are considered illegal (e.g. *heroin* cocaine *cannabis*) is by no means clear-cut or based on firm *evidence*. Within the United Kingdom, for example, a number of commentators have suggested that given the fact that both alcohol and tobacco are associated with many more deaths than all of the currently illegal drugs it is illogical to proscribe certain drugs whilst leaving alcohol and tobacco as legal substances (Nutt, 2012). Similarly there has been a wide-ranging and now long-standing dispute as to the placement of cannabis within many countries' drugs legislation given a perception held by some commentators that it is a relatively harmless drug (Nutt *et al.*, 2007).

Legislation is also evident at the international level with various conventions setting out shared laws governing the production transportation and use of certain substances. The various international conventions set out under the auspices of the United Nations, for example, seek to differentiate between appropriate use and availability of certain painkilling narcotic drugs and the proscribed sale and use of the same substances for illegitimate purposes. It has been suggested, however, that the international regulation of drugs should be more appropriately a matter for the World Health Organization to determine than the United Nations Office on Drugs and *Crime* and the International Narcotics Control Board (Nickerson and Attaran, 2012).

Various countries have tried to develop some level of legal acceptance covering what were regarded as formerly illegal drugs. These initiatives are multiple in nature and on occasion confusing in their specifics. For example, the term 'decriminalization' tends to refer to the retention of the criminal law in relation to drugs trafficking but the acceptance that the criminal law will not be used in cases of actual drug use. By contrast the term 'legalisation' is often taken to be the complete withdrawal of the criminal law from any aspect of drug production, trafficking, transportation and consumption. The two broad terms of decriminalization and legalisation, however, have been supplemented in some areas with the use of such concepts as de-penalization being used to refer to the situation in which the use of criminal penalties for drug use has been removed in favour of the use of more civil penalties (e.g. referral to a drugs *prevention* session).

The strongest case which advocates make for a change in the laws relating to drug use tend to be that the persistence and in some areas the steady increase in the use of various illegal drugs stands as clear evidence that the existing drug laws have failed to curb drug use. The claim is also made that it is unfair for many young people to be criminalized as a result of what may in fact be only occasional use of a substance that is anyway less harmful than either tobacco or alcohol which are legal. However the opponents of the calls for legalisation or decriminalization often point out that the fact that none of the currently illegal drugs are being consumed at a level approximating the legal drugs of alcohol and tobacco that far from the drugs laws being a failure they have been a success.

KEY TEXTS
- Kleiman, M., Caulkins, J. and Hawken, A. (2011) *Drugs and Drug Policy What Everyone Needs to Know* (Oxford: Oxford University Press)

- Nutt, D. (2012) *Drugs without the Hot Air: Minimising the Harms of Legal and Illegal Drugs* (England: UIT Cambridge)
- Travis, A. (2012) 'Case for Drug Decriminalisation Rests on Failure of 40 year Old Law', *Guardian*, Monday, 15 October
- United Kingdom Drug Policy Commission (2012) *A Fresh Approach to Drugs: Final Report of the UK Drug Policy Commission* (London: UKDPC)

m

maturing out

SEE ALSO gateway thesis; normalization; recovery; spontaneous
remission; stages of change; stigma

In 1962 Charles Winnick published what was to become the first
study of the process of 'maturing out' of *addiction*. At the time that
Winnick undertook his *research,* there had been a number of studies
looking at the onset of drug-using behaviours but no research into
the cessation of those behaviours. The perception at that time was
that the chances of recovery from narcotic addiction was very low
and that once individuals had become addicted they were likely
to remain so until they died. The phrase 'once and addict always'
conveyed the predominant view at that time. Winnick's research
was to fundamentally overturn that perception by introducing the
notion that many addicts do indeed mature out of their addiction
(Winnick, 1962).

The research which Winnick undertook involved examining the
records of all of the narcotic addicts referred to the Federal Bureau of
Narcotics in 1955 and identifying those cases that had not reappeared
within the statistics by the end of 1960. According to Winnick it would
have been virtually impossible for anyone to have remained an addict
over that period and not have come to the attention of law *enforcement*
agencies. On that basis Winnick surmised that those whose details
failed to reappear could be considered to have ceased their addiction.
Of the 42,329 individuals whose details were recorded by the Bureau
of Narcotics in 1955, there were a total of 7,234 individuals whose
details did not reappear within the Bureau's statistics over the five-
year period. When Winnick looked at the data in terms of the addicts'
ages what he saw was that there was a clustering of inactive narcotic
addicts in the 26 to 43 age range with three-quarters of addicts having
dropped out of the statistics by the age of 36.2. Winnick speculated
at the possible reason why so many addicts appeared to have ceased

their drug use by the time of their mid-30s. It may have been, he suggested, that the individuals started their drug use in their late teens as a way of coping with multiple difficulties in their personal lives that may have been resolved by their mid-30s.

In the period following Winnick's research there have been a number of studies that have built upon the notion of an addiction career and charted the journey to *recovery* (Maddux and Desmond, 1980; Waldorf, 1983; Biernacki, 1986; McIntosh and McKeganey, 2000). For McIntosh and McKeganey the process of recovery (maturation) was seen to consist in the development of a non-addict *identity* on the part of the drug user (McIntosh and McKeganey, 2000). Other researchers have described the process of recovery or maturation as the addicts having reached a 'rock bottom' where they are confronted with the realization that they can fall no lower and that they must now either cease their drug or *alcohol* use or face the end of their life.

KEY TEXTS
- Biernacki, P. (1986) *Pathways from Heroin Addiction: Recovery without Treatment* (Philadelphia: Temple University)
- McIntosh, J. and McKeganey, N. (2002) *Beating the Dragon: The Recovery from Dependent Drug Use* (London: Pearson Education)
- Winnick, C. (1962) 'Maturing Out of Addiction', *Bulletin of Narcotics,* 14: pp. 1–7

media

SEE ALSO **evidence; politics**

It is no exaggeration to say that the media loves drugs – or at least loves stories about drugs and drug users. Pick up a newspaper on any day of the week and in all probability there will be a handful of stories to do with illegal drugs. Similarly, watch any of the 'cops with cameras' television programmes that follow *police* officers as they go about their day-to-day work and within a few minutes of the opening titles you will be watching the arrest of some inner-city male found in possession of a small amount of *cannabis* or *heroin*. And who has not seen the televized drugs raid in which body-armoured police bring their own version of shock and awe to the urban landscape as a drug dealer watches in stunned disbelief as their worldly goods are meticulously examined in the search for illegal drugs. Whether fact or fiction the media is only one story away from a drugs headline.

In terms of factual reporting there are four ways in which the media has a major influence on the drugs issue. First there is the near daily reporting of some aspect of the drugs trade whether it is the result of a major drug seizure or the details of some celebrities drug use. Second there are the calls made in and through the media to either strengthen or weaken the countries drugs laws. Simon Jenkins, writing in the *Guardian*, is one of the journalists who consistently argues for the legalization of illegal drugs and in his terms the costly failure of the war on drugs:

> It is wrecking the government of Mexico. It is financing the Taliban in Afghanistan. It is throwing 11,000 Britons into jail. It is corrupting democracy throughout Latin America. It is devastating the ghettoes of America and propagating Aids in urban Europe. Its turnover is some £200bn a year, on which it pays not a penny of tax. Thousands round the world die of it and millions are impoverished. It is the biggest man-made blight on the face of the earth. 'No, it is not drugs ... The curse is different: the declaration by states that some drugs are illegal and that those who supply and use them are criminals. This is the root of the evil. (Jenkins, 2010)

The journalist Peter Hitchens has accused the UK government of waging a phoney war on drugs in which there is no genuine attempt to use the criminal law to tackle the drugs problem but instead a liberal acceptance of the inevitability of individuals' drug use that is glossed over by little more than the rhetoric of tough action:

> They (those who argue for decriminalization) also say that a campaign of stern prohibition has failed and so must be abandoned. But it has not failed. It could not have failed, because it has not been tried. It cannot be abandoned because it does not exist. Advocates of *decriminalisation* have pretended – for propaganda purposes – that the existing state of affairs is cruel, repressive and draconian ... Drugs decriminalization, by its very nature, will make it harder to sustain a competent, thoughtful, self-disciplined, hard working and efficient society.

It will also create contentment and apathy where discontent and a passion for reform should be. (Hitchens, 2013, p. 11; emphasis added)

The third way in which the media exerts a powerful influence in relation to drugs is through the language used to characterize those who are using illegal drugs. Campaigning groups and researchers have drawn attention to the way in which the media often uses the language of 'junkies' and 'addicts' to stigmatize those who are using illegal drugs. Rod Liddle, a senior journalist working for the *Sunday Times*, in criticizing a report on *stigma* from the UK Drug Policy Commission, has maintained that:

It is not a good thing to be a junkie. That is why we stigmatise it – not because we are thick or unenlightened or right-wing. (Liddle, 2010)

However perhaps the greatest influence that has been claimed the media exerts on the drugs issue is in the fear it instils in politicians who favour legalization or decriminalization in private but who could never articulate those views in public for fear of attracting the critical attention of the 'right-wing' press (Dean, 2011).

KEY TEXTS

- Coomber, R., Morris, C. and Dunn, L. (2000) 'How the Media Do Drugs: Quality Control and the Reporting of Drug Issues in the UK Print Media', *International Journal of Drug Policy*, 11: 217–225
- Dean, M. (2011) *Democracy under Attack: How the Media Distort Policy and Politics* (Bristol: Policy Press)
- Jenkins, S. (2010) 'Our "War on Drugs" Has Been an Abysmal Failure. Just Look at Mexico', *Guardian*, 9 September.
- Liddle, R. (2010) 'My Daily Fix Is to Stigmatise These Smackheads', *The Sunday Times*, 19 December
- United Kingdom Drug Policy Commission (2010) 'Press Reporting of Issues Relating to Illicit Drug Use UK Drug Policy Commission Submission to the Leveson Inquiry', available at http://www.ukdpc.org.uk/wpcontent/uploads/

methadone

SEE ALSO **chronic relapsing condition; recovery; treatment**

Methadone is the drug prescribed more widely than any other for the *treatment* of opiate dependency. Developed in Germany in 1937 as a pain reliever it came into its own as a treatment for opiate dependency in 1965 when Drs Vincent Dole and Marie Nyswander published a paper in the *Journal of the American Medical Association* (JAMA) reporting on their observations of having used methadone in the treatment of 22 *heroin* addicts (Dole and Nyswander, 1965).

Dole and Nyswander found that by *prescribing* methadone along with supportive counselling to long-term heroin addicts it was possible for the drug users to experience a marked reduction in their craving for heroin, and to achieve a level of stability in their lives that had been absent during the many years of their heroin *addiction*. Treated with methadone, these long-term addicts managed to rebuild their relationships with long-estranged *family* members, to enrol in educational classes, and to achieve stable *employment*. These were impressive achievements on the part of individuals whose lives for years had revolved around their search for, and use of, illicit heroin.

In the period following publication of this small study methadone has become the default treatment for heroin dependency in countries across the globe. Indeed just about the only country where methadone is not available as a major (if not the major) treatment for heroin dependency is Russia, where the government and medical establishment remain unconvinced that prescribing a highly addictive synthetic opiate to individuals who have become opiate dependent amounts to treatment in the conventional sense of the word. In many other countries the vast majority of heroin addicts in treatment are being prescribed the drug. Within Scotland, for example, it has been estimated that approximately 22,000 problematic drug users are being prescribed the drug. Since Scotland is thought to have between 55,000 and 59,000 problematic drug users in total (both in treatment and out of treatment) this would suggest that the vast majority of addicts in contact with treatment services in Scotland are being prescribed methadone (on the basis that it is unlikely that more than half of the total addict population are in contact with drug treatment services). Within England it is thought that around 170,000 heroin addicts are being prescribed methadone out of a total treatment sample of around 220,000.

Methadone is typically prescribed to dependent drug users in one of two ways. One way is by prescribing methadone on a short-term basis to wean addicts off heroin – with the expectation that over a matter of weeks the individual will cease or markedly reduce his or her heroin use and their methadone use. The other, and more controversial way in which methadone is prescribed to dependent drug users is on a maintenance basis. Prescribed in this way the individual may remain on a methadone prescription for many years. Dole and Nyswander drew a parallel between methadone prescribed to the addict and the prescription of insulin provided to a diabetic patient. Within both cases it is assumed the individual will remain on the medication for the remainder of their lives.

Because of the controversy around methadone the drug has been subjected to more *research* than any other treatment within the addictions. The body of *evidence* has shown that addicts prescribed methadone are less likely to experience a fatal drug *overdose* than those who are not prescribed the drug (Kimber *et al.*, 2010), they are more likely to reduce their use of illicit drugs (Condellie and Dunteman, 1993; Powers and Anglin, 1993), likely to commit fewer crimes (Ball and Ross, 1991; Powers and Anglin, 1993; Gossop *et al.*, 2000), less likely to share *injecting* equipment (Ball *et al.*, 1998; Abdul-Quader *et al.*, 1987), and more likely to engage with drug treatment services and remain in contact with those services than are those drug users who are not prescribed methadone (Faggiano *et al.*, 2003).

There are concerns that the drug has been shown to be associated with a growing number of deaths amongst addicts (McIntosh, 2013; Webster, 2005; Johnson, 2012). Within Scotland, for example, methadone has been shown to be associated with 47% of addict deaths whilst in some parts of the country there are now more addict deaths associated with methadone than are associated with heroin (National Statistics for Scotland, 2012).

Along with the concerns at the rising number of deaths linked to methadone there has also been a growing concern at the length of time (often measured in years) that an individual will remain on methadone (BBC, 2005; Easton, 2009). It has been suggested that all too often individuals have effectively been 'parked on methadone', indicating that they are remaining on the drug long after it has ceased to provide any benefit for them. The grounds for that concern have been illustrated in *research* from Scotland undertaken by Kimber and colleagues (Kimber *et al.*, 2010). In this study the researchers were able to show that prescribing methadone to opiate addicts had a positive impact on reducing the risk of premature *death*:

> For each additional year of opiate substitution treatment the hazard of death before long-term cessation fell 13% (95% confidence interval 17% to 9%) after adjustment for *HIV*, sex, calendar period, age at first injection, and history of *prison* and overdose. (Kimber *et al.*, 2010; emphasis added)

However, this important study also identified what was described by the researchers as an 'inverse relationship' between the provision of opiate substitution treatment and the likelihood of drug users achieving long-term cessation in their drug use. Drug users who were prescribed methadone remained drug dependent for substantially longer than those who were not prescribed the drug.

The worry here is that a drug prescribed to dependent drug users with the aim of reducing some of the health harms associated with opiate misuse may be extending rather than shortening the period over which individuals remain drug dependent. The challenge facing prescribing services in the light of the Kimber data is to ensure that drug users are provided with access to medications that can reduce their risk of a wide range of adverse outcomes, whilst at the same time maximizing the chances of their eventual *recovery*.

Finally, there are concerns that by providing drug users with access to methadone on a maintenance basis drug treatment services may be adding to the sum total of the substances individual drug users are consuming rather than replacing one substance (heroin) with another (methadone). The evidence for this concern is to be found in those studies that have identified very high proportions of drug users on methadone combining their prescribed medication with street purchased drugs. Bloor and colleagues found that more than 80% of drug users were topping up their methadone prescriptions with additional illicit drugs (Bloor *et al.*, 2008).

The UK government identified the weaknesses in past approaches to addictions treatment (including methadone) that had failed to enable more drug users to become drug free, and which had left them in a state of continuing drug dependency for many years:

> Substitute prescribing continues to have a role to play in the treatment of heroin dependence, both in stabilising drug use and supporting detoxification ... However, for too many people currently on a substitute prescription, what should be the first step on the journey to recovery risks ending there. This must change. (HM Government, 2010, p. 18)

In 2010 the UK National Treatment Agency gave a clear indication of the sea change in attitudes towards maintenance methadone prescribing:

> No one should be parked indefinitely on methadone or similar opiate substitutes without the opportunity to get off drugs. New clinical guidance has introduced strict time limits to end the practice of open-ended substitute prescribing in prisons. This principle will be extended into community settings. (National Treatment Agency Business Plan, 2010–2011, p. 3)

The United Kingdom has seen a dip in the political popularity of long-term methadone maintenance prescribing with the discourse of drug abuse treatment in 2012 being all about recovery rather than maintenance on state provided substitute medication. What such a change means in reality, however, is far from clear. Methadone is prescribed by *doctors* not by politicians and it is by no means evident that the numbers of drug users being prescribed methadone has reduced, or that there has been a whole-scale shift away from maintenance prescribing as a result of the language of politicians.

KEY TEXTS

- Dole, V. and Nyswander, M. (1965) 'A Medical Treatment for Diacetylmorphine (Heroin) Addiction. a Clinical Trial with Methadone Hydrochloride', *Journal of the American Medical Association*, 193 (8): pp. 646–650
- Dole, V. and Nyswander, M. (1967) 'Heroin Addiction – A Metabolic Disease', *Archives of Internal Medicine*, 120, July: pp. 19–24
- Kimber, J. *et al.* (2010) 'Survival and Cessation in Injecting Drug Users: Prospective Observational Study of Outcomes and Effect of Opiate Substitution Treatment', *British Medical Journal*, 341: p. c3172
- National Treatment Agency (2012) *Medications in Recovery Reorienting Drug Dependence Treatment* (UK: NTA)

- Robertson, J.R. and Daniels, A.M. (2012) 'Methadone Replacement Therapy: Tried Tested Effective? Current Controversies', *Journal of the Royal College of Physicians of Edinburgh*, 42: pp. 133–142

morality

SEE ALSO **evidence; harm reduction; politics; religion**

According to the British journalist Peter Hitchens a country's drug laws should above all else express a moral disapproval about the use of illegal drugs. In the absence of a moral dimension, Hitchens has questioned, whether the drug laws have any purpose. Speaking of the laws proscribing the use of *cannabis* Hitchens has written, for example, that:

> The only reason for the existence of a law of this kind is a moral disapproval of the drug's effects on those who use it. If it does not embody and express such a disproval, then what is or was its purpose? (Hitchens, 2012, pp. 253–254)

Despite Hitchens's views that morality should underpin the drug laws in fact the moral dimension is largely absent from most countries drug laws. Within the United Kingdom, for example, there have been frequently repeated exhortations from influential bodies to the effect that drug laws and drugs policies should be based above all else on science and *evidence* rather than morality and personal preference. Similarly, whilst successive UK drug strategies have talked about the need to reduce the harm associated with illegal drug use, to support families, to protect young people, to encourage *recovery* on the part of those who have become drug dependent, and to punish those who are trading in illegal drugs these strategies have had virtually nothing to say on the morality of illegal drug use. In fact the public discourse around illegal drugs is largely devoid of any notion of morality with the predominant paradigm being that individuals should be informed about the harms of the various substances involved and largely left to decide themselves whether they will use the drugs that are being sold in most parts of the country.

The fact that possession of the substances involved is a criminal act has not for the most part led to a clear moral case being made by government or other bodies as to the immorality of illegal drugs use. Indeed to even speak of the immorality of illegal drug use will be puzzling to many people.

The lack of a moral dimension in relation to drug use is somewhat puzzling given that in other areas of public life we are very much inclined to emphasize the importance of morality. For example, in sex *education* provided to young people it is often stressed that it is important to show respect to the other person, to not make demands upon other people and to accept the individuals' right to choose whether or not they wish to engage in sexual behaviour. Within such education what is being stressed is a very strong moral code governing how individuals interact with each other. This is very different from what happens with illegal drug use where there is very little emphasis on the idea that individuals 'should' seek to avoid using illegal drugs and remain drug free. Perhaps the key difference here is the fact that we have a very clear sense of how people can be victimized by the demands of others and pressured into unwanted sexual contact. In relation to drug use, by contrast, there is very little sense of a victim – indeed drug use is frequently seen as a victimless *crime* such that there is no need for a moral view emphasizing the need to protect the individual.

The notion that drug use is a matter of individual consumption largely devoid of morality is itself somewhat odd. We know that the trade in illegal drugs has had a hugely negative effect on the economies of drug producer countries such as Colombia and Afghanistan and that in many ways the growth in the demand for illegal drugs has largely shaped the development of those countries. Similarly, we are well aware of the multiple ways in which drug *addiction* and drug dependence can wreak havoc on the lives of individuals, families, and whole communities. We are equally aware of the ways in which the drugs trade is linked to other forms of serious and organized criminality and in some instances is being used to fund terrorism. It is striking that aware as we are of the huge harm that is being caused by drugs misuse that we should choose to view drugs consumption (if not drug trafficking) as a victimless, almost harmless crime.

KEY TEXTS
- Euchner, E. *et al.* (2013) 'From Morality Policy to Normal Policy: Framing of Drug Consumption and Gambling in Germany and the

Netherlands and Their Regulatory Consequence', *Journal of European Public Policy*, 20 (3): pp. 372–389
- Hitchens, P. (2012) *The War We Never Fought* (London: Bloomsbury)
- McKeganey, N. (2011) 'Where Is the Morality in UK Drugs Policy', *Criminal Justice Matters*, 84 (1): p. 36
- Szasz, T. (1987) *The Morality of Drug Controls*, available at Drugtext.org

motivational interviewing

SEE ALSO **brief interventions; recovery; spontaneous remission; stages of change; twelve-step programmes**

Motivational interviewing is an approach that derives principally from the work of clinical psychologists William Miller and Stephen Rollnick, and which has been widely used within the addictions field. The approach involves a style/technique of interviewing that is designed to change how the individuals see his or her circumstances and which develops the individual's inner motivation to change. Rollnick and Miller have defined the approach in the following way:

Motivational interviewing is a directive client centred counselling style for eliciting behaviour change by helping clients to explore and resolve ambivalence. Compared with non-directive counselling it is more focussed and goal directed. The examination and resolution of ambivalence is its central purpose and the counsellor is intentionally directive in pursuing this goal. (Rollnick and Miller, 1995, p. 326)

The approach of motivational interviewing resonates with the *Stages of Change* model set out by Prochaska and DiClemente within which the motivation to change is a key stage in the *recovery* journey. Within motivational interviewing the notion is that individuals who may not yet see the need to change (pre-contemplation) can still be helped to develop the motivation to change by being encouraged, through a process of motivational interviewing, to focus upon their circumstances. This may include encouraging the individuals to focus on what aspects of their current behaviour (e.g. drug and *alcohol* use) may be impeding realizing their personal goals. The process of stimulating the motivation to change is not seen to come about through the therapist being highly confrontational or by being wholly non-directive. The aim instead is to work with the clients in jointly exploring their situation, and through an empathic process to stimulate the clients' motivation to change (Rollnick and Miller, 1995).

Within the addictions field clients undergoing motivational interviewing could be encouraged to focus on the place of alcohol, drugs, or *tobacco* within their life, to look at how the substance may be shaping their experience in an adverse way, and to begin to develop a sense that they can exert control over their substance use. Within this model of counselling the individual would not be chastized or challenged as a result of his or her drug or alcohol use, or badgered into giving up drugs, rather the aim is to work with the clients and to encourage the development of their own motivation to change, at a pace which the client himself or herself feels is appropriate but with the therapist retaining a clear sense of direction.

It would be impossible to overstate the influence that motivational interviewing has had in the area of counselling and behaviour change. There is probably no behaviour where some practitioners have not sought to use the approach of motivational interviewing to positive effect. The popularity of motivational interviewing is probably a result of the positive evaluations that have been carried out of the approach by a range of researchers. Rubak and colleagues (2005) undertook a systematic review of 72 randomized control trials into the use of motivational interviewing in relation to a wide range of disease conditions. These researchers reported a positive effect for motivational interviewing in 74% of the randomized controlled trials reviewed. Further, the researchers found that the motivational interviewing approach was particularly effective when it came to interventions targeting alcohol abuse *addiction* and other psychiatric diagnoses in which the motivational interviewing interventions outperformed traditional advice giving in 75% of the studies reviewed.

Similar positive results were identified by McCambridge and Strang (2004) in relation to the use of motivational interviewing with young people using illegal drugs. In this evaluation, 200 16 to 20 year olds using illegal drugs were randomly assigned to receive either motivational interviewing or a standard (non-motivational interviewing) educational intervention. The results from this study were particularly striking: in relation to smoking, the control group (i.e. non-motivational interviewing group) were found to have increased their mean frequency of cigarettes per week over the three months of the study by 12% compared to a 21% reduction in mean number of cigarettes smoked over the three-month-study period on the part of the motivational interviewing group. In relation to *cannabis* use the motivational interviewing group reduced their weekly consumption by 66% compared to an increase of 27% in the control group.

Given those results it is not hard to see why there should have been such widespread adoption of the motivational interviewing approach within the health field. However, one would also have to say that in some respects the results are almost too good to be true. This is not to suggest that the studies are fundamentally flawed so much as to note that if drug-using behaviours could be so easily reduced one might wonder why there is even a drug and alcohol problem at all. It may well be that whilst the motivational interviewing approach can facilitate change in individual's behaviour in the short term, this is not the same thing as ensuring that those changes become a permanent part of the individual's world.

KEY TEXTS

- Miller, W.R. and Rollnick, S. (2002) *Motivational Interviewing: Preparing People to Change Addictive Behaviour* (New York: The Guilford Press)
- Rollnick, S. and Miller, W. (1995) 'What Is Motivational Interviewing?' *Behavioural and Cognitive Psychotherapy*, 23: pp. 325–334
- Rollnick, S. *et al.* (2010) 'Motivational Interviewing', *British Medical Journal*, 340, April: p. c1900
- West, R. (2008) 'Time for a Change: Putting the Transtheoretical (Stages of Change) Model to Rest', *Addiction*, 100 (8): pp. 1036–1039

n

naloxone

SEE ALSO harm reduction; injecting; overdose; prison

Naloxone has been described as a Lazarus-like drug that can dramatically reverse the effects of a *heroin overdose* by blocking the receptor in the brain targeted by opiates and immediately inducing a state of withdrawal in those who have had the drug administered to them.

Research is currently underway within the United Kingdom, funded by the Medical Research Council, evaluating the impact of providing prisoners with naloxone kits prior to their release. Previous research has shown that prisoners are at high risk of overdose in the period immediately following their release if they resume their prior pattern of drug use. In this research random samples of prisoners will be given either active naloxone-loaded syringes or placebo-loaded syringes for administration in the event that the individual experiences or witnesses a potentially fatal drug overdose. The researchers will undertake repeat interviews with prisoners over an extended period of time to assess whether provision of the drug has resulted in a statistically significant reduction in the number of addict overdose deaths.

There are concerns around the use of naloxone even given its impressive capacity to reverse the effects of a heroin overdose. One of those concerns has to do with the possibility that some individuals may be willing to inject larger quantities of opiate based drugs in the knowledge that they have ready access to overdose reversal medication. At present it is not known whether this unintended outcome could occur but a parallel may be drawn with the provision of contraceptive methods – the possession of which will in some instances enable sexual contact to take place that, in the absence of which may not have occurred. There is also the difficulty of establishing how effective naloxone has been with regard to preventing overdose. While there is little doubt that providing drug users with naloxone will result in the drug being used, this does not necessarily mean that it will have been used appropriately or on those occasions when the drug user might otherwise have died. There is a strong likelihood that on some occasions the drug will be administered to injectors who appear to be overdosing but who in reality might have revived without the drug being administered to them. This is important because it suggests that simply knowing the number of occasions naloxone has been administered is not the same thing as being able to assess how effective the drug has been. The more demanding assessment is to establish, at a population level, that provision of the medication has resulted in an overall reduction in the number of addict deaths.

There is a further area of concern around naloxone which has to do with the fact that the overdose reversal effect of the drug is effective for only a limited period of time (approximately 40 minutes) such that it remains very important once the individual has revived, having had the drug administered to them, that they access appropriate medical services. What is extremely risky would be for the individual instead to inject further opiate drugs since what would then happen, once the effects of the naloxone drug wore off, would be for the individual to slip into an even deeper drug overdose.

KEY TEXTS

- Advisory Council on the Misuse of Drugs (2012) *Consideration of Naloxone* (London: HMSO)
- Maxwell, S. *et al.* (2006) 'Prescribing Naloxone to Actively Injecting Heroin Users: A Program to Reduce Heroin Overdose Deaths', *Journal of Addictive Diseases*, 25 (3): pp. 89–96
- Sporer, K. and Kral, A. (2007) 'Prescription Naloxone: A Novel Approach to Heroin Overdose Prevention', *Annals of Emergency Medicine*, 49 (2): pp. 172–177
- Strang, J. *et al.* (1996) 'Heroin Overdose: The Case for Take-Home Naloxone', *British Medical Journal*, 312: p. 1435

normalization

SEE ALSO **learning to become a marijuana user; set and setting; stages of change**

The notion that some forms of drug use have become normalized is most closely associated with the work of Howard Parker and colleagues at the University of Manchester (Measham, 1994; Parker *et al.*, 1999, 2000). In the early 1990s Parker's *research* team surveyed a representative sample of 14 to 15 year olds in the north of England. The survey revealed a world within which some forms of drugs misuse had become commonplace: 59% of the young people surveyed had been offered illegal drugs with *cannabis* being the most frequently offered drug (52% of the sample had been offered the drug), 36% had been offered LSD, 26% had been offered amphetamines, 7% had been offered cocaine and 4% had been offered *heroin* (Measham *et al.*, 1994); 27% of the young people surveyed had used cannabis in the last year, 11%, had used LSD, 9% had used solvents, 10% had used magic mushrooms and 10% had used amphetamines. Overall 31% had used at least one drug in the last year. Extrapolating these drug use levels to the wider population, Measham and colleagues suggest that up to 200,000 young people in the north east of England had used drugs.

According to Parker and his colleagues what was happening in the north east of England was that some forms of drugs misuse were becoming increasingly normalized. Normalization in this context referred to young people's growing accessibility to illegal drugs, the increasing availability of illegal drugs, the increasing rates of drug-trying, the increasing rates of drug use, the development of increasingly favourable attitudes towards recreational drug use, and finally a level of cultural accommodation and acceptance of the fact of illegal drug use (Parker *et al.*, 2002).

Influential as the normalization thesis has been it has not been without its critics. Shiner and Newburn suggested that the view that drug use has become increasingly normalized did not accord with how the young people interviewed in their own research talked about their own and others' drug use. Amongst these young people drug use was seen as something about which they felt guilty, and with many young people articulating views that were steadfastly against illegal drug use (Shiner and Newburn, 1997). According to Shiner and Newburn the image of increasing levels of drug use that Parker and his team were portraying was largely dependent upon lifetime measures of drug use, which tend to give an erroneous impression that drug use is widespread when in reality it remains a minority activity amongst young people.

Other critics have suggested that the normalization thesis has ignored more structural determinants of young people's drug use (MacDonald and Marsh, 2002; Pilkington, 2006). In response to the criticism one of the lead authors of the normalization thesis (Measham) and one of the leading critics (Shiner) published a joint paper in 2009 in which they sought to identify the common ground between their own divergent views as to the worth and accuracy of the normalization thesis (Measham and Shiner, 2009)

KEY TEXTS

- Measham, F. and Shiner, M. (2009) 'The Legacy of Normalisation: The Role of Classical Contemporary Criminological Theory in Understanding Young People's Drug Use', *International Journal of Drug Policy*, 20 (6): pp. 502–508
- Measham, F., Newcombe, R. and Parker, H. (1994) 'The Normalisation of Recreational Drug Use amongst Young People in North West England', *British Journal of Sociology*, 45 (2), pp. 287–312
- Parker, H., Aldridge, J. and Measham, F. (1999) *Illegal Leisure: The Normalization of Adolescent Recreational Drug Use* (London: Routledge)
- Parker, H., Williams, L. and Aldridge, J. (2002) 'The Normalization of "Sensible" Recreational Drug Use Further Evidence from the North West England Longitudinal Study', *Sociology*, 36 (4) November: pp. 941–964
- Pilkington, H. (2006) 'Beyond Peer Pressure: Rethinking Drug Use and Youth Culture', *International Journal of Drug Policy*, 18 (3): pp. 213–224

O

overdose

SEE ALSO methadone; naloxone; prevention; recovery

In the mind of many people overdose is a predictable fact of life for those who are drug dependent. In a survey of 312 *injecting* drug users in London, Powis and colleagues found that just over a third (38%) had experienced a drug overdose and just over half (54%) had witnessed a drug overdose (Powis *et al.*, 1999). In this study the factors associated with increased risk of overdose included being female, regular use of *alcohol* alongside other drugs, injecting benzodiazepines and having injected for longer (i.e. length of injecting career). Gossop and colleagues identified a slightly lower figure for the number of overdoses in their study of 438 *heroin* users – in this study 23% of respondents had overdosed in the past with an average of 3.6 overdoes per person. Amongst the heroin users who were injecting the proportion that had overdosed in the past rose to 31%. According to the drug users interviewed 55% of the overdoses were explained in terms of the individual having used more heroin than they typically used, 30% were explained in terms of the heroin being stronger than in the past, 28% in terms of the individual using heroin after a period of abstinence and in 10% of cases because the individual was deliberately attempting to overdose (Gossop *et al.*, 1996). In a study that involved attending hospital accident and emergency clinics when an individual was admitted following a non-fatal drug overdose Neale interviewed 77 drug users and found that 49% had suicidal thoughts before overdosing (Neale, 2000).

More recent information on the extent of overdoses amongst injecting drug users has been provided by Evans and colleagues (2012) who examined the risk of *death* amongst a sample of 644 young injectors (under aged 30) who were recruited in San Francisco in 1997 and followed to December 2007. Over that period there were 38 deaths recorded amongst the injectors, 10 times higher than would have been expected for the general population; 57% of those deaths were associated with fatal drug overdose. Similarly Coffin and colleagues reviewed all overdose deaths in New York between 1990 and 1998 – a total of 7451 accidental overdose deaths amongst whom 97.6% were caused by opiates, cocaine or alcohol (Coffin et al., 2003).

In a review of coronial files in London for the year 2003 Hickman and colleagues (2007) identified 148 overdose deaths; 78% of which were classified as accidental or injury by misadventure and 12% as *suicide*. Significantly 92% of the cases showed *evidence* of drug dependence and in 70% of cases there was evidence of injecting drug use; in 66% of cases there was evidence of recent heroin use, in 42% there was evidence of recent cocaine use, and in 32% there was evidence of recent *methadone* use. This study also showed that the typical pattern of overdose death involved the use of multiple drugs; amongst the 146 deaths for which drug use information was available there were 69 different drug use combinations involved in the deaths. Just under half of the heroin related overdose deaths had evidence of concurrent use of cocaine and a quarter had evidence of concurrent methadone use. One of the key factors associated with overdose deaths amongst addicts is unquestionably the combining of different substances in a pattern of poly drug use.

Interestingly this study was also able to show that in 80% of fatal overdose cases the individual had been in contact with services (accident and emergency, general practitioners or specialist drug *treatment* service) in the month prior to the individual's death. On that basis one would have to say that there was at least an opportunity for services to have identified those individuals who were at heightened risk of a fatal drug overdose and to have intervened at an earlier point. The authors of this report also emphasized the importance of drug users exercising a duty of care for themselves and their peers given that in the majority of cases (66%) the death occurred with other drug users present.

The close link between poly drug use and drug overdose belies the appealing but misleading impression that the overdose phenomenon itself is simply a matter of the individual having used more of particular drug than they have in the past. The term overdose is somewhat misleading since the death may have arisen as a result of the combination of drugs used rather than as a result of the quantity of any single drug ingested. As Darke has put it: 'An injection of heroin or cocaine that may be well tolerated when sober may well kill when drunk' (Darke, 2003, p. 711).

KEY TEXTS

- Bird, S. and Robertson, R. (2011) 'Toxicology of Scotland's Drugs-Related Deaths in 2000–2007: Presence of Heroin, Methadone, Diazepam and Alcohol by Sex, Age Group and Era', *Addiction Research and Theory*, 19 (2): pp. 170–178
- Merrall, E. *et al.* (2010) 'Meta-Analysis of Drug-Related Deaths Soon after Release from Prison', *Addiction*, 105 (9) September: pp. 1545–1554
- Neale, J. (2000) 'Suicidal Intent in Non-Fatal Illicit Drug Overdose', *Addiction*, 95 (1): pp. 85–93
- Powis, B. *et al.* (1999) 'Self Reported Overdose among Injecting Drug Users in London: Extent and Nature of the Problem', *Addiction*, 94 (4): pp. 471–478

P

parental drug use

SEE ALSO addiction; family; recovery; relapse; stigma

In 2003 the UK Advisory Council on the Misuse of Drugs estimated that there were between 205,300 and 298,900 children in England and Wales with drug dependent parents and between 40,000 to 50,000 children in Scotland (ACMD, 2003). There has been no official update on those figures although researchers have estimated that there are around 3.3 million children in the United Kingdom living with at least one parent who is a binge drinker, and 957,666 living in a household where both parents are binge drinkers. The estimate for the number of children living with a parent who has used illegal drugs in the last year is 978,205 for England and Wales and 47,631 for Scotland (Manning *et al.*, 2009).

It is impossible to know how many of these children are being harmed as a result of their parent's drug and *alcohol* use. According to the Advisory Council on the Misuse of Drugs 57% of drug-using parents do not have their dependent children living with them. In Scotland it has been estimated that as few as 13% of drug dependent fathers are actually living with their young children (ACMD, 2003). The extent of *family* breakdown evident from those figures provides an indication of the impact that parental drug and alcohol problems can have on young children. The 2008 UK drug strategy Drugs: Protecting Families and Communities highlighted that impact:

> Drug misuse can prevent parents from providing their children with the care and support they need and greatly increases the likelihood that their children will grow up to develop drug problems themselves. (Drugs Protecting Families and Communities, 2008, p. 8)

Professor Sharon Dawe, one of the leading researchers studying the impact of parental substance misuse, has observed that:

The outcomes for children raised in families in which either or both parents use illicit substances are generally poor. Such children are at high risk of child abuse and neglect, and early conduct and behaviour problems, school failure and adolescent substance abuse. (Dawe *et al.*, 2003, p. 299)

Street and colleagues undertook a five-year follow-up of 71 infants born to drug dependent mothers matched with 142 babies born to non-drug dependent mothers. The results of this study led the authors to pose a particularly challenging question:

One could question whether drug *addiction* and adequate parenting are mutually incompatible. A key marker of good enough parenting is the ability to put the child's needs above one own need. Addiction entails a need to satiate one's own needs above all else. (Street *et al.*, 2007, p. 206; emphasis added)

Although most of the *research* in this area has focused on the drug-using parents, some studies have sought to obtain the views of the children and young people involved. Kroll and Taylor, for example, undertook one such study and found that many of the young people were clear about the impact of their parent's drug use on their life:

The young people's data reflect the long shadow cast by the emotional and physical impact of parental drug misuse and its consequences for felt security, sense of safety, and day-to-day life. The majority (of young people) were in no doubt that using drugs and caring for children did not mix and had come to believe that drugs came first and were more important than they were. (Kroll and Taylor, 2008, p. 2)

Professor Marina Barnard is one of the few UK researchers to have undertaken detailed cross-generational qualitative research with families affected by substance misuse having interviewed parents, grandparents, and siblings (Barnard, 2007). Within the studies that Barnard undertook there was little doubt that the drug dependent parents loved their children, although there was equally little doubt as to how big an impact the parent's drug dependency was having on their children. Children within these families would often accompany their parents (most often their mother) in the daily search for drugs; they were frequently witness to their parents' drug use and frequently exposed to the illegality associated with their parents' drug use:

> The very people whom they looked for care, for certainty and security in their developmental journey through childhood were often those least able to provide it. The world they learned about through their parental relationships was not a safe benign place. It could be unpredictable, was often dangerous and frightening and it was difficult to know whom to trust. (Barnard, 2007, p. 99)

Bancroft and colleagues interviewed the adult survivors of parental drug and alcohol problems and described in detail the long-term impact of being exposed repeatedly as a child to the nature of parental substance abuse (alcohol and drugs). For example:

> Parents were reported as often wanting to discuss their own emotional issues with their children when they had been drinking heavily. Some respondents also spoke about emotional blackmail by their alcohol-misusing parents often in the form of *suicide* threats. Drunken declarations of leave and caring were resented as meaningless. (Bancroft *et al.*, 2004, p. 12; emphasis added)

As shocking as the impact of parental drug and alcohol problems undoubtedly is, there is at least some comfort in the knowledge that once these problems are known about services can intervene to ensure that the children involved can be helped. The research in this area though is by no means that positive in terms of how much services are able to repair the damage that families can inflict upon young people. Interventions provided to drug and alcohol dependent parents typically involve a combination of counselling, parent training, childcare assistance, and financial assistance. Most of the interventions are focused on the parents themselves with a much smaller number being focused on the children involved. Where these programmes have been evaluated the level of success in tackling the deficiencies that have been evident in the parenting practices are generally modest. One such programme (Focus on Families) was evaluated by Catalano and colleagues in the United States. This programme was pretty intensive with parents receiving 53 hours of small group training, five hours of family retreat and 32 twice-weekly 90-minute meetings. Children were involved within this programme and individual case managers supported the family over a nine-month period with one home visit and two telephone calls per week.

On evaluation this programme was found to have been helpful in building household routines, in reducing parents' drug and alcohol use, and in reducing family conflict. However the programme was found to have had relatively little impact on the children with some indication that the older children were more resistant to the intervention (Catalano *et al.*, 2002).

The modest impact that services can have in remedying the deficits arising from parental drug and alcohol use has given rise to one of the most ethically challenging questions that family services face, such as how long children should be left within an environment that is causing them harm and potentially long-term damage? Clearly, it would be a gross breach of both the child, and the parent's human rights, to automatically remove children where there are indications of parental drug and alcohol problems. Equally, however, it amounts to no less of a breach to leave children in situations that are causing them severe harm. There are no clear answers to this dilemma. Within the United States the Adoption and Safe Families Act initiated in 1997 sought to assist children living in circumstances where they were being harmed by parents. One of the elements of this act was to require state authorities to seek the termination of parental rights where the parent's drug or alcohol problem had resulted in their children being placed in foster care for 15 of the last 22 months. The aim here was to present drug and alcohol misusing parents, who were not managing to look after their children, with a clear ultimatum to address their substance abuse problem within a fixed time period or to give up their children for adoption.

Within the United Kingdom there is no equivalent time frame attached to the question of how long children should be left with drug or alcohol dependent parents. The policy view is rather that these families should be helped for as long as is required. However the sheer number of children in the United Kingdom now living in circumstances where they are being adversely affected to some degree by their parent's drug or alcohol problem means that the majority of these children are in all probability still being left to find their own way through the adversity of their family circumstances.

KEY TEXTS

- Advisory Council on the Misuse of Drugs (2003) *Hidden Harm Responding to the Needs of Children of Problem Drug Users* (London: HMSO)
- Barnard, M. (2007) *Drug Addiction and Families* (London and Philadelphia: Jessica Kingsley)
- Barnard, M. and McKeganey, N. (2004) 'The Impact of Parental Problem Drug Use on Children: What Is the Problem and What Can Be Done to Help?' *Addiction*, 99 (5) May: pp. 552–559
- McKeganey, N., Barnard, M. and McIntosh, J. (2002) 'Paying the Price for Their Parents Addiction: Meeting the Needs of the Children of Drug Using Parents Drugs', *Education Prevention and Policy*, 9 (3): pp. 233–246

police

SEE ALSO **corruption; crime; enforcement; politics**

In every country in the world, including those that have decriminalized drugs for personal use, law *enforcement* agencies are engaged in responding to drugs, drug users and drugs traffickers. Despite the ubiquity of drugs enforcement, however, the level of *research* directed at the impact of enforcement is only a fraction of that directed at the impact of drugs *treatment*. Whilst it would be misleading to describe drugs policing as an *'evidence* free zone' nevertheless given the level of public funding invested in drugs policing it is surprising that there is not a body of evidence as to the effectiveness of drugs policing that is at least the equal of that relating to the effectiveness of drugs treatment (United Kingdom Drugs Policy Commission, 2009).

Policing in relation to drugs, drug users and those involved in drugs production and trafficking involves a multitude of agencies ranging from those that have a generic policing role through to specialist drugs enforcement teams. Whilst in the past in the United Kingdom there has been a tendency in many police force areas to develop specialist drugs squads, increasingly this is seen as a responsibility spread across all branches of law enforcement encompassing individual officers providing community policing responsibilities through to specialist forensic accountants specializing in tracking drugs money often through complex international transactions involving multiple banking systems across different countries.

In terms of the street policing of problem drug users Lister and colleagues looked at the range of encounters between police officers and drug users and found that these were broadly of three types. First there were what the researchers described as informal encounters that served the purpose of 'communicative surveillance'. In these encounters problem drug users who were known to the police and who were encountered by the police in an unplanned way in the course of their day-to-day work in a local area would be asked questions about where they were going, what they were doing, and generally how they were getting on. These largely unplanned encounters were seen by the police as providing valuable ongoing intelligence about what was happening in their local area. In addition such questions also conveyed a clear message to the drug users themselves that they were under surveillance with the police knowing who they were and interested in where they were going and what they were doing. Only rarely, however, did these encounters result in the use of formal police powers – rather they were an informal way of demonstrating the power relationship between the police and problem drug users. The second type of encounter between police and problem drug users had a more direct and focused intelligence-gathering role with the police often seeking out specific drug users and requesting information on specific issues of local criminality. Finally, there were a range of more formal encounters between police and problem drug users which could include 'stop and search' activities, arrests for drugs possession. Typically, however, street policing of problem drug users tended to involve what the researchers described as an approach of 'managing drug users and the problems they were seen to present'. Often the element of management here involved identifying which drug users were present in any given area and frequently moving them on to another area. One of the drug users interviewed by Lister and his team described the experience of being managed in this way in the following terms:

If I walk up the high street, whenever, I'm being watched; and I don't even shoplift on that high street any more. I wouldn't shoplift in town any more but I still get followed. I get put on the radio-link and they follow me about everywhere. (Lister *et al.*, 2008, p. 26)

Typically the drug users interviewed by Lister and colleagues described their encounters with police officers as constituting something of an 'occupational hazard' which 'neither deterred them from taking drugs nor committing offences'.

In contrast to viewing encounters with the police as amounting to an 'occupational hazard' McKeganey and colleagues interviewed drug users who had personal experience of being involved in drugs raids (McKeganey *et al.*, 2012). Typically the drug users in this research described in detail the 'shock and awe' of being woken, often in the early hours of the morning, as the police raided their home:

> I hated it. It was nothing to do with me, I was just in the wrong place at the wrong time, and I got handcuffed and dragged up the stairs, strip searched, bend over, part your cheeks, you're like that 'Oh my God', you're just glad you're not black, your snatch is clean, you've shaved your legs and all that… The two women were big fat ugly bastards so I was like 'who cares man. I've no drugs on me', I just wanted it over as quickly as possible. (Site B: Interviewer; McKeganey *et al.*, 2012)

Such raids could be particularly stressful when, as often happened, there were small children within the property being raided:

> Scary mate. They come through me door about ten of them and I had me kids with me and that. And like I was bollock naked on the bed with me bird, you know me wife was there, the door opened like that, I was scared and the kid was screaming it was horrible, proper scary. I mean they wouldn't even let me go to my wean (child) who was in the toilet when the door went in. They've come straight in and they've cuffed me and they've cuffed the missus and they left me sitting and I says 'look mate', I says, 'my weans in the toilet, barricaded the door'. I says, 'I want to go'. 'No you sit there, I'll go and see her'. I says 'no mate let me, you do what you want but I'm going to go and get my wean'. I says 'you go in there she's kind of wanting help, it's really a horrible, horrible thing because the weans going, 'I don't

want you to go to jail', that's what really gave me a kick in the teeth'. (McKeganey *et al.*, 2012)

There is little doubt that through the power and authority which they can exercise the police can have a dramatic and in some cases lasting impact on the lives of drug users. There will be occasions undoubtedly when the experience of being arrested and gaoled can act as a catalyst for the individual increasing the possibility that the individual may begin to see the necessity of changing their lives. Equally there can be little doubt that the exercise of formal police powers, including the fear of arrest can result in drug users being less not more likely to contact drug treatment services (Lister *et al.*, 2008). Indeed the potentially negative impact of policing on the lives of drug users has led some researchers to suggest that particularly robust forms of policing may be a public health nuisance in themselves increasing rather than decreasing drug users' health related risk behaviour – for example, resulting in drug injectors hurrying the administration of their drugs as a way of reducing the likelihood of their being arrested (Fitzgerald, 2005). Whilst it may well be accepted that some forms of policing can result in adverse outcomes for individual drug users it is important to recognize at the same time that the police are also serving a community function in seeking not simply to assist the drug user into *recovery* but actually reducing the impact of illegal drugs on the wider society. The balance between the traditional policing concerns of protecting the community and the more newly adopted concerns of meeting the needs of drug users is reflected in the adoption of a more *harm reduction* focus on the part of the police and other enforcement agencies (see enforcement).

KEY TEXTS
- Aitken, C. *et al.* (2002) 'The Impact of a Police Crackdown on a Street Drug Scene: Evidence from the Street', *International Journal of Drug Policy*, 13 (3): pp. 193–202
- Lister, S. *et al.* (2008) *Street Policing of Problem Drug Users* (UK: Joseph Rowntree Foundation)
- May, T. *et al.* (2002) *Times They Are a Changing: Policing of Cannabis* (UK: Joseph Rowntree Foundation)
- May, T. *et al.* (2007) *Policing Cannabis As a Class C Drug: An Arresting Change?* (UK: Joseph Rowntree Foundation)

politics

SEE ALSO classification of drugs; evidence; strategies

Politicians have had a key role in shaping drugs policy for as long as drugs policy has existed though whether that involvement has been illustrious or flawed is a question that remains unanswered. Perhaps the most well-known example of the involvement of politicians within drugs policy was the passing of the National Prohibition Act (Volstead Act) in the United States in 1919 which outlawed the production, sale and transport of intoxicating liquor. Another example is the US President Richard Nixon, who has been described as the architect of the 'War on Drugs'. Within the United Kingdom politicians were involved in downgrading the classification of *cannabis* from Class B to Class C (and its subsequent return to Class B) and the development of a *recovery* focus in drug *treatment* policy and provision.

Whether one views these involvements in positive or negative terms depends to a large extent on whether one shares the political viewpoint underpinning the decisions taken. In the case of the so-called War on Drugs there are many commentators who would argue that the development of prohibitionist *legislation* in relation to illegal drug use has been a failure of public policy (indeed some would argue that it has been the single greatest costly failure in public policy) whilst others who would argue that prohibitionist drug laws have meant that drug use *prevalence* remains only a fracture of that of the legal drugs (*tobacco* and *alcohol*). Similarly, the classification and reclassification of cannabis by successive Home Secretaries within the United Kingdom may be seen either as a classic example of the provision of clear political leadership on a difficult and sensitive issue or the denial of the *evidence* in favour of political expediency. The development of a recovery focus in drug treatment policy and the downgrading of emphasis given to *harm reduction* will be seen as a positive development by those commentators who favour abstinence and a retrograde step by those who favour some form of drugs decriminalization.

The involvement of politicians in determining national drug policy has been extended to the international arena in the development of the international drug conventions, which have sought to enshrine in international law prohibition of the production, trafficking, transport, and use of banned substances. Whilst there are some commentators who celebrate the international drug conventions as the high water mark of cross-national cooperation in tackling a difficult social issue there are others who regard the conventions as an unwelcome imposition upon countries' individual capacity to develop their own drug laws. The Global Commission on Drug Policy, for example, has called for a replacement of the 'global drug prohibition regime' that would allow individual countries to 'experiment with models of legal regulation of drugs to undermine the power of organized *crime* and safeguard the health and security of their citizens' (Global Commission on Drugs, 2011, p. 2; emphasis added). It could be argued, however, that enabling individual countries to experiment with various forms of drugs decriminalization and legalization would undermine the very principle of shared responsibility that has sat at the heart of international drug control since its very inception (see international drug treaties).

There is little doubt that politicians will continue to have a role to play in shaping drugs policy, or that such a role will continue to be disputed by those who have a different view to that of the politicians in power at any one time. Equally, although there have been calls to remove the political dimension from drugs policy and to base policy in this area on scientific evidence it is doubtful that there will ever be a time when policy itself will be regulated solely by the available evidence.

KEY TEXTS
- Dean, M. (2012) *Democracy under Attack* (Bristol: Policy Press)
- MacGregor, S. (2013) 'Barriers to the Influence of Evidence on Policy: Are Politicians the Problem?' *Drugs Education Prevention and Policy*, doi: 10.3109/09687637.2012.54403
- Stevens, A. (2011) *Drugs Crime and Public Health: The Political Economy of Drug Policy* (London: Routledge)

prescribing

SEE ALSO **harm reduction; methadone; treatment**

The prescription of substitute medication is a key part of the *treatment* of drug dependency in most countries. By far the greatest proportion of drug users who are being prescribed substitute drugs are receiving *methadone* in response to a *heroin* problem with a much smaller proportion being prescribed Buprenorphine (with or without the inclusion of *naloxone* to reduce concurrent opiate misuse). *Research* has shown that those drug users who had been prescribed methadone have reduced *HIV* related risk behaviour (Ball *et al.*, 1998), they commit few crimes (Gossop *et al.*, 2000), they have a reduced risk of fatal *overdose* (Clausen *et al.*, 2008; Kimber *et al.*, 2010) and they remain in contact with drug treatment services for longer (Faggiano *et al.*, 2003). The UK National Institute for Health and Clinical Excellence reviewed both methadone and Buprenorphine and recommended that both treatments should be available with the *prescribing* doctor deciding which medication to use in each individual case. However NICE also stated that because Buprenorphine was the more expensive of the two drugs that methadone should ordinarily be the first line of treatment for opiate dependency:

> [T]he Committee concluded that the decision about which drug to use should be made on a case by case basis and should consider a number of clinical and patient factors including the persons history of opioid dependence, their commitment to a particular long term management strategy and an estimate of the risks and benefits made by the responsible clinical in consultation with the person. However, the Committee was mindful that methadone is cheaper than buprenorphine and therefore concluded that, if both drugs are equally suitable for a person, methadone should be prescribed as first choice. (NICE, 2007, p. 25)

Whilst there are clear benefits associated with methadone, research has also shown that drug users who have been prescribed the medication on a long-term maintenance basis may remain drug dependent for longer than their peers who have not been prescribed the medication. Kimber and colleagues, for example, found an inverse relation between being prescribed substitute medication (principally methadone) and the cessation of *injecting* drug use with those drug users who had been prescribed the drug having a substantially longer injecting career than those drug users who were not prescribed the drug (Kimber *et al.*, 2010). There has also been growing concern within the United Kingdom and elsewhere at the rising number of fatal drug overdoses amongst injecting drug users involving methadone. In Scotland, for example, methadone was found to be associated with approaching half (47%) of all addict deaths (General Register Office for Scotland, 2012).

In response to concerns at the scale of drug related deaths involving methadone attention has focused on the possible wider use of Buprenorphine which when combined with naloxone (as in the drug Suboxone), reduces the individual's need for heroin and their risk of overdose in the event that they were to use street based heroin on top of their prescribed medication. Research has also shown that those drug users prescribed Buprenorphine appeared to be psychologically clearer and more able to function than those prescribed methadone (Tanner *et al.*, 2011). Where the individual drug user is committed to his or her *recovery* it may well be that Buprenorphine is a more appropriate drug than methadone. However not all drug users either want or are able to cope with the greater level of psychological clarity that may be associated with Buprenorphine and at least some individuals may prefer the more psychologically dulled state often associated with methadone (Tanner *et al.*, 2011).

One of the enduring controversies to do with prescribing drugs to dependent drug users has to do with how long such prescriptions should be maintained. Although there have been periodic discussions about placing a time limit on the use of substitute medication (e.g. limiting methadone prescriptions to two years) in fact the most recent guidance from the UK National Treatment Agency has advised against placing time limits on the use of prescribed substitute medication whilst encouraging *doctors* to ensure that where drugs are being prescribed to dependent drug users that this is done with a view to enabling the individual to become drug free at some point in the future (National Treatment Agency, 2012).

KEY TEXTS
- Bell, J. *et al.* (2013) 'Evidence and Recovery: Improving Outcomes in Opiate Substitution Treatment', *British Journal of Medical Practitioners*, 6 (1)
- Clausen, T., Anchersen, K. and Waal, H. (2008) 'Morality Prior to, during and after Opioid Maintenance Treatment: A National Prospective Cross-Registry Study', *Drug and Alcohol Dependence*, 94 (1–3): pp. 151–157

- Hickman, M. *et al.* (2011) 'Promoting Recovery and Preventing Drug Related Mortality: Competing Risks', *Journal of Public Health*, 33 (3): pp. 332–334
- National Treatment Agency (2012) *Medications in Recovery: Re-orientating Drug Dependency Treatment* (UK: NTA)

prevalence

SEE ALSO **evidence; research**

Research to establish the prevalence of *alcohol* and smoking within societies has typically involved the use of social surveys in which individuals of differing ages are asked about the nature and extent of their *tobacco* and alcohol use. In contrast to the use of social surveys to establish the extent of smoking, alcohol and recreational drug use, establishing the prevalence of more problematic forms of drugs misuse has been a good deal more challenging. The reasons for this are not hard to fathom; in the case of *heroin* use, for example, there is a much greater likelihood of individuals concealing the fact of their heroin use when asked about this by a researcher. Within general population surveys that ask individuals about whether they have used heroin it is common to find that the number of people reporting such drug use is less than the number of heroin users in contact with drug *treatment* services – thereby indicating a substantial level of under-reporting. Within the 2010/2011 British *Crime Survey* it is estimated that there are between 43,000 and 83,000 people in England and Wales that have used heroin (National Statistics, 2011). Data from the National Drug Treatment Monitoring System for England, however, has indicated that opiates were the primary drug of use of 100,433 people accessing drug treatment services in the year 2010–2011 (National Treatment Agency for Substance Misuse, 2011). On the basis of these figures household surveys cannot be regarded as providing an accurate picture of the prevalence of drug use at the harder end of the spectrum even if they are accepted as providing a reasonably accurate picture of the prevalence of other forms of drug use and misuse.

There is another reason why the social survey approach is not an effective means of establishing the prevalence of problem drug use, which has to do with the relative infrequency of the behaviour. In the case of alcohol we know that the proportion of the adult population consuming the drug is well above 50%. On that basis it can be reasonably assumed that almost any survey one carries out is likely to identify that around half of the people surveyed will have consumed alcohol. In the case of heroin use because the overall prevalence of consumption is so low (less than 1%) there is a very strong likelihood that any social survey one undertakes of the general population will simply fail to identify anybody that has used the drug – unless the sample being studied is very large. For these reasons it has generally been accepted that the social survey approach is not a realistic means of assessing the prevalence of the harder forms of drugs misuse.

One alternative method for calculating prevalence has been to base the estimate of the total number of problematic drug users on the number of addict deaths within a given area. Such a calculation is only possible where there is reasonably accurate information on the percentage of addicts expected to die over a given time period. De Angelis and colleagues used information on the number of addict deaths in England to provide an estimate of long-term trends in the incidence and prevalence of opiate use and *injecting* drug use (De Angelis *et al.*, 2004). The researchers on this study were able to draw upon data from large addict cohorts to estimate both the rate at which individuals were ceasing their drug use (moving out of the addict population) and the rate at which they were dying (estimated to be 0.75% per year). This information was combined with the known number of addict deaths during 1968–2000 to plot the curve of increasing incidence and prevalence of opiate/ injecting drug use over that time period within England. On the basis of their calculations De Angelis and colleagues suggested that the prevalence rate of opiate and injecting drug use in England in 2000 ranged from 100,000 to 150,000 (0.5%–0.7% of those aged between 15 and 44).

The capacity to use data on addict deaths to estimate the prevalence of problem drug use relies on the accuracy of the *death* data being used. If the percentage of addicts dying has been over or under estimated then the error in that estimate will be transferred into the prevalence estimate and lead to an over/underestimate of drug use prevalence. In view of the difficulties of relying on information on drug related deaths to estimate problem drug use prevalence, researchers have developed other ways of estimating drug misuse prevalence with one of the most widely used being the 'capture recapture' or 'mark recapture' approach. This method is widely regarded as the gold standard for estimating the prevalence of hidden populations and is similar to the techniques used by field ecologists to estimate wild animal, bird and fish populations. In essence what field ecologists do to produce their estimates is to capture, tag, and then release a sample of the population they are seeking to estimate. By recapturing a second sample, field ecologists are able build an estimate of the overall population of the animals they are studying on the basis of the proportion of tagged animals that are recaptured in the second sample. If the second sample of wild animals contains a large number of the animals that had been previously tagged it suggests that the population of wild animals within the area being studied is small. Conversely if the number of tagged animals in the second sample is very small the suggestion is of a much larger number of animals within the study area. By repeating this series of capture, tag, and recapture over a number of cycles field ecologists are able to build up a picture of the likely size of the population they are estimating.

Researchers within the addictions have used a variant of the same approach to provide estimates of the number of problem drug users and sex workers within a given area. In one such study the researchers regularly walked round the red-light area in Glasgow talking to as many female prostitutes as possible and maintaining a nightly log of the total number of women they saw working, whether each woman they spoke to was someone who was new to them or someone whom they had spoken to on a previous night. By analysing the pattern of new and repeat contacts over the multiple nights of fieldwork, the researchers were able to statistically model the likely size of the street working population in Glasgow that had produced the particular pattern of new and repeat contacts (McKeganey et al., 1992).

Hay and colleagues have used a variant of the 'capture recapture' approach to provide successive estimates of the prevalence of problem drug use in England and in Scotland (Hay et al. 2009a,b). Other researchers have used the same approach to provide estimates of problem drug misuse prevalence in the Netherlands (Korf et al., 1994), in Australia (Larson et al., 1994), in Italy (Abeni et al., 1994), in Asia (Mastro et al., 1994) in Barcelona (Domingo-Salvany *et al.*, 1995). The researchers in these studies reviewed multiple lists of drug users held by different agencies in each of the countries studied. By studying the pattern of overlaps between different agencies' lists of drug users (i.e. individuals who appear in more than a single database) the researchers were able to statistically model the overall size of the drug-using population in each of the geographical areas they were studying.

By producing serial estimates of the prevalence of problem drug use it has been possible to monitor changes in prevalence over time and to use this information to assess the impact of drug treatment and *prevention* services in reducing prevalence. In addition, the prevalence estimates have also proved invaluable in assessing the financial costs of problematic drug use within societies (Godfrey *et al.*, 2002).

KEY TEXTS
- European Monitoring Centre for Drugs and Drug Addiction (1997) *Estimating the Prevalence of Problem Drug Use in Europe, Monograph No 1* (Lisbon: EMCDDA)
- Hay, G. *et al.* (2010) 'Opiate and Crack Cocaine Use: A New Understanding of Prevalence', *Drugs-Education Prevention and Policy*, 17 (2): pp. 135–147
- Hickman, M. *et al.* (2004) 'Estimating Prevalence of Problem Drug Use: Multiple Methods in Brighton', Liverpool and London Home Office Online Report 36/04

prevention

SEE ALSO **education; harm reduction; strategies**

Prevention is a key component of how most countries are tackling the problem of drug use. Prevention in this context tends to mean either preventing the onset of substance use or preventing the escalation in individual's substance use. In the period following the identification of *HIV* as a major public health concern prevention also came to mean not so much the prevention of substance use itself but the prevention of the risk behaviours associated with the spread of infection:

A key issue in shaping drug policies is the choice that has been posed between two targets: between the prevention of HIV

transmission and the prevention of drug abuse. Preventing
the physical disease of AIDS has now been given priority over
concerns with drug problems. In this paradigm prevention
takes on a new meaning – the key prevention task is not the
prevention of drug use but the prevention of HIV infections and
transmission. (Stimson, 1990, p. 33)

Fear at what was felt to be the imminent epidemic of HIV reshaped
the meaning of drug prevention to mean prevention of HIV.
Government funding within the United Kingdom, and in many
other countries, was directed at supporting the development of new
services aimed at reducing *injecting* drug users HIV related risk
behaviour (i.e. sharing injecting equipment, *prostitution*). Services
such as needle and syringe exchange, outreach counselling on safer
injecting techniques, bleach distribution for the sterilization of
injecting equipment, substitute *prescribing, heroin* prescribing, and
safe injecting centres became the front line in the prevention of HIV
infection. Drug prevention, for much of the period from the late
1980s, became the poor relation of HIV prevention.

As concerns over the spread of HIV receded in the face of lower
than feared levels of HIV infection amongst injecting drug users,
preventing the onset and progression in drug use increased in
importance. The means for preventing the onset and progression
in young peoples' drug use are multiple in type and focus. These
range from student drug *testing* (widely used within the US), drugs
education in schools, use of the *media*, use of diversionary activities
including the promotion of football, basketball and other sports as
a way of directing young peoples' energies and interests away from
drug use, actively rewarding young people for avoiding becoming
involved in drug and alcohol abuse, the use of peer education
approaches to bolster young peoples' resistance to drug and alcohol
use and the use of former and recovering addicts and the *police*
in drugs prevention education. Drug prevention approaches have
been targeted at a range of levels with some initiatives directed at
the individual, some directed at the *family*, and some directed at the
wider society.

Despite the clear importance of ensuring the development of
effective and well-targeted approaches to drugs prevention the
evidence identifying the most successful types of drugs prevention

is by no means well founded. Within the United Kingdom the largest evaluation of drugs prevention was the government-funded Blueprint project. This project, led by Professor Gerard Hastings at the University of Stirling, sought to evaluate the effectiveness of multiple approaches to drug and alcohol prevention in a number of local areas within England. The *research* involved qualitative and quantitative interviews with young people as well as with teachers, shopkeepers, and other local community members. At the start of this study the expectations were high as to what the research would reveal. However when the study team published the findings it was conceded that because the sample size used in the study had been too small they were unable to assess the impact of the prevention approaches studied. The limitations of the Blueprint study design led to substantial criticism of the funding of the research and its execution (Goldacre, 2009).

It has been pointed out by critics that much of the drugs prevention education in schools presents too agnostic a picture to young people providing largely factual information on the effects of different drugs and leaving young people to make up their own mind as to whether to use various different substances. Such critics have suggested that it would be more appropriate, given the harms associated with various different substances and the illegality of the drugs involved, for schools to adopt a much clearer anti-drug stance actively discouraging drug use rather than leaving it to the child to determine whether they want to become involved in such use (Gyngell, 2012).

KEY TEXTS
- European Monitoring Centre for Drugs and Drug Addiction (2008) *Insights Prevention of Substance Abuse No 7* (Lisbon: EMCDDA)
- Stead, M. *et al.* (2007) 'Implementation Evaluation of the Blueprint Multi-Component Drug Prevention Programme: Fidelity of School Component Delivery', *Drug and Alcohol Review*, 26 (6) November: pp. 653–664

prison

SEE ALSO community sentences; contingency management; methadone; recovery

It would be impossible to overestimate the impact of illicit drugs on life within prisons over the last 20 or so years. David Blakey, a former chief constable, who undertook a report for the UK government on the impact of drugs in prison has commented that

> Prisoners going into prison have been taken from a world where the use of illicit drugs is endemic. Many, probably a majority, will be problem drug users. Drugs may well be the reason, or one of the reasons why they are incarcerated. They will view the use of drugs to 'relieve boredom' or 'cope with stress' as normal. It would be remarkable indeed if they did not attempt to bring their 'normality' into prison. (Blakey, 2008, p. 7)

As Blakey pointed out, the capacity of prisoners to smuggle drugs into prison may have been aided in the past by a perception on the part of some staff that a drug-using prison is a more easily managed prison:

> Some staff with long experience in the Service accepted that decades ago the smell of *cannabis* throughout a prison on a Friday evening might have suggested a quiet weekend for the staff. (Blakey, 2008, p. 7; emphasis added)

Successive surveys in a wide range of countries have identified the substantial proportion of prisoners who have a drug problem and whose offending is related to their drug dependency. Stewart (2009) surveyed 1457 prisoners across 49 prisons within England: 28% had used *heroin* in the previous four weeks before arriving in the prison, 25% had used crack cocaine, 15% had used cocaine powder, and 46% had used cannabis. Significantly 81% of those that had used heroin in the preceding four weeks had used the drug on a daily basis as had 59% of those that had used crack cocaine in the preceding four months. From Scotland, Carnie and Broderick (2011) found that just under half of the prisoners they surveyed had been under the influence of drugs when they committed the offence that had led to their imprisonment.

Given the extent of drug misuse amongst prisoners it is hardly surprising that a number of commentators have emphasized the importance of ensuring that prisons are able to provide effective and accessible drug *treatment* services:

As far as treatment is concerned the opportunity that prison provides for intervening with problem drug users is potentially so valuable to the individual and society as a whole, that it would be remiss not to attempt to exploit it as far as possible. (McIntosh and Saville, 2006, p. 240)

However, prisons are not principally therapeutic settings and it is by no means a straightforward matter for prison staff to combine their custodial responsibilities with a commitment to provide treatment to drug dependent inmates. McIntosh and Saville (2006) quote one of the prison staff they interviewed as being illustrative of the perception which some prison officers had as to the relative priority in their work between security and treatment:

'First and foremost I always see myself as a prison officer. My discipline duties will always come first'. According to the officers this latter priority applied boundaries to the extent to which they could develop therapeutic relationships with prisoners. It also meant that drug service officers had to strike a difficult and delicate balance between being supportive and sympathetic on the one hand and maintaining order and discipline on the other. (McIntosh and Saville, 2006, p. 239)

Whilst there is a clear need to ensure that prisoners have access to drug treatment services within prisons, attention has also focused on the period immediately surrounding prisoners' release from prison which has been seen to be a time of heightened risk of drug *overdose*. Farrell and Marsden (2007) reviewed a national sample of 48,771 male and female prisoners released during 1998–2000. By November 2003 there had been a total of 261 drug related deaths amongst the released prisoners. Crucially this study showed that the odds of a female drug-using offender dying within the first week following release was ten times greater than at week 52 whilst amongst males the figure was eight times greater.

In an attempt to reduce the level of drug related mortality amongst recently released prisoners two controversial programmes have been developed within the prison service in the United Kingdom. The first involves the provision of the opiate reversal drug *naloxone* to prisoners just prior to their release in order that they can administer this drug (or have it administered to them) in the event that they experience or witness a drug overdose following their release. The second more controversial programme involved reintroducing drug-using prisoner to opiate based drugs in the period prior to their release as a way of increasing their tolerance to opiates thereby reducing their risk of overdose should they resume their previous level of drug use on liberation from the prison. The retoxification programme attracted considerable adverse publicity when details of its existence became public knowledge, and it raised questions about whether the role of drug treatment within prisons was principally about reducing prisoners' level of drug use or reducing their risk of overdose once they had left the prison (MacDougall, 2002). If it was the former then clearly it made no sense at all to be reintroducing prisoners to opiate based drugs prior to their release, however if it was the latter then the programme made some sort of sense even if it seemed to make it pointless to have attempted to reduce prisoners' drug use whilst they remained incarcerated.

KEY TEXTS

- Bahr, S., Masters, A. and Taylor, B. (2012) 'What Works in Substance Abuse Treatment Programs for Offenders', *The Prison Journal*, 92 (155): pp. 154–174
- Blakey, D. (2008) 'Disrupting the Supply of Illicit Drugs into Prisons: A Report for the Director General of National Offender Management Service', available at http://www.drugscope.org.uk/Resources/Drugscope/Documents/PDF/Good%20Practice/blakeyreport.pdf
- Hedrich, D. *et al.* (2012) 'The Effectiveness of Opioid Maintenance Treatment in Prison Settings: A Systematic Review', *Addiction*, 107 (3) March: pp. 501–517
- McIntosh, J. and Saville, E. (2006) 'The Challenges Associated with Drug Treatment in Prison', *Probation Journal*, 52: pp. 230–246
- Patel Report (2010) *Prison Drug Strategy Review Group* (Department of Health)

project match

SEE ALSO **recovery; relapse; treatment; UKATT**

The idea that some addictions treatments are more effective than others and that it makes sense to try to ensure that people get the *treatment* that most closely matches their needs is the thinking that lay behind the single most costly study ever undertaken into the effectiveness of treatment for *alcohol* dependency. Project Match was a \$27 million, eight-year, multi-site study that aimed to iden- tify which treatments worked best with which people and go on to guide the future direction of alcohol treatment within the United States and internationally. There could have been fewer studies that started with higher expectations than Project Match and ended with such modest outcomes.

The study design sought to compare three distinct types of alcohol treatment: (1) cognitive behavioural coping skills therapy, (2) motivational enhancement therapy, (3) 12-step abstinence based peer support therapy. The study began in 1989 with researchers recruiting 1726 alcohol dependent patients into the two wings of the trial. One wing received their treatment on an outpatient basis and the other wing received their treatment on an inpatient or day hospital basis followed up with aftercare in the community.

The *research* demonstrated that patients across each of the treat- ment types improved in increasing the number of abstinent days, reduced number of drinks consumed on drinking days, improved liver function, reduced drug use, and that these improvements were maintained across the 12 months of the data collection. Crucially, however, the study failed to identify whether the treat- ments differed in their capacity to facilitate positive behaviour change. In a press release from the funding agency Professor Thomas Babor, one of the leading Project Match researchers, pointed out that 'the striking differences in drinking from pre- treatment levels to all follow-up points suggest that participating in any of the MATCH treatments would be associated with marked positive change' (NIH, 1996). The positive spin placed on the finding that all treatments were broadly equally effective could not fail to dilute the feeling that what the results actually meant was that it did not make much difference what treatment you were given when you were seeking help for an alcohol problem. Those who were looking to Project Match for guidance as to what types of treatments to make more widely available to meet the needs of problem drinkers in the United States and elsewhere could hardly have been inspired by the findings.

Following the main published reports from Project Match there has been a steady stream of critical comment that have identified major weaknesses in the study design – the chief of which was the lack of a no-treatment control group. In the absence of a no-treatment group it was impossible for the researchers to measure how much of the improvement they identified would have occurred in the absence of any treatment provided, and how much of the improvement could be attributed specifically to the treatment delivered.

Project Match also revealed another fundamental fact about the nature of research aiming to evaluate the effectiveness of different treatments. Namely, whilst one can design a study that can evaluate the effectiveness of a specific treatment, nevertheless the same treatment delivered in a different city, or in a different clinic, by different staff, with different attitudes and training, could produce very different results. The reason for this is the simple observation that delivering a behaviourally based treatment is always going to have a high level of variation even where the treatment itself is tightly specified. When it comes to evaluating a treatment service the range of factors that can influence the effectiveness of the treatment are so numerous that it is virtually impossible to know what impact these factors may be having on the outcomes of any particular treatment.

Following the modest outcomes of Project Match some researchers have called for an end to the funding of large-scale treatment evaluation studies (Buhringer and Pfeiffer-Gersche, 2008).

KEY TEXTS

- Babor, T. and Del Boca, F. (2002) *Treatment Matching in Alcoholism: International Research Monographs in the Addictions* (Cambridge: Cambridge University Press)
- Buhringer, G. and Pfeiffer-Gerschel, T. (2008) 'COMBINE and MATCH: The Final Blow for Large Scale Black Bock Randomized Controlled Trials', *Addiction*, 103 (5) May: pp. 708–710
- Orford, J. (2008) 'Asking the Right Questions in the Right Way: The Need for a Shift in Research on Psychological Treatments for Addiction', *Addiction*, 103 (6) June: pp. 875–885
- Peele, S. (1998) 'Ten Radical Things NIAAA Research Shows about Alcoholism', *The Addictions Newsletter* (The American Psychological Association, Division 50), 5 (2) Spring: pp. 6, 17–19

prostitution

SEE ALSO **harm reduction; heroin; injecting; recovery**

In the 1980s and early 1990s, attention focused on the link between prostitution and drug use as a result of fears that *injecting* drug-using women working within the sex industry might be at particularly high risk of acquiring, and spreading, *HIV* to their commercial sex partners. Outreach health projects were developed in many countries targeted at the women in the sex trade aiming to ensure that they had access to barrier *contraception* and, where they needed it, sterile injecting equipment.

Research in this area has typically concentrated upon a relatively narrow range of topics, establishing the level of HIV and other infections amongst sex workers; establishing and promoting the use of barrier protection in prostitute and client relationships; understanding the dynamics of the prostitute–client relationship including the propensity for violence within those relationships; and identifying the factors that facilitate or impede the use of condoms.

Within Scotland, researchers attempted to measure the extent of the link between prostitution and injecting drug use by carrying out extensive fieldwork within the Glasgow's major red-light areas. The work involved providing all of the women and men identified as working on the streets with a range of health related resources including condoms and sterile injecting equipment. By maintaining a detailed record of which sex workers requested which resources (injecting equipment, condoms) it was possible to build up a picture of the numbers of women who requested the injecting equipment and on that basis to estimate the total number of women working on the streets who were injecting drug (McKeganey and Barnard, 1996). By combining this information from data obtained from having requested a saliva sample from the women it was also possible to calculate a rate of HIV positivity for both drug injecting and non-drug injecting women.

The results of this research showed that within this single city over a two-year period the percentage of street based female sex workers injecting drugs ranged between 71% and 74%. Other research, in different cities, has similarly reported on the extent of injecting drug use amongst female sex workers. For example, Tran *et al.* (2005) reported that 32% of female sex workers were injecting drugs in Hanoi Vietnam, Chen *et al.* (2005) identified that 58% of female sex workers within Yunan province in China were injecting drug, Shannon *et al.* (2008) identified an injecting drug use rate of 56% amongst female sex workers in Vancouver, and Van de hoek and colleagues (1989) have reported a figure of 82% of female sex workers in Amsterdam injecting drug.

Within the Glasgow study out of 158 women who provided a saliva sample only a single woman was found to be HIV positive producing an HIV infection rate amongst female street-working prostitutes in the city of just 0.6%. In the second year of the study 127 women were tested amongst of whom only a single woman was found to be HIV positive, producing an HIV *prevalence* rate of 0.8% (McKeganey and Barnard, 1996). This research showed that whilst injecting drug use was widespread amongst the women working on the streets in Glasgow, HIV remained very low. Through qualitative interviewing with the women it was also established that the majority of women insisted on their clients wearing a condom prior to providing sex to them (McKeganey and Barnard, 1996).

Whilst the Glasgow research identified low level of HIV infection amongst female sex workers, other research has identified much higher levels of HIV infection amongst female sex workers in different cities. Strathdee and colleagues, for example, found that 5.3% of a sample of 620 injecting drug-using female sex workers from the border region between Mexico and the United States were HIV positive (Strathdee *et al.*, 2012). This study also found that over half of the female HIV positive injecting drug-using sex workers reported injecting drugs directly with their clients – further increasing their risk of acquiring and spreading HIV infection. Research undertaken by Sarkar and colleagues, on brothel based sex workers in Kolkata, India, identified that 27.7% of the sex workers aged between 16 and 20 were HIV positive with the figure reducing to 8.4% for those aged over 20. The overall prevalence of HIV amongst the sex workers in this study was 9.6% (Sarkar *et al.*, 2005). In this study all of the women, when asked about condom use, reported consistently using condoms with their clients although on closer questioning 44% of the women indicated that they had not used a condom with their most recent client.

Whether or not sex workers are able to insist on condom usage with their clients depends to an extent on the question of who holds the power within prostitute–client interactions. Where the sex worker is in a position of power over the client there is an increased likelihood of consistent condom use. By contrast, where the sex worker is in a relatively powerless position in relation to the client, then condom use is likely to be less consistent.

The issue of power within prostitute–client encounters is highly variable. Whilst it should not be assumed that simply because a sex worker is an injecting drug user that their power over their clients is reduced; there is a possibility that where sex workers are working in a state of acute drug withdrawal or drug intoxication their capacity to insist on the client using a condom may be compromised. It is perhaps significant in this respect that almost half of the women interviewed by Strathdee and colleagues reported earning more money for unprotected sex than for protected sex, indicating that there was a powerful economic inducement coming from clients for unprotected sex (Strathdee *et al.*, 2012).

Along with a focus on the link between sex work and HIV, research has also focused on the nature, extent and determinants of violence involving sex workers. Although this research is by no means limited to the United Kingdom, interest in the results of this work has been fuelled by a number of murders of female sex workers that have been widely covered in the UK *media* (Telegraph, 2008). In a study that looked at violence to female sex workers operating from indoor and outdoor locations, Church and colleagues found that of 115 outdoor sex workers surveyed, 50% had experienced client violence in the last six month, 47% had been slapped, punched or kicked, 24% had been threatened with a weapon, 25% had been held against their will, and 28% had a client attempt to rape them. With regard to the 125 indoor sex workers surveyed, 26% had experienced client violence in the last six months, 14% had been slapped, punched or kicked, 17% had experienced a client who attempted to rape them, and 15% had been held against their will. Violence, or the threat of violence, was an everyday occurrence for these women (Church *et al.*, 2000). Further confirming these research findings Beattie and colleagues (2010) reported that from nearly 4000 sex workers surveyed in India 31.5% of those who began working aged under 20 had been beaten or raped in the last year.

Decker and colleagues (2011) surveyed 815 sex workers in Thailand and report that 25% of those who began working aged between 14 and 17 had been beaten or raped in the last year.

There has been considerable research around the issue of whether societies should identify areas where the trading of sex for money can take place without the women and the clients fearing arrest by the *police* (prostitute tolerance zones). The two countries that represent the polar extremes of this topic are the Netherlands (where commercial sex is decriminalized) and Sweden where commercial sex is seen as a serious criminal offence and where both the sex worker and the client can be subject to criminal prosecution.

KEY TEXTS

- Bloor, M., McKeganey, N. and Barnard, M. (1990) 'An Ethnographic Study of HIV-Related Risk Practices among Glasgow Rent Boys and Their Clients: Report of a Pilot Study', *AIDS Care: Psychological and Socio-Medical Aspects of AIDS/HIV*, 2 (1)
- Cusick, L. *et al.* (2011) 'Exiting Drug Use and Sex Work: Career Paths Interventions and Government Strategy Targets', *Drugs Education Prevention and Policy*, 18 (2): 145–156
- Kinell, H. (2008) *Violence and Sex Work in Britain* (UK: Willan Publishing)
- Maher, L. (2000) *Sexed Work Gender Race and Resistance in a Brooklyn Drug Market* (Oxford: Oxford University Press)
- McKeganey, N. and Barnard, M. (1996) *Sex Work on the Streets: Prostitutes and Their Clients.* (Philadelphia: Open University Press)

r

rapid assessment

SEE ALSO research

Research in any area is often a lengthy and drawn out process of designing the study, securing the funding, collecting and analysing the data, and writing up the findings. As well as being costly in terms of time, research is also costly in financial terms. For these reasons most of the research in the human sciences is undertaken within the rich economies of the developed world even though many of the most urgent health problems are occurring within the developing nations.

In an attempt to redress that imbalance researchers within the addictions (and in other spheres) have developed the techniques of rapid assessment and response. Whilst it may not be possible to secure the funding for a three-year research study to look at the drug-using behaviour of individuals within developing countries, rapid assessment and response studies are cheaper, quicker and can assist health and other agencies to formulate interventions that can address particular local problems. The aim here is not to undertake world-class science but to produce socially relevant knowledge that can assist agencies in tackling specific problems. Rapid assessment project are designed to be conducted quickly and to identify new, effective, and inexpensive interventions that have a high probability of being adopted, and sustained at the local level (US DHSS, 1999)

Since the 1990s, largely as a result of work led by the Centre for Research on Drugs and Health Behaviour at the University of London, the approach of rapid assessment and response has been widely applied in the substance misuse field to study, amongst other areas, *HIV* related risk behaviour on the part of drug users, drug injectors and sex workers (Stimson *et al.*, 1998; Stimson *et al.*, 2001). Rapid assessment and response projects have been developed in relation to the burgeoning drug problem within South Africa where it has been found that local drug users have relatively poor knowledge of the health risks associated with their drug use and how these may be reduced (dos Santos *et al.*, 2011). Ezard and colleagues have used rapid assessment and response methods to collect detailed information on *alcohol* and other drug use related problems amongst displaced persons in conflict zones in Africa and Asia (Ezard *et al.*, 2011).

Within these studies the aim is not to undertake research over a number of years, but to rapidly identify a small numbers of key individuals, to draw upon a range of local information (including local *media* reports, policy documents) and to formulate in as short a time as possible a clear enough picture of what is happening to provide guidance on how local agencies may tackle the health problem that the rapid assessment project has identified. According to Fitch and colleagues rapid assessment projects take an average 125 days to complete (Fitch *et al.*, 2004).

Whilst the methods of rapid assessment and response have been promoted by national and international organizations, including the World Health Organization, the approach has not been without its critics. It has been pointed out that research on difficult and hard to reach populations that is rapidly undertaken in countries where there is little pre-existing experience of social research methods may lead to the wrong conclusions being drawn, misplaced interventions being developed, and the further marginalization of excluded groups within those societies where the methods are being applied (McKeganey, 2002; Friedman, 2000).

Despite concerns around the scientific merits of rapid assessment and response methods it is easy to see why the approach has proven to be so popular in countries where there would be little chance of undertaking long-term studies to shed light on important health challenges. It seems likely that these methods will continue to expand leading to a twin track body of research in which the more established methods of social science research are applied in the developed economies, and the more rapid assessment and response methods are applied in the developing economies. In time this bifurcation of knowledge may lead to further marginalization of the developing countries and to the perception that the social and health related problems within the developing countries are simply not worth the level of investment in research directed at the problems within the developed nations.

KEY TEXTS

- Fitch, C. *et al.* (2004) 'Rapid Assessment: An International Review of Diffusion Practice and Outcomes in the Substance Use Field', *Social Science and Medicine*, 59: pp. 1819–1830
- McKeganey, N. (2002) 'Rapid Assessment: Really Useful Knowledge or an Argument for Bad Science', *International Journal of Drug Policy*, 11: pp. 13–18
- Stimson, G., Fitch, C. and Rhodes, T. (1998) *The Rapid Assessment and Response Guide to Injecting Drug Use* (Geneva: World Health Organization)

recovery

SEE ALSO addiction; brief interventions; motivational interviewing; project match; relapse; strategy; UKATT

Within the last five years a near revolution has occurred in UK drug *treatment* policy in the importance that is now being given to ensuring that drug treatment services are focused on maximizing the opportunities for recovery. Increasingly from the late 2000s the key drug treatment policy debate within the United Kingdom has had to do with the importance of ensuring that drug treatment services are focused on enabling their clients to become drug free. This shift in policy has come about within the context of a growing concern that the previous emphasis on *harm reduction* within drug policy has led to a marginalization of the idea that individual's contacting drug treatment services ought to be being helped to become drug free (Wardle, 2012). As a result of that concern the UK government issued a new drug strategy in 2010 'Reducing Demand Restricting Supply, Building Recovery: Supporting People to Live a Drug Free Life' (HM Government, 2010). In the introduction to that strategy the Home Secretary outlined the distinctive approach the government was taking and the shift away from the previous strategy's focus on reducing the harm associated with individuals' drug use:

A fundamental difference between this strategy and those that have gone before is that instead of focussing primarily on reducing the harms caused by drug misuse, our approach will be to go much further and offer every support for people to choose recovery as an achievable way of dependency. (HM Government, 2010, p. 2)

The strategy contains a clear commitment to promoting abstinence and drug free outcomes:

Our ultimate goal is to enable individuals to become free from the dependence; something we know is the aim of the vast majority of people entering drug treatment. Supporting people to live a drug free life is at the heart of our recovery ambition. (HM Government 2010, p. 18)

One of the controversies that has characterized debate around drug treatment within the last few years has had to do with the definition of recovery and the extent to which recovery is taken to mean the complete cessation of the individual's drug use. Within the United States, the Betty Ford Centre has provided one definition of recovery that has been particularly influential within the addictions field:

Recovery from substance dependence is a voluntarily maintained lifestyle characterised by sobriety, personal health, and citizenship. (Betty Ford Consensus Panel, 2007, p. 221)

'Sobriety' within this definition means abstaining from using drugs or *alcohol*, 'personal health' encompasses the individual's physical and psychological health. 'Citizenship' refers to 'living with regard and respect for those around you' (Betty Ford Consensus Panel, 2007). Recovery here is a multidimensional notion that consists in a good deal more than the simple cessation in the individual's drug use.

The United Kingdom Drug Policy Commission, an independent charitably funded organization influenced by the ideas of harm reduction, has offered a contrasting definition of recovery as:

The process of recovery from problematic substance use is characterised by voluntarily sustained control over substance use, which maximises health and wellbeing and participating in the rights, roles and responsibilities of society. (UKDPC, 2008, p. 6)

Like the Betty Ford Centre consensus panel, the UKDPC defines recovery beyond the simple issue of the individual's drug use to include an element of participation within the rights, roles and responsibilities of society. However the UKDPC included within the definition of recovery the idea of 'voluntarily-sustained control over substance use'. What this means in effect is that recovery as a goal can sit alongside the individual's continued drug use – sobriety or abstinence is not then a core element of the UKDPC definition of recovery.

The advantage of the UKDPC definition is that it enables a much larger group of people to be designated as 'in recovery' than would be the case if the definition were closely tied to the notion of abstinence. In effect the UKDPC definition includes all of those who have ceased their drug use as well as those who are continuing to use drugs but in a controlled way. The problem with the UKDPC definition, however, is the inherent difficulty of defining what 'control' in this context actually means, and whose definition of 'being in control' applies, that is, is it the individual drug user who defines whether he or she is in control of his or her drug use or somebody else? It could also be argued that the simple fact that the individual is continuing to engage in a form of drug use that involves purchasing drugs that are illegal and of unknown purity means that they are not in control of their drug use.

Within a context in which increasing attention is being given to ensuring that drug treatment services are working towards drug users' recovery and *rehabilitation*, some supporters of the harm reduction approach have complained at what they see as the erosion of a previous government commitment to harm reduction. Gerry Stimson, former executive director of the International Harm Reduction Association, has been particularly forceful in his criticism of government policy in this area:

> Recovery is relevant to a tiny proportion of drug users ... Many treatment providers and the National Treatment Agency have however pre-emptively rewritten their aims to be consistent with the new goal of abstinent recovery ... No one challenges this; seemingly happy to follow the way the wind blows. Where are the critics and the critical thinkers? Why are our treatment providers, clinicians and public health experts' not sounding

warning bells to government about the risks they are taking with the public health? (Stimson, 2010, pp. 14/15)

Other commentators have expressed the fear that the ground won in developing harm reduction services in the United Kingdom may be lost by the growth of abstinence focused treatment services (McDermott, 2010; Drugscope, 2010).

Recovery from dependent drug use is a long-term process and with around 200,000 drug users in treatment in the United Kingdom it is questionable whether the treatment system has anything like the capacity to provide the intensive, recovery oriented, support to all of those clients. In addition, it is by no means certain that the current drug treatment workforce is appropriately skilled to deliver intensive high-quality abstinence and recovery oriented support that could sustain a whole-scale shift in emphasis from harm reduction to abstinence and recovery. Many drug users currently in contact with drug treatment services may not wish to engage with a recovery focused treatment system even if that system were widely available. As a result it is more probable that the future will involve a combination of abstinence recovery and harm reduction oriented interventions than the complete dismantlement of the harm reduction approach to drug treatment that some commentators have feared.

One possible area of difficulty in combining recovery and harm reduction agencies may have to do with the question of how to allocate drug users to either the intensive, recovery focused, services or to the more harm reduction oriented services. To do this might entail some form of differentiating between those drug users who might benefit from the more costly, recovery oriented services, from those for whom recovery is not yet a realistic possibility, and who would benefit from continued contact with harm reduction services. Within the United Kingdom this segmenting option is currently being considered by the National Treatment Agency (NTA, 2010). However this work is likely to be hampered in part by the lack of *research* within the United Kingdom (as opposed to the US) on the criteria that may be used to direct drug users into appropriate treatment (Mee-Lee, 2001).

Although the segmenting option might offer a possible solution to the inability of the drugs treatment system to provide intensive, recovery oriented support to the estimated 200,000 drug users currently in treatment, the degree to which this will succeed in practice will depend on whether the segmenting exercise is able to reduce the number of drug users who need the intensive recovery oriented services to a manageable size. If, after having undertaken a segmenting exercise, one is still left with a very large number of drug users seeking to become drug free then the issue may still arise as to the capacity of the drug treatment system within the United Kingdom to deliver abstinence focused support to clients even despite the level of governmental support for such a shift.

KEY TEXTS

- Best, D. and Lubman, D. (2012) 'The Emergence of a Recovery Movement Alcohol and Drug Dependence', *Australia and New Zealand Journal of Psychiatry*, 46 (6): p. 586
- Best, D. *et al.* (2012) 'Wellbeing and Recovery Functioning among Substance Users Engaged in Post Treatment Recovery Support Groups', *Alcoholism and Treatment Quarterly*, 30 (4): pp. 397–406
- Hunt, N. (2012) 'Recovery and Harm Reduction: Time for a Shared Development Oriented Programmatic Approach', in R. Pates and D. Riley (eds), *Harm Reduction in Substance Use and High Risk Behaviour* (Chichester: Wiley-Blackwell)
- Neale, J., Nettleton, S. and Pickering, L. (2011) 'Recovery from Problem Drug Use: What Can We Learn from the Sociologist Erving Goffman?' *Drugs Education Prevention and Policy*, 18 (1): pp. 3–9
- White, W. and Kelly, J. (2011) 'Recovery Management: What If We Really Believed That Addiction Was a Chronic Disease', *Current Clinical Psychiatry*, Part 1, 67–84, doi: 10.1007/978-1-60327-960-4_5
- Yates, R. and Malloch, M. (2010) *Tackling Addiction Pathways to Recovery* (London: Jessica Kinglsey)

rehabilitation

SEE ALSO **recovery; residential rehabilitation**

Rehabilitation is distinct from *recovery* in that whilst recovery typically refers to the reduction and or cessation in the individual's drug or *alcohol* use (reduction in levels of dependency) rehabilitation tends to refer to the building or rebuilding of the individual's life and the taking on of roles and responsibilities that are associated with wider citizenship. Those roles and responsibilities may typically include paid *employment*, parenting, *education*. In addition there is also an expectation that rehabilitation is also associated with the reduction or cessation in lifestyle behaviours that are injurious to communities and individuals, for example, reducing involvement in criminal and other anti-social behaviours. Rehabilitation can also include reducing the visible signs of a prolonged drug habit (e.g. improving drug users dental health) as a way of reducing the individual's marginalization, *stigma* and enhancing the individual's likelihood of being reintegrated into the wider society.

Whilst recovery and rehabilitation can be seen to be associated with different elements it is inevitably the case that there is considerable overlap between the two. Recent definitions of recovery, for example, have often stressed not simply the cessation or reduction in the individual's drug or alcohol consumption but the assumption of wider rights and responsibilities associated with full citizenship. The United Kingdom Drug Policy Commission, for example, has defined recovery in terms that encompass some notion of rehabilitation:

> The process of recovery from problematic substance use is characterised by voluntarily-sustained control over substance use which maximises health and wellbeing and participation in the rights roles, and responsibilities of society. (UKDPC, 2008, p. 6)

Similarly the world-renowned Betty Ford Centre has also produced a definition of recovery which combines the traditional element of drug and alcohol reduction with some element of rebuilding the individual's life and the assumption of wider societal roles:

> Recovery from substance dependence is a voluntarily maintained lifestyle characterized by sobriety, personal health, and citizenship. (Betty Ford Consensus Panel, 2007, p. 222)

The inclusion of sobriety within the Betty Ford consensus definition of recovery clearly relates to the cessation in the individual's drug or alcohol use whilst the notion of citizenship relates to the assumption of the wider responsibilities that are associated with full societal membership.

KEY TEXTS

- Betty Ford Institute Consensus Panel (2007) 'What Is Recovery? A Working Definition from the Betty Ford Institute', *Journal of Substance Abuse Treatment*, 33: pp. 221–228
- United Kingdom Drug Policy Commission (2008) *The UK Drug Policy Commission Recovery Consensus Group: A Vision of Recovery* (London: UKDPC)

relapse

SEE ALSO **chronic relapsing condition; recovery**

It is almost impossible to imagine the *recovery* from any dependency without at the same time considering the issue of relapse. Whilst there are individuals who manage to overcome their dependency without relapsing, relapse is a common component of most peoples' journey to recovery. Indeed the currently preferred characterization of drug dependency as a *'chronic relapsing condition'* elevates the notion of relapse to the position of being a defining element of the condition itself. Research on the process of recovery has identified a range of factors that are associated with relapse, for example, being exposed to cues that are associated with the individual's former drug or *alcohol* use. Those cues can include either sight of the substances which the individual became dependent upon, contact with acquaintances whom they associate with their past drug or alcohol use, situations within which their drug or alcohol use typically occurred.

Support provided to individuals to reduce the likelihood of their relapse includes working to identify alternative ways of responding to drug related cues, identifying and avoiding the situations in which the individual is likely to be exposed to drug or alcohol related cues, recognition of the early signs of craving, and identifying alternative ways of dealing with stressful situations that might otherwise result in the individual resuming some level of drug or alcohol use.

Along with talk-based therapies that aim to reduce the likelihood of relapse there are also a range of pharmaco-therapies that are similarly designed to reduce the risks of relapse. In the case of opiate dependency, for example, prescription of the drug naltrexone in either oral or injectable form is one such *treatment* that blocks the receptor in the addict's brain that is targeted by *heroin*. In the case of alcohol dependency prescription of the drug disulfiram (antabuse) results in the individual experiencing a range of unpleasant symptoms (nausea, vomiting) in the event that they consume alcohol. By inducing these unpleasant reactions it is hoped to boost the individual's resistance to the temptation to use alcohol.

Whilst relapse is often a feature of the early stages of recovery from drug and alcohol dependence there are indications that even in situations where the individual has been abstinent for many years there is still a possibility of relapse occurring (White and Schulstead, 2009).

KEY TEXTS

- Marlatt, G. and Donovan, D. (2005) *Relapse Prevention Maintenance Strategies in the Treatment of Addictive Behaviours* (New York: Guildford Press)
- Sinha, R. (2011) 'New Findings on Biological Factors Predicting Addiction Relapse Vulnerability', *Current Psychiatry Reports*, 13: pp. 398–405
- Welbeing, L (2011) 'Addiction Putting Relapse into Context', *Nature Reviews Neuroscience*, 12 April: p. 186
- White, W. and Schulstead, M. (2009) 'Relapse Following Prolonged Addiction Recovery: Time for Answers to Critical Questions', *Counselor*, 10 (4): pp. 36–39

religion

SEE ALSO **project match; recovery; twelve-step programmes**

On the face of it one might well wonder what possible connection there could be between substance misuse and religion; surely these two domains sit as far apart as it is possible to get. However in a sense it is perhaps the distance between these domains that explains the wealth of *research* showing that religion and religiosity is a protective factor against drug use. In reviewing the literature on drug use and religion Benson, for example, notes that:

> Negative correlations between religiousness and substance use have been consistently reported among both males and females ... Overall there is a persistent tendency for religion to be inversely related to substance use. (Benson, 1992, p. 214)

Other research has shown that those young people who have a defined religious affiliation or *identity* are at much reduced risk of using a range of licit and illicit drugs (Koenig *et al.*, 2001; Leigh *et al.*, 2005). Although research has identified a negative association between religion, religiosity, spirituality and substance misuse it is by no means clear what factors may explain that negative association – the how and why it is that levels of drug use should be lower amongst those with a religious affiliation. It may be that those with a strong religious affiliation are more likely to have a clear moral sense in which various forms of drug and *alcohol* use are prescribed; equally it may be that the social norms amongst religious groups act as a barrier to individual's drug use (Cook, 2009).

As a result of the link that has been identified between drug use and religion, it is hardly surprising that many drug *treatment* centres (particularly the abstinence focused centres) often have a strong religious element to their programme focusing, for example, on the importance of a higher power (as in the case of Alcoholics Anonymous) and/or encouraging the addict to strive from some form of repentance for his or her former drug use.

Where research has been undertaken to try to assess the contribution of faith based programmes to drug treatment there are clear signs that by strengthening or bolstering individuals' sense of religiosity or spirituality that it is possible to enhance individuals' chances of recovery from dependent drug use. *Project Match*, for example, evaluated the contribution of a faith based 12-step approach to recovery alongside two other forms of counselling and psychological support. The faith based programmes were seen to achieve a level of sustained recovery on the part of patients that was comparable to the other treatment programmes evaluated and with some indication in certain areas of slightly improved outcomes (Project Match Research Group, 1998)

KEY TEXTS

- Cook, C. (2006) *Alcohol Addiction and Christian Ethics* (Cambridge: Cambridge University Press)
- Cook, C. (2009) *Substance Misuse in Spirituality and Psychiatry* (London: Royal College of Psychiatrists), pp. 139–168
- Cook, C., Goddard, D. and Westall, R. (1997) 'Knowledge and Experience of Drug Use amongst Church Affiliated Young People', *Drug and Alcohol Dependence*, 46: pp. 9–17

- Humphreys, K. and Gifford, E. (2006) 'Religion Spirituality and the Troublesome Use of Substances' in W.R. Miller and K. Carroll (eds), *Rethinking Substance Abuse: What the Science Shows and What Should We Do about It* (New York: Guilford), pp. 257–274
- Jarusiewicz, B. (2000) 'Spirituality and Addiction: Relationship to Recovery from Chemical Dependency', *Journal of Addictions and Offender Counselling*, 13: pp. 58–61

research

SEE ALSO **prevalence; project match; rapid assessment**

Longitudinal research studies have made a major contribution to research in the substance misuse field identifying those factors associated with the onset and development in individual's drug and *alcohol* use. Longitudinal research is particularly suited where the research questions posed have to do with the impact of social or individual factors over an extended period of time. In assessing the impact of *cannabis* smoking, for example, it is necessary to be able to follow individuals over an extended period of time; to study both those who have smoked cannabis and those that have not, in order to identify whether cannabis consumption is associated with particular health outcomes.

Where the statistical likelihood of developing particular health problems is relatively small it is necessary to follow large samples of individuals over time to be sure of picking up enough instances of the adverse health outcome to identify the possible causal pathway involved. Understanding how particular health problems have evolved and their connection to particular substances is particularly difficult within the addictions as a result of the fact that people differ so much not only in what drugs they use, the quantities of the drugs used, the frequency of use, what combinations of drugs are used and the situations in which the drugs are used. Each of these sources of variation can exert a powerful influence on the likelihood of any particular adverse health outcome occurring and the degree to which it is associated (whether causally or not) with the specific substances consumed.

Whilst longitudinal studies have a played a key role in addressing major issues within the addictions (e.g. does cannabis cause schizophrenia) they are amongst the most difficult studies to undertake because they can involve following people over an extended period of time. These studies tend to be costly and there may be many years before data that has been collected can be analysed to shed light on the topics being studied. As a result, whilst longitudinal studies represent one of the most powerful methodological designs for researchers their use in reality is relatively rare.

Within the United Kingdom there has never been a single longitudinal study on the health impact of cannabis consumption. To understand the long-term impact of the use of this drug it has been necessary to turn to longitudinal studies that have been undertaken in countries such as the Netherlands, New Zealand, Australia, the United States, and Sweden. Andreasson and colleagues from Sweden, for example, looked at all 45,570 conscripts to the Swedish military in the year 1969/70. The conscripts completed two anonymous questionnaires that requested a range of biographical and drug use data. Individuals were followed up over a 13-year period by reviewing the Swedish national register of psychiatric care. In this study the researchers identified a strong association between the level of cannabis exposure at conscription and the development of schizophrenia during the follow-up period; with clear *evidence* of a dose response relationship between the amount of cannabis smoked and the likelihood of developing schizophrenia (Andreasson *et al.*, 1987, p. 1484).

Van-Os and colleagues from the Netherlands have similarly used a longitudinal study design to look at the mental health impact of cannabis. In this instance they carried out a three-year follow-up survey of 4,045 people who were free of any psychosis at baseline, and 59 people who had a diagnosis of a psychotic disorder at baseline. Individuals were followed up at year one and year three to see if they had developed psychotic symptoms and if so whether there was any clear association with cannabis consumption. The researchers on this study found that at the follow-up points those who had developed a psychotic illness were much more likely to have consumed cannabis and further that the risk of psychotic illness increased significantly as the level of the individuals' use of cannabis increased. The researchers also found that respondents with a diagnosed psychosis at baseline, and who smoked cannabis during the period of follow-up, increased their vulnerability to further illness (van-Os *et al.*, 2002).

Longitudinal research designs have been of enormous value in enabling us to understand the development of dependency, the relative likelihood that those with a drug or alcohol problem will die as a result of their substance use, the length of time that individuals typically remain drug dependent, and the relative proportions of those who find a route out of their drug use over time either with or without the assistance of drug *treatment* services.

Stimson and Oppenheimer undertook one of the first longitudinal follow-up studies of *heroin* addicts in the United Kingdom when they tracked 128 individuals over a ten-year period (Stimson and Oppenheimer, 1982). The researchers found that whilst some of their study subjects were living the life of the typical addict (on the streets and suffering from multiple adversities) others were leading relatively ordinary lives. Amongst the latter were individuals whose drug use remained invisible to those around them and who appeared to suffer few of the problems typically thought to characterize the life of a heroin addict.

Rathod and colleagues undertook what is undoubtedly the longest follow-up study of heroin addicts when they mounted a 33-year follow-up study of heroin addicts treated in a small town in the south east of England. The individuals in this study were treated for the most part without recourse to substitute opiate medication. As a result, the study is perhaps the clearest examples of what might have happened within the United Kingdom had opiate substitution treatment not become the default treatment for opiate dependency. At the first follow-up point (six years from recruitment into the study) 13% of the 79 people had ceased their drug use and 51% were continuing to inject. By the time of the 33-year follow-up point 42% of their study subjects had ceased their drug use, 10% were still using and 22% had died. Remarkably the attrition rate in this study was as little as 8%. The clinicians who conducted this study drew a conclusion from their research that was as radical as the study they had accomplished:

> we were struck by the number of premature deaths in people taking *methadone* and also by the negative perceptions of life amongst those who are currently prescribed this opioid. Our study findings suggest that equally satisfactory results are possible without recourse to long term *prescribing* of opioid. (Rathod *et al.*, 2005; emphasis added)

Within the United States one of the classic long-term follow-up studies was conducted by George Vaillant who, for 20 years, followed 100 opiate addicts who had contacted treatment services in New York in 1952. By 1970, 25% of the original cohort were still using drugs and between 35% and 42% had become drug free with around 23% having died as a result of their drug use (Vaillant, 1973).

Longitudinal studies have produced unique insights into the trajectory of drug dependency and have shattered many of the beliefs about the lack of *recovery* (the view that 'once an addict always an addict') as well as identifying key factors in influencing in the development of drug-using behaviours and the likelihood of experiencing serious adverse consequences as a result of individual's drug use.

Just as longitudinal studies have made a major contribution to research in the addictions so to have qualitative studies where the emphasis is not on recruiting large numbers of study subjects, and subjecting them to the same set of questions, but to building up close links with a smaller number of respondents and seeking, through observation and interview, to develop a detailed picture of their lives, their drug use, and their risk behaviour. Researchers using qualitative approaches are akin to anthropologists studying their own societies. Some of the earliest qualitative studies in the addictions took place in the United States in the 1960s and 1970s when the country was experiencing a drug culture that at that time had not manifested in other areas.

In contrast to the focus of previous research which viewed drug users as either 'mad or bad' the qualitative researchers in the 1960s were interested in describing the life of an addict on the streets in more positive terms; vividly portraying in observational field notes and interview transcripts what it was like to be a drug user within an urban environment; chasing down drugs, getting the money to buy drugs, avoiding the *police* and generally living the life of an addict. Within these studies the world occupied by the drug user was an urban under-land shunned by conventional society but providing a fascinating sub-culture in its own right. The most notable study exemplifying that view was carried out by Preble and Casey in the article 'Taking Care of Business the Heroin Users Life on the Streets' (1969). In the aftermath of Preble and Casey's study there was a slew of articles reporting on the world of the drug user as seen through the eyes of the addicts themselves (Cavan, 1972; Feldman, 1973; Agar, 1973; Weibel, 1979; Adler, 1985).

The tradition of urban ethnography within the addictions has continued to the present time with Philip Bourgois, for example, producing his classic study 'In Search of Respect: Selling Crack in El Barrio' (Bourgois, 2003) very much in the tradition that Preble and Casey had established 30 years previously.

The world that these researchers were portraying was, as other researchers were quick to point out, almost entirely rooted in the experience of male drug users and addicts. As a corrective to that focus, Marsha Rosenbaum produced her classic 'Women on Heroin' focusing on the world of the female drug user and challenging the invisibility of the female addict that was prevailing at that time (Rosenbaum, 1981). Similarly in her book *Sexed Work Gender, Race, and Resistance in a Brooklyn Drug Market* anthropologist Lisa Maher (1997) described how the drug use 'choices' of the women she was studying were largely shaped by their economic position and marginal status. Earlier Marina Barnard had shown how female *injecting* drug users were particularly at risk of *HIV* as a result of the greater likelihood that they would be involved with male partners who were also injecting drugs and with whom they were sharing injecting equipment (Barnard, 1993).

In addition to documenting the social world of the drug user, qualitative studies have also proven to be useful in exploring the addict's journey to recovery. In the late 1980s Patrick Biernacki (1986) undertook qualitative research with recovering addicts to show how the addict's sense of their own drug use, and their life trajectory, could impact on their decision to cease or continue their drug use. The sense of the addict facing 'rock bottom' reflecting on how far they had fallen from the person they had hoped to be, and the resolution to change their lives were seen as key to their eventual recovery from *addiction*. McIntosh and McKeganey continued that focus in their own ethnographic account of the recovery from dependent drug use 'Beating the Dragon: The Recovery from Dependent Drug Use' in which they drew upon Erving Goffman's notion of a 'spoiled *identity*' to look at the addicts' attempts at managing their own eventual recovery (McIntosh and McKeganey, 2001).

KEY TEXTS

- Andreasson, S. *et al.* (1987) 'Cannabis and Schizophrenia: A Longitudinal Study of Swedish Conscripts', *Lancet*, 26 December: pp. 1483–1485
- Denzin, N. and Lincoln, Y. (eds) (2000) *Handbook of Qualitative Research* (London: Sage Publications)
- Hammerley, M. and Atkinson, P. (1983) *Ethnography Principles in Practice* (London: Tavistock Publications)
- Pope, C. and Mays, N. (2000) *Qualitative Research in Health Care* (London: BMJ Books)
- Rathod, N., Addenbrooke, W. and Rosenbach, A. (2005) 'Heroin Dependence in an English Town', *British Journal of Psychiatry*, 187: pp. 421–425
- Silverman, D. (2011) *Interpreting Qualitative Data* (London: Sage Publications)
- Stimson, G. and Oppenheimer, E. (1982) *Heroin Addiction treatment and Control in Britain* (London: Tavistock Publications)
- Vaillant, G. (1973) 'A 20 Year Follow Up of New York Addicts', *Archives of General Psychiatry*, 29 (2): pp. 237–241

residential rehabilitation

SEE ALSO **maturing out; recovery; therapeutic communities; twelve-step programmes**

Residential rehabilitation services involve individuals with a drug or *alcohol* problem spending an extended period of time within a residential facility participating within daily therapy programmes. These programmes often involve a combination of prescription medication and intensive counselling. The length of time that individuals may remain within such facilities varies considerably but is often measured in months rather than days or weeks although in some instances can involve years. The *treatment* programmes within these facilities are typically focused on complete abstinence with many (although not all) following a treatment programme based either loosely or more tightly on the twelve-step abstinence programme developed by Alcoholics Anonymous.

Over the last few years within the United Kingdom there has been a steady decline in the number of residential rehabilitation centres as a result of a government policy that has favoured community based drug treatment programmes in which *methadone* is made available to drug users on a maintenance basis. Residential rehabilitation services are thought to be considerably more expensive than community based *prescribing* services although the economic comparison between these treatment modalities rarely moves beyond a superficial comparison of unit cost. Since in reality an individual may remain on a methadone programme for many years whilst an individual may remain within a residential facility for only a number of months, the comparison between the two treatment modalities needs to compare the full accumulated costs of the two treatments. In addition, any robust assessment of the relative cost of residential rehabilitation services and community based prescribing services needs to include an estimate of the cost saved to society as a result of the individual ceasing his or her drug use as opposed to their drug use continuing.

Within the United Kingdom, one of the largest studies comparing treatment provided on a residential and community basis was the National Treatment Outcomes *Research* Study led by researchers from the University of London National *Addiction* Centre (Gossop *et al.*, 2001). This study tracked the progress of a large sample of drug users who began treatment in 1995 and followed up as many of the original sample as possible over a five-year period. At the outset to the study 13% of clients were receiving inpatient treatment, 26% were receiving residential rehabilitation services, 18% were receiving methadone reduction programmes and 43% were engaged in methadone maintenance programmes.

The proportion of clients within the residential rehabilitation agencies that were free of opiates (the main drug that had caused them a problem) increased from 19% at intake to a high of 47% at five years. In the case of the methadone clients, by comparison, the proportion free of opiates at the five-year point was 35% compared to 6% at the outset to the study. On the basis of this study residential rehabilitation services had achieved a higher rate of recovery (abstinence) than the community based methadone programmes.

These positive results were further confirmed by research in Scotland using a similar design to the National Treatment Outcome Research Study (NTORS) study and involving, following a cohort of drug users beginning a new episode of addictions treatment. In the

Scottish equivalent of the NTORS study (DORIS – Drug Outcome Research in Scotland) 29.4% of those who had been provided with access to residential rehabilitation services were abstinent at the 33-month follow-up point compared to 3.4% of those that had received methadone maintenance (McKeganey *et al.*, 2006). As with the NTORS study the greater proportion of positive outcomes on the part of the residential rehabilitated clients could not be explained by reference to those clients having been healthier at the outset of the study. In fact the residential rehabilitated clients in the DORIS study were slightly more drug dependent than their methadone treated counterparts.

Whilst these findings do not provide incontrovertible proof that residential rehabilitation services are more effective than community based services in delivering drug user abstinence, they are a powerful indication that for many drug users residential rehabilitation services may well assist their journey towards recovery. In reality, however, only a tiny proportion of drug users are provided with access to residential rehabilitation services. Within England less than 5% of drug users in treatment are provided with access to residential rehabilitation services whilst in excess of 70% are provided with access to methadone maintenance services.

KEY TEXTS

- Chessor, D. (2013) 'Effectiveness of a Group Residential Intervention Program for Young Men with Drug and Alcohol Addiction', *Addiction Research and Therapy*, 4 (1): pp. 2–7
- Mooney, H. (2011) 'Think Tank Criticises Payment by Results for Treating Drug', *British Medical Journal*, 342 (3), June
- Perez, D. (2012) 'Applying Evidence Based Practices to Community corrections Supervision: An Evaluation of Residential Substance Abuse Treatment for High Risk Probationers', *Journal of Contemporary Criminal Justice*, 25 (4): pp. 442–458
- Stolzfus, K. and Cecil, D. (2013) 'A Different Atmosphere of Love: A Qualitative Study of the Experiences of Participants in Evangelical Substance User Rehabilitation Programmes in the Russian Federation', *Substance Use and Misuse*, 48 (6): pp. 421–428

risk factors for onset of drug use

SEE ALSO **education; prevention**

There has been extensive *research* undertaken with the aim of identifying the risk factors associated with the development of young peoples' drug use. Much of the research that has been undertaken has been carried out within the United States where there have been a number of large-scale longitudinal studies that have tracked samples of young people over extended periods of time to identify the point at which their drug use begins and the various risk factors that predate and may explain their drug use.

There is no one factor that in itself provides an explanatory model for young people's drug use – rather what has been identified is a range of risk factors that often coincide in the lives of young people and which increase the risk of young people using different drugs. The risk factor literature has identified the following factors that seem to be influential in the development of young people's drug use:

- *Family*
- School
- Peers
- Conduct disorders
- Mental health
- Deprivation
- Age of onset

In relation to the influence of family factors research has shown that where young people are living within a family where one or both parents have a drug problem, or where there are siblings with a drug problem, young people are at increased risk of developing a pattern of substance use themselves. It has been shown that family discord, family disruption and broken family are associated with an increased risk of drug use. Similarly the relationships between parents and children has been shown to be significant with concern being expressed in those situations where parents seem remote from children, overly authoritarian or overly lax, or where there is inconsistency in their parenting. Child abuse and neglect have similarly been shown to increase the risk of young people's drug use.

In relation to the school, research has shown that pupils who are truanting or who are excluded from school are at increased risk of drug use. In relation to the influence of peers research has shown that associating with peers who are displaying conduct problems increases the likelihood of young people developing a pattern of drug use. The contribution of peers in explaining young people's drug use is by no means straightforward with uncertainty as to how much young people are selecting their peers (peer preference rather than peer influence) with a view to enabling their engagement in a range of problem behaviours. What is certainly very clear is the diminishing influence of the family and increasing influence of peers as young people age.

Research has also shown that young people who are engaged in a range of conduct problems: fighting shoplifting, running away from the home, vandalism are at increased risk of developing a pattern of drug use. Mental health problems and growing up in an area of multiple social deprivation have been shown to increase the risk of drug use. Finally, research has shown that the early use of *tobacco* and *alcohol* by young people increases the risk of the progression to other forms of drug use.

Whilst research has sought to identify the factors associated with young people's increased risk, there has also been attention directed at the factors that may protect young people and enhance their resilience in circumstances where they are exposed to this range of risk factors. Key here are such factors as forming a close relationship with at least one adult who can provide consistent, warm, caring attention, forming a link with someone outside the family who can similarly provide supportive input to the young person, developing strong communication skills and having an easy-going temperament, developing confidence and a strong sense of self-esteem, having positive role models, and developing some level of religious affiliation or belief. To an extent these protective factors can be seen to be the opposite of the risk factors that may enhance a young person's likelihood of developing a pattern of drug use.

KEY TEXTS

- Lloyd, C. (1998) 'Risk Factors for Problem Drug Use: Identifying Vulnerable Groups', *Drugs: Education Prevention and Policy*, 5 (3): pp. 217–232
- McLeod, J. *et al.* (2012) 'Early Life Influences on the Risk of Injecting Drug Use: Case Control Study Based on the Edinburgh Addiction Cohort', *Addiction*, 108 (4): pp. 743–750
- Robbins, L. and Rutter, M. (eds) (1990) *Straight and Deviant Pathways from Childhood to Adulthood* (Cambridge: Cambridge University Press)

S

safe injecting centres

SEE ALSO decriminalization; harm reduction; injecting; recovery

There are few more controversial services provided to those with a drug dependency problem than the supervised *injecting* centres. These are settings where injecting drug users are able to inject black market drugs under some level of medical supervision. The thinking behind safe injecting centres is simple enough – injecting drug use carries multiple health risks many of which can be reduced if the injecting takes place in a hygienic environment under some level of supervision. Safe injecting centres are a clear example of the *harm reduction* policy that has been hugely influential within the addictions over the last 20 years.

Described in these terms, safe injecting centres seem straightforward and uncontroversial. However it must also be acknowledged that where a government is supporting the provision of a safe injecting centre, they are also by definition coming very close to supporting illegal drug use itself. Providing a centre where illegal drugs can be used under supervision is tantamount to providing a degree of approval for an illegal activity.

There are thought to be over 70 safe injecting centres in cities across the world with the two most famous centres being based in the Lower East Side of Vancouver, Canada, and the Kings Cross area of Sydney, Australia. Where safe injecting centres have been set up they have typically been granted a limited exemption from the countries' existing drug laws on the basis that they are providing an important public health service although at the same time and somewhat incongruously they tend to be framed as operating solely on a pilot or demonstration project basis.

Such centres have often been the subject of sustained legal challenge in the countries where they have been developed. Within

Vancouver, for example, whilst the safe injecting centre (Insite) has enjoyed the unwavering support of the city administration it has been subjected to legal action from the federal government seeking its closure. In 2011 the Vancouver Supreme Court signalled the end of that political opposition in a 9–0 ruling in favour of the injecting centre remaining open (BBC, 2011).

The Vancouver safe injecting centre opened in 2003 within a context of rampant *HIV* and *Hepatitis C* infection amongst local injecting drug users. The original aims of the centre were to increase drug users' access to health care and *addiction* services, to reduce the level of drug related fatalities, to reduce the transmission of HIV and other blood borne infections, to reduce injection site problems and to improve public order.

Between March 2004 and April 2005 staff within the Canadian facility intervened in 336 *overdose* events, which represented around 1.33 overdoses per 1000 visits to the centre. An ambulance was called in 39% of cases but in only 8.3% of cases was the individual taken to a hospital. There were no recorded overdose deaths within the facility (Kerr *et al.*, 2006). From April 2004 to March 2006 staff within the centre made a total of 4084 referrals 40% of which were for addiction counselling and 368 were for detoxification. The annual cost of operating the safe injecting centre within Vancouver was estimated in 2007 to be $3000,000 or around $1380 per visitor to the centre.

In a review of the *evidence* on safe injecting centres undertaken for the *European Monitoring Centre for Drugs and Drug Addiction* Hedrich concluded that:

> The *research* evidence on the impact of consumption rooms, although still incomplete, suggests that consumption rooms do achieve some of the specific purposes for which they were set up. They reach a population of long-term problem drug users with various health and social problems. They provide a hygienic environment for drug use and, for regular attenders at least a decrease exposure to risks of infectious disease. They contribute to a reduction in levels of risk taking amongst their clients and increase access for specific hard to reach target populations of drug users to health, welfare, and drug *treatment* services. (Hedrich, 2004, p. 83; emphasis added)

Other publications have presented a much more critical assessment of the contribution of safe injecting centres in realizing their various goals. A review of the published evaluations of the Canadian safe injecting centre in Vancouver, for example, claimed that:

> Serious problems are noted in the evaluations' reporting and interpretation of findings. Specifically, the published evaluations and especially reports in the popular *media* overstate findings, downplay or ignore negative findings, report meaningless findings and overall, give an impression the facility is successful, when in fact the research clearly shows a lack of program impact and success. The published findings actually reveal little or no reductions in transmission of blood-borne diseases or public disorder, no impact on overdose deaths in Vancouver, very sporadic individual use of the facility by individual clients, a failure to reach persons earlier in their injecting careers and very little or no movement of drug users into long-term treatment and recovery. (Mangham, 2008; emphasis added)

There is little doubt that it is possible to develop services that can reduce individual's injecting related health risks. It seems equally beyond challenge that such services can assist individuals by facilitating their access to other health and addictions treatment services. The controversy surrounding safe injecting centres has less to do with what those centres can achieve by way of reducing drug injectors' health related risk behaviour, as to whether public agencies should take on the responsibility of facilitating individual's drug use through providing centres where illegal drug use can occur. The answer to that question depends upon the relative importance one places on meeting the health related needs of dependent drug users or tackling the problem of illegal drug use within society. For those who elevate the needs of vulnerable people over other societal goals it is highly likely that they will support the provision of safe injecting centres even if only on a pilot and demonstration project basis (Wright and Tomkins, 2004). For those who maintain that the greater responsibility lies with the need to reduce the level of illegal drug use within society it is likely that such centres will receive a more critical response. The International Narcotics Control Board, responsible for monitoring the application of the UN conventions on narcotic drugs, has remained a steadfast critic of such centres (INCB, 2004). Similarly whilst the UK government has supported the wider use of *heroin prescribing* and other harm reduction measures it has rejected the development of safe injecting centres.

KEY TEXTS

- DeBeck, K. *et al.* (2011) 'Injection Drug Use Cessation and Use of North America's First Medically Supervised Safer Injecting Facility', *Drug and Alcohol Dependence*, 113 (2/3): pp. 172–176
- Hedrich, D. (2004) *European Report on Drug Consumption Rooms* (Lisbon: EMCDDA)
- Independent Working Group on Drug Consumption Rooms (2006) 'Report of the Independent Working Group on Drug Consumption Rooms', Joseph Rowntree Foundation.
- Kerr, T. *et al.* (2006) 'Impact of a Medically Supervised Safer Injection Facility on Community Drug Use Patters: A before and after Study', *British Medical Journal*, 332: pp. 220–222
- Mangham, C. (2008) 'A Critique of Canada's INSITE Injection Site and Its Parent Philosophy: Implications and Recommendations for Policy Planning', *Journal of Global Drug Policy and Practice*, http://www.globaldrugpolicy.org/Issues/Vol%201%20Issue%202/A%20 critique%20of%20Canada's%20INSITE.pdf.

set and setting

SEE ALSO **addiction; brief interventions; harm reduction; safe injecting centres**

The notion of drug 'set' and 'setting' was originally set out by psychiatrist Norman Zinberg on the basis of his work with recreational *heroin* users in the 1970s. For Zinberg, it was impossible to understand the nature of individual's drug-using behaviour by paying attention solely to the drug itself. Rather, he argued, of equal importance is the set (i.e. the individual's state of mind) and the setting (i.e. the context within which the drug-using behaviours are occurring). In relation to the ready availability of heroin within Vietnam, for example, Zinberg wrote:

> Ready availability of heroin seems to account for the high *prevalence* of use, but it alone does not explain why some individuals became addicted and others did not, any more than

the availability of *alcohol* is sufficient to explain the difference between the alcoholic and the social drinker. Availability is always intertwined with the social and psychological factor that create demand for an intoxicant... In the case of both heroin use in Vietnam and psychedelic use in the 1960's the setting determinant including social sanctions and rituals is needed for a full explanation of the appearance magnitude and eventual waning of drug use. (Zinberg, 1984; emphasis added)

Drug set and setting are likely to be influential not only in the development of drug-using behaviours and dependency but also in the *recovery* from drug dependency. One of the clearest examples of this involved *research* led by Lee Robbins on soldiers returning to the US after having served in Vietnam where many had developed a pattern of regular opiate use (Robbins, 1974; Robbins *et al.* 1974, 1975, 1980, 1993).

Concerned at the growing problem of heroin use in the 1970s, Robbins was asked by the US drug czar to undertake a study to establish the level of drug use amongst serving soldiers and to find out what happened to those soldiers once they returned to the United States. The initial results from Robbins and her team were striking enough in showing that just over a third of soldiers had tried heroin and that a fifth thought that they were addicted to opiates, 80% were using *cannabis*.

The truly surprising element of Robbins's research though came when she followed up the soldiers on their return. On interviewing, and drug *testing* the soldiers one year after they had returned to the United States, Robbins found that only 5% of those who had been addicted to opiates within Vietnam were still addicted. Similarly, when Robbins followed up the same sample some three years later she found that only 12% of those who had been addicted within Vietnam had been addicted at any time in the last three years in the United States. Crucially it was not the provision of drug treatment that explained the remarkable rate of recovery amongst the returning Vietnam veterans, since only a third of those who had been addicted within Vietnam had received even rudimentary addictions treatment on their return. Nor was the veterans' recovery dependent on their never having used heroin once they had returned to the United States – since around half of those who had been addicted to heroin within Vietnam used the drug on their return although of those only 6% became re-addicted.

Robbins's findings came to be seen as a powerful illustration of the fact that drug use and drug dependence are highly influenced by the social setting in which they occur. Whilst heroin was common-place within Vietnam leading to widespread use, its availability within the United States was much more restricted leading to many fewer individuals consuming the drug even when they had been dependent upon it within Vietnam (Robbins, 1993).

KEY TEXTS

- Peele, S. (1998) *The Meaning of Addiction: An Unconventional View* (San Francisco: Jossey-Bass)
- Robbins, L., Helzer, J. and Davis, D. (1975) 'Narcotic Use in Southeast Asia and Afterward: An Interview Study of 898 Vietnam Returnees', *Archives of General Psychiatry*, 32 (8): pp. 955–961
- Robbins, L. *et al.* (1980) 'Vietnam Veterans Three Years after Vietnam: How Our Study Changed Our View of Heroin' in L. Brill and C. Winnick (eds), *Yearbook of Substance Use and Abuse* (New York: Human Science Press)
- Zinberg, N. (1986) *Drug, Set, and Setting: The Basis for Controlled Intoxicant Use.* (New Haven, CT: Yale University Press)

spontaneous remission

SEE ALSO maturing out; recovery; relapse

The notion that some individuals are able to recover from their drug or *alcohol* dependency with little or no input from drug and alcohol *treatment* services seems both remarkable and potentially under-mining of the very notion of *addiction* as being something over which the individual has very little control. Spontaneous or unas-sisted *recovery* has been described by some commentators as one of the taboos of the addictions field (Chiauzzi and Liljegren, 1993). Despite the reticence of some commentators, academics, and clini-cians to even accept the notion that it is possible to overcome drug or alcohol dependency spontaneously a growing number of studies have reported on the phenomenon.

In a large-scale survey of over 4500 individuals in recovery and who had been classified as alcohol dependent, only one-quarter had actually sought help for their alcohol problem (Dawson *et al.*, 2006). An even larger Swedish study of individuals in recovery from alcohol dependency estimated that as many as 80% of those studied had recovered without any contact with drug treatment services (Blomquist *et al.*, 2007). However, on the basis of a review of the various *research* studies that have claimed to report on the phenomenon of spontaneous, unassisted recovery Sobell and colleagues (2000) have raised concerns about the methodological quality of much of the research in this area.

Where research has been undertaken it would appear that spontaneous recovery is more common amongst those with an alcohol problem than with an opiate problem, and further, that the likelihood of spontaneous recovery is greater where the nature of the drug or alcohol problem is less severe.

Mocenni and colleagues (2010) have suggested that spontaneous or unassisted recovery might come about in four distinct ways: (1) as a result of the individual choosing to go 'cold turkey', that is to simply cease his or her drug or alcohol use without any external reason impacting on that decision; (2) as a result of the individual initiating cold turkey due to an external event or reason; (3) on the basis that the individual gradually reduces his or her drug or alcohol intake; (4) where the individual finally gives up drugs or alcohol following a number of prior failed attempts at recovery. Despite the attempt to characterize recovery in this way we still know relatively little about how individuals come to the decision to cease or reduce their drug and alcohol intake, and what resources they are able to draw upon in turning that motivation into a reality of long-term abstinence. Within the last few years, for example, there has been interest in the notion of 'recovery capital' within which it is recognized that the resources (psychological, interpersonal, financial etc) that individuals have access to varies substantially from one individual to the next with those who have access to greater recovery capital standing a much better chance of facilitating their recovery (Best and Laudet, 2010; Best *et al.*, 2012).

Other researchers have given greater weight to cognitive changes in how the individuals appraise their past drug and alcohol using behaviour and their sense of the future. Cunningham *et al.* (2005) suggested that those who were able to successfully overcome their alcohol dependence tended to have reassessed the pros and cons of their addiction and reached the conclusion that the negatives outweighed the positives. Although the notion of individuals rationally weighing the pros and cons of their addiction may sound rather 'too rational to be true', other researchers have shown how many individuals in recovery reach a crisis point in their lives where they feel they are at a crossroads and in which they can go in one of two ways – either they continue with their drug use to the eventual destruction, or they choose the other path of recovery and abstinence. Such a perceptual or cognitive shift in the individual's assessment of their life does indeed appear to be an important part of the process of successful recovery (Best *et al.*, 2008).

On the basis of the research that has been carried out there is little doubt that many individuals are able to overcome their addiction without the input of *treatment* services, and further that the numbers of such individuals may well be greater than we might have expected. Potentially the phenomenon of spontaneous and unassisted recovery could contribute a great deal to improving the effectiveness of drug treatment services.

KEY TEXTS

- Best, D. *et al.* (2008) 'Breaking the Habit: A Retrospective Analysis of Desistance Factors among Formerly Problematic Heroin Users', *Drug and Alcohol Review*, 27 (6): pp. 619–624
- Klingemann, H. (1991) 'The Motivation for Change from Problem Alcohol and Heroin Use', *Addiction*, 86 (6): pp. 727–744
- Klingemann, H., Sobell, M. and Sobell, L. (2010) 'Continuities and Changes in Self-Change Research', *Addiction*, 105 (9): pp. 1510–1518
- Stall, R. and Biernacki, P. (1986) 'Spontaneous Remission from the Problematic Use of Substances: An Inductive Model Derived from a Comparative Analysis of the Alcohol, Opiate, Tobacco, and Food/Obesity Literatures', *Substance Use and Misuse*, 21 (1): pp. 1–23

stages of change

SEE ALSO **brief interventions; motivational interviewing; recovery; relapse**

One of the most influential models of the journey to *recovery* from dependent drug and *alcohol* use was developed by James Prochaska and Carlo DiClemente in the 1970s. Interested in the process through which smokers were able to overcome their dependence on *tobacco*, Prochaska and DiClemente identified a series of stages, which, they argued, individuals tend to progress through in the journey to their eventual recovery. Stage 1 (Pre-contemplation) is the point at which the individual does not yet acknowledge that he or she has a substance dependency problem. In this stage the individuals may see their drug use as a non-problematic part of their everyday life. Stage 2 (Contemplation) is where the individual is beginning to consider that they have a problem but they are not yet at the point of determining that their behaviour and substance use have to change. Stage 3 (Preparation) is the point at which the individuals have made a decision to change their substance use and they are beginning to make small changes in their behaviour that are indicative of their move towards a determined attempt at abstaining from the behaviour that is causing them a problem. Stage 4 (Action/Willpower) is the point at which the individual is making a determined attempt to cease their drug or alcohol use and trying to maintain the changes in their behaviour. Stage 5 (Maintenance) is the point at which the individual is seeking to and embed the changes in their drug or alcohol use that they have implemented. Finally Stage 6 (*Relapse*) is the period where the individual resumes some level of drug or alcohol use, even if only temporarily, before recommitting to the goal of abstinence.

Influential as the stages of change model has been in describing the process of recovery from drug and alcohol use as well as dependency on other problematic behaviours (e.g. domestic violence) (Levesque *et al.*, 2009) criticism of the approach has focused on the degree to which the journey to recovery can be characterized as a series of discrete stages or rather a much more fluid process. Little and Girven (2002, 2004) reviewed a wide range of applications of the stages of change model, across different behaviours, and could find little *evidence* of the operation of discrete stages and the authors suggest that the real value of the model may be as an heuristic device than a characterization of the actual process of recovery.

Adams and White (2003) reviewed a range of studies to assess whether the stages of change model had been effective in interventions aimed at increasing the level of physical activity on the part of subjects. The authors found that in 11 of the 15 studies, reviewed projects that had integrated the stages of change approach were found to have been more effective in facilitating behaviour change than those interventions that had not been based on the stages of change approach. However, where the researchers followed up people for longer than six months the results were much less impressive with only two of the seven studies reviewed identifying a positive effect for the interventions based on the stages of change model. Other evaluations of interventions that used the Stages of Change approach have similarly found little evidence of a sustained longer-term effect compared to interventions that have not been based on the stages of change approach (Riesma et al., 2002). In a randomized control trial evaluation with 2471 smokers, Aveyard and colleagues compared the relative effectiveness of stages of change-based interventions against control interventions with regard to smoking cessation (Aveyard et al., 2008) and found little to differentiate the treatments in terms of their effectiveness.

In an editorial in *Addiction* Robert West, one of the world's leading tobacco researcher, has set out one of the most far-reaching criticisms of the stages of change model. The title of West's editorial gave an indication of what he felt about the model: 'Time for Change: Putting the Transtheoretical (Stages of Change) Model to Rest'. According to West the model is flawed 'even in its most basic tenet, the concept of the stage' in which arbitrary lines are drawn in the sand drawn between stages. Second, according to West, the approach assumes that individuals 'make coherent and stable plans' when in reality there is considerable instability in intentions and plans. Third, the stage model focuses too much on conscious decision-making when in reality behaviour is also shaped by such factors as habituation, reward and so on. As a result of its focus on conscious decision-making the stages of change model is unable to cope with the idea of spontaneous recovery in which the individual seem able to recover without passing through a series of discrete stages. According to West the stages of change model 'has been little more than a security blanket for researchers and clinicians' (West, 2005, p. 1037).

Despite these criticisms the stages of change model survives intact perhaps in part because of the intuitive appeal of a narrative that provides a clear structure out of the chaos and fluidity that more often than not typifies most individual lives.

KEY TEXTS

- Armitage, C. (2010) 'Is There Utility in the Transtheoretical Model?' *British Journal of Health Psychology*, 14 (2) May: pp. 195–210
- Prochaska, J., DiClemente, C. and Norcross, J. (1992) 'In Search of How People Change: Applications to Addictive Behaviours', *American Psychologist*, 47 (9): pp. 1102–1114
- Riesma, R. *et al.* (2002) 'A Systematic Review of the Effectiveness of Interventions Based on Stages of Change Approach to Promote Individual Behaviour Change', *Health Technology Assessment*, 6 (24)
- Riesma, R. *et al.* (2003) 'Systematic Review of the Effectiveness of Stage Based Interventions to Promote Smoking Cessation', *British Medical Journal*, 326: p. 1175
- West, R. (2008) 'Time for a Change: Putting the Transtheoretical (Stages of Change) Model to Rest', *Addiction*, 100 (8): pp. 1036–1039

stigma

SEE ALSO **harm reduction; maturing out; media; parental drug use**

In a provocatively titled paper 'In Praise of Stigma' the American psychiatrist Dr Sally Satel caused something of a storm in 2007 when she wrote that she could imagine few behaviours more deserving of stigmatization than those associated with *addiction*:

> Fighting stigma is all the rage nowadays. But the stigma abolitionists rarely say what exactly it is they wish to strip of shame: addictive behaviour, seeking help, or addition *treatment* itself? I vigorously applaud help seeking; encourage attendance at a twelve-step group; and believe treatment should be accessible, respectful and competent. But we don't have to neutralize the moral valence of addiction-fuelled behaviour to destigmatize the treatment process. (Satel, 2007, p. 147; emphasis added)

There are few more unwelcome heresies in the world of addictions than the proposal that stigma may be beneficial. According to the American sociologist Erving Goffman (1963), stigma occurs when a person possesses some undesirable characteristic that marks them off from others and negatively impacts upon their capacity to function in their social world.

There is little doubt that stigma is associated with drug use and drug addiction or that stigma runs very deep in people's attitudes towards those who are using illegal drugs. The stigma associated with substance use has a number of components. There is the notion that those with a drug or *alcohol* problem have brought their misfortune upon themselves by failing to take control of their behaviour. In the 2009 UK Scottish Social Attitudes Survey, asked a number of questions about peoples' attitudes towards those using illegal drugs. In this survey 45% of respondents said that they agreed with the statement 'most people who end up addicted to *heroin* only have themselves to blame' (Ormston *et al.*, 2010). In addition to the notion that the drug users are largely responsible for their own problems, the stigma associated with drug use and drug addiction is also based upon the notion that the addict is likely to engage in a range of behaviours that have a profoundly negative impact on other people. There is a perception that the individual who is drug or alcohol dependent is less reliable than others, less caring for their own health and the health of others, and focused almost entirely on their own drug dependency needs. For these various reasons the addict often comes to be seen as someone who you would not wish to associate with, be seen with, be linked to or be reliant upon. They are seen as people who in some fundamental way fail in almost every area of their personal and social responsibilities.

There can be little doubt that the addict's experience of being stigmatized is deeply painful. The vast majority of people would be deeply upset if they experienced only a fraction of the stigma directed towards the addict on a daily basis. In other areas of human behaviour (e.g. mental illness) there has been a determined effort to reduce the stigma directed at those with a mental health problem. The stigma of psychiatric illness has been tackled in part by persuading us that mental health problems can befall anybody – to stigmatize the mentally ill then is in a sense to stigmatize ourselves, our loved ones, our communities. By challenging the notion that mental illness only affects 'other people' the stigma associated with the condition has been reduced, even if it has not been entirely eradicated.

There have been similar attempts to reduce the stigma associated with drug use and drug dependency. Within the United Kingdom, for example, the drug user rights organization 'Release' sought to tackle the stigma directed towards drug users by sponsoring an advertising campaign on London buses that proclaimed in large letters 'nice people take drugs'. Whilst the aim of the campaign was to challenge the idea that those who are using drugs are always unclean, untrustworthy, and undesirable, the campaign foundered in the face of complaints that the claim 'nice people take drugs' could be seen as encouraging and promoting the use of illegal drugs. In the face of that criticism the campaign was eventually withdrawn (O'Hara, 2009).

In a review of the impact of stigma on problematic drug users, Charlie Lloyd has outlined the multiple ways in which stigma can impact negatively on drug users' access to health and social support services (Lloyd, 2010). Drug users attending pharmacies may experience stigma especially where they are required to consume their medication (*methadone*) within the public space of the pharmacy, under the direct gaze of the pharmacy staff and other customers. Faced with that experience individuals may be less likely to make use of a much needed service. According to Hilary Klee and colleagues (Klee *et al.*, 2002) stigma can also have an adverse impact on drug users' ability to secure paid *employment*. Klee's team found that amongst a sample of employers interviewed there were negative attitudes towards drug users that would undoubtedly have impacted upon the employer's likelihood of offering employment to an individual with a current or past drug problem. Drug users were seen by the employers as being untrustworthy, unreliable, moody and as 'generally tarnishing the company's image' (Klee *et al.*, 2002, p. 35). Other researchers have described the negative attitudes of the *police* towards drug users. Lister and colleagues (2008) have recounted how the drug users they interviewed frequently felt targeted by the police, stopped and searched for no better reason than the fact that they were known to the police as someone with a drug problem.

There is a sense in which stigma can be seen to offend a very basic sense of fairness that many of us possess. It seems fundamentally wrong that an individual should be judged not on the basis of who they are, but rather on what they have done or what they are thought likely to do in the future. Stigma resonates with a notion of prejudice in which the individual is somehow characterized not by the multiple roles they may play in their life (brother, father, sister, employee) but by a single master status (that of the drug user or the addict). The challenge faced by those who are seeking to tackle the stigma associated with drug use and drug dependence is the fact that in many ways the prejudicial judgements the stigma is based upon accord with the reality of being an addict. This is not to suggest that everybody who is drug dependent will be unconcerned with their own welfare or the welfare of others, or that every individual who is drug dependent will be unreliable.

But is stigma necessarily a bad thing? And may there be some forms of the stigma that one might wish to retain even if one is sympathetic to the overall importance of reducing drug users' experience of stigma? McIntosh and McKeganey undertook research with individuals who had been drug dependent for many years but who had eventually managed to overcome their addiction. Interestingly the drug users interviewed in this study did not ascribe their eventual *recovery* to the contribution of drug treatment services rather they explained it much more in terms of their own needs to change their sense of *identity*. What was important within the drug users' own narratives of recovery was the fact that they had reached a point where they recognized, through the negative reactions of others, that their own identity had been spoiled as a result of the many years of their drug use and drug addition. Faced with that knowledge powerfully conveyed through the stigma directed at them from other people they determined to change their lives and cease their drug use. In this sense whilst the stigma that the drug users were experiencing was unquestionably unpleasant, deeply negative, and profoundly unwelcome it did at the same time eventually galvanize the individuals into changing their lives and assist in the realization of their recovery. By reducing the stigma that the individual may experience as a result of his or her drug dependency one might make the life of the drug user more bearable but in doing so one may also be undermining one of the most powerful catalysts to the individual's eventual recovery.

There is a further sense in which it might not be entirely appropriate to seek to reduce the stigma associated with the use of illegal drugs that has to do with the importance of drug *prevention*. According to Furst *et al.* (1999) the negative image of the 'crack head' in the 1990s may have been one of the factors that led to a gradual decline in the numbers of crack smokers. Stigma though painful for the individual drug user may still be an important tool within the broader domain of drug prevention.

KEY TEXTS

- Anstice, S., Strike, C.J. and Brands, B. (2009) 'Supervised Methadone Consumption: Client Issues and Stigma', *Substance Use and Misuse*, 44 (6): pp. 794–808
- Hunt, N. and Derricott, J. (2001) 'Smackheads, Crackheads and Other Junkies: Dimensions of the Stigma of Drug Use' in C. Carlisle *et al.* (eds), *Stigma and Social Exclusion in Healthcare* (London: Routledge)
- Lloyd, C. (2010) *Sinning and Sinned Against: The Stigmatisation of Problem Drug Users* (London: United Kingdom Drug Policy Commission)
- McKeganey, N. (2010) 'Bad Stigma ... Good Stigma?' *Drink and Drugs News*, 15 February.
- Satel, S. (2007) 'In Praise of Stigma' in J.E. Henningfield, P.B. Santora and W.K. Bickel (eds), *Addiction Treatment: Science and Policy for the Twenty-First Century* (Baltimore: John Hopkins University Press)

strategies, drug

SEE ALSO decriminalization; international treaties; recovery

Since the late 1980s successive UK governments have published a series of drug strategies setting out the goals of the various policies directed at tackling the problem of illegal drug use. For the most part those strategies have represented a blend of three elements: *treatment*, *enforcement* and *prevention* with the specific weight given to each component reflecting the predominant orientation of the government of the day.

From the late 1980s and early 1990s the focus of UK government policy on drugs was very much to do with tackling the emerging threat of *HIV* infection. Within its 1998 drug strategy 'Tackling Drugs to Build a Better Britain', the UK Labour government outlined its commitment to four key policy areas: these were young people (reduce the proportion of young people using illegal drugs), communities (reduce the extent of reoffending by drug users), treatment (increase the numbers of young people in treatment) and availability (reducing young people's access to illegal drugs).

'Tackling Drugs to Build a Better Britain' emphasized the importance of *harm reduction* within the general approach to tackling illegal drug use prioritizing to some extent treatment over enforcement. David Blunkett, the then Home Secretary, further endorsed the importance of harm minimization initiatives in his introduction to the Updated Drug Strategy in 2002:

All problematic users must have access to treatment and harm minimization services both within the community and through the criminal justice system. (Updated Drug Strategy, 2002, p. 3)

So central were the ideas of harm minimization that the updated drug strategy even re-named the fourth pillar of the strategy 'Treatment and Harm Minimization' illustrating how widespread the ideas and practices of harm reduction had become by 2002. By the time of the 2010 drug strategy 'Reducing Demand, Restricting Supply, Building Recovery: Supporting People to Build a Drug Fee Life' the importance of harm reduction had waned substantially such that the term was not even mentioned within the strategy. Instead the government gave much greater prominence to the commitment to ensure that individuals who had become addicted were being helped to become drug free.

The strategic importance being given to drug user recovery within the 2010 drug strategy from the Conservative Liberal coalition government echoed a similar commitment on the part of the Scottish Nationalist government in Scotland in 2008 which had already stressed the importance of ensuring that drug users were being helped to become drug free:

This is the purpose of this new strategy. To signal a step change in the way that Scotland deals with its drug problem. To explain how we need to change our way of thinking about drug use, and to set out what actions are effective in tackling it. Above all, to set out a new vision where all our drug treatment and *rehabilitation* services are based on the principle of recovery. (Scottish Government, 2008; emphasis added)

The direction and content of the UK drug strategy has been a source of substantial comment and criticism particularly in relation to the balance between treatment and enforcement. In an editorial in the influential *British Medical Journal* Professor John Strang, one of the UK Government's most senior advisors on drug misuse, wrote about his and others' mounting concern at the growing politicization of the drugs issue in the late 1990s:

It is good news that the new Labour government is evidently serious about the growing national and international drug problem ... But there is a grave danger that the increased political attention could backfire, producing a more politicised approach to the problem and causing the new czar's dominant orientation to be one of control. *Crime* dominated posturing would lead to a damaging dissociation between the public appeal of the policy and actual *evidence* of effectiveness. (Strang *et al.*, 1997, p. 325; emphasis added)

Professor Gerry Stimson, a long-time advocate for harm reduction was similarly critical at what he saw as the increasingly punitive tone of political statements on drugs and drug users:

Between 1987 and 1997 we had a public health approach. The aim was to help problem drug users to lead healthier lives, and to limit the damage they might cause to themselves or others. When we did interfere for the sake of the wider community it was done in a spirit of facilitation and respect. We had a healthy drug policy. We don't have one now. Drugs policy has now focused down on the link between drugs and crime. If we do things to drug users, it is because of the effect they have on others. We are witnessing the introduction of a punitive and coercive ethos. (Stimson, 2010)

Much of the controversy generated in discussions over the various drug strategies has had to do with what is seen as the balance between a predominantly criminal justice focus or a health focus within the strategy documents and political announcements. However as Reuter and Stevens have pointed out it is by no means clear that these strategies (whatever their actual content) have ever been particularly influential:

There is little evidence from the UK, or any other country, that drug policy influences either the number of drug users or the share of users who are dependent. There are numerous other

cultural and social factors that appear to be more important.
(Reuter and Stevens, 2007, p. 10)

In terms of the drug strategies of other countries the mix is similarly very much one of combining treatment, enforcement, and prevention in varying amounts. In Sweden in the 1960s, for example, drug policy was fairly liberal with a widespread acceptance of *cannabis* smoking and relatively little emphasis on criminal justice interventions. Drug treatment policy within Sweden encompassed the *prescribing* of *heroin* and other drugs to addicts (Chatwin, 2011). From the 1970s through to the 1980s drug policy in Sweden became increasingly more hard line under the influence of Professor Nils Bejerot who advised the Swedish government that the only way in which Sweden would avoid the epidemic of illegal drug use which was sweeping through Europe would be by adopting a much tougher *zero tolerance* policy comprising widespread treatment for those who were dependent, vigorous enforcement directed at those involved in drug trafficking, and an approach to drug prevention that sought to involve all members of Swedish society. Drug policy within Sweden remains focused on the goal of achieving a drug free society. Although that goal has not been reached Sweden certainly enjoys one of the lowest levels of illegal drug use anywhere in Europe (EMCDDA, 2011).

In contrast to the zero tolerance approach to illegal drugs in Sweden the Netherlands has one of the most liberal drug policies anywhere in Europe with cannabis consumption being increasingly tolerated and openly sold in coffee shops throughout the country. Over the last ten years there has been increasing pressure upon the Netherlands to dilute its policy of drugs toleration and to develop drug laws and drug policies that are more congruent with other European states. Calls have been made to limit the sale of cannabis in Dutch coffee shops solely to Dutch nationals as a way of reducing the number of foreign tourists travelling to the Netherlands specifically to use recreational drugs. In recent years there has also been a marked reduction in the number of coffee shops licensed to sell cannabis within the Netherlands.

Drug treatment policy within the Netherlands has been very much influenced by the ideas of harm reduction allowing the development of heroin prescribing schemes as a way of attempting to stabilize the lives of long-term addicts, reduce their chances of acquiring and spreading HIV and other infections, and reduce drug related criminality.

In Portugal, possession of any drug for personal use has been decriminalized. Where an individual's drug use comes to official attention the individual is referred to a local 'drug dissuasion committee' whose members (social worker, lawyer and psychiatrist) can, if they judge it to be appropriate, require the individual to access treatment facilities. Such committees can also impose civil penalties where the individual's drug use is seen to compromise their capacity to discharge *employment* responsibilities. Drug trafficking and drug dealing remain a criminal offence within Portugal despite the acceptance of all forms of personal drug use.

Drug policy within Switzerland, like most other countries. is a blend of treatment, enforcement, prevention, with a distinctive fourth element comprising a commitment towards harm reduction. In terms of drugs prevention the Swiss drug policy stresses the importance not only of preventing the onset of drug use but of preventing the various harms associated with drug use and of discouraging individual's escalation from recreational to more dependent forms of drug use. Treatment within Switzerland encompasses heroin prescribing coupled with a commitment to seek to reintegrate drug users into the wider society and to improve their physical and mental health. Enforcement within Switzerland is very much targeted at those involved in drug trafficking, drug production and money laundering. The harm reduction pillar within Swiss drug policy has enabled the widespread development of such measures as needle and syringe exchange and *safe injecting centres* where individuals are legally allowed to consume drugs purchased on the street under some level of medical supervision.

Drug policies and drug strategies within Central and South America have become the focus of worldwide attention and discussion over recent years as leaders of various countries have sought to develop policies that are seen to be moving away from their former prohibitive stance. Within Mexico, for example, there has been a recent shift from the previous administration's crackdown on the drug cartels in an attempt to explore other policies based on a greater degree of acceptance as to the inevitability of some forms of illegal drug use. Similarly, within Colombia the government has vociferously argued that the prohibitive stance on illegal drugs has failed and that some other form of government regulation of drug markets needs to be considered.

KEY TEXTS

- Buchanan, J. and Young, L (2000) 'The War on Drugs – A War on Drug Users?' *Drugs: Education, Prevention and Policy*, 7 (4), 1 November: pp. 409–422
- Chatwin, C. (2011) *Drug Policy Harmonization and the European Union* (Basingstoke: Palgrave Macmillan)
- Monaghan, M. (2012) 'The Recent Evolution of UK Drug Strategies: From Maintenance to Behaviour Change', *People Place and Policy*, online 6/1: pp 29–40
- Reuter, P. and Stevens, A. (2007) *An Analysis of UK Drug Policy*. A Monograph Prepared for the UK Drug Policy Commission

suicide

SEE ALSO **dual diagnosis**

It is perhaps inevitable that suicide should be a significant factor in the lives of dependent drug users given the stresses and strains of the drug-using lifestyle and the overlap between substance use and mental health problems. Having said that it is often very difficult to establish whether a *death* in an individual with a history of dependent drug use is a case of suicide or an unfortunate outcome of the risks associated with their drug use. In terms of the scale of non-drug related suicide amongst those with a drug dependency problem Merrall and colleagues identified that 10% of non-drug related deaths were classified as suicide (Merrall *et al.*, 2013). Similarly, Backmund and colleagues (2011) looked at suicide attempts amongst individuals admitted to a drug *treatment* service in Germany between 1991 and 1997. These researchers identified that of the 1049 individuals admitted for treatment, 20% had attempted suicide in the past (Backmund *et al.*, 2011).

According to Harris and Barraclough, suicidal death amongst those with a drug dependency problem is six times greater than that found in non-drug-using peers (Harris and Barraclough, 1997). Darke and colleagues looked at admissions to an Australian therapeutic community and found that 34% had a history of self-harm with 20% having self-harmed on more than a single occasion (Darke *et al.*, 2012). Within the German study the risk factors associated with suicide attempts included being female, being unemployed, having initiated drug use at a younger age and being divorced or separated and frequent benzodiazepine use. In this study there was *evidence* that counselling provided to dependent drug users could significantly reduce individuals' risk of suicide.

KEY TEXTS

- Darke, S., Campbell, G. and Popple, G. (2012) 'Self-Harm and Attempted Suicide among Therapeutic Community Admissions', *Drug and Alcohol Review*, 31, June: pp. 523–528
- Haw, C. and Hawton, K. (2011) 'Problem Drug Use Drug Misuse and Deliberate Self Harm: Trends and Patient Characteristics with a Focus on Young People Oxford 1993–2006', *Social Psychiatry and Psychiatric Epidemiology*, 46: pp. 85–93
- Kokkevi, A. *et al.* (2012) 'Multiple Substance Use and Self Reported Suicide Attempts by Adolescents in 16 European Countries', *European Child* and *Adolescent Psychiatry*, doi 10.1007/s00787–012–0276–7

t

testing

SEE ALSO **stigma**

The technology of drug testing has developed considerably over recent years with the capacity to test a wide range of materials (urine, saliva, blood, sweat, hair, nail clippings) for *evidence* that an individual has used a range of legal and illegal drugs. Drug testing, applied within educational, *employment*, medical and sport settings, has generated controversy in virtually every facet of its use, from how the drug testing takes place, that is who is selected for drug testing, who carries out the drug test, what samples are taken to show drug use, whether it is ethical to require compliance with testing regimes, what to do in the event that the person provides a positive drug test and whether that information should be revealed to others and if so to whom?

In relation to drug testing within educational settings this has formed a key part of approaches to drugs *prevention* within the United States. The 2004 US national Drug Control Strategy, for example, extolled the benefits of student drug testing and the government's commitment to supporting such testing.

While student drug testing has become a commonplace element of many school programmes in the United States, student drug testing has remained a rarity within the UK educational sector – occasionally being used within private schools but rarely within state schools. One reason for this may be the fact that the UK government has not provided funding for the development of drug testing programmes.

Student drug testing is highly controversial – welcomed by supporters and railed against by critics in equal measure. In relation to the evidence as to whether student drug testing actually works the data are far from clear-cut. Supporters of drug testing have assembled evidence that shows lower levels of drug use within drug testing schools compared to non drug-testing schools. Similarly, it has been suggested by the supporters of drug testing that the educational attainment of students in schools that use drug testing are greater than in those schools that do not have a testing programme. By contrast, other research has questioned whether there are any statistically significant differences in the levels of student drug use between drug testing and non-drug testing schools. A large survey of both drug testing and non-drug testing schools undertaken in the United States by Yamaguchi and colleagues concluded that:

> school drug testing was not associated with either the *prevalence* or the frequency of student marijuana use or of other illicit drug use. Nor was drug testing of athletes associated with lower than average marijuana use and other illicit drug use by high school male athletes. (Yamaguchi *et al.*, 2003, p. 164; emphasis added)

Other researchers, however, have asserted that:

> Random drug testing policies appear to provide a strong tool for schools to use in the battle to reduce *alcohol* and drug usage amongst teens. (McKinney, 2004, p. 4; emphasis added)

Student drug testing is controversial not simply in terms of the dispute as to whether it works but also in terms of a range of ethical and practical difficulties associated with such testing. Because of the fact that any test carries with it a risk of identifying false positives (test results that are positive when in fact the individual has not used an illegal drug) and false negative (test results that are negative even where an individual has used an illegal drug) testing can give rise to the ethical dilemma of what one does in the case of someone who has been wrongly accused on the basis of a test result. There are concerns that imposing a drug testing regime on young people might undermine their trust in their teachers and other adults, that individuals who are identified as having used an illegal drug might come to be labelled as 'drug users' even though their drug use may have been only occasional and episodic; there are issues to do with how to respond to a young person who declines to provide a drug test and whether such a response should be taken (as it is in the case of elite athlete testing) as the equivalent of having provided a positive drug test; there are concerns that testing programmes may encourage young people to switch from using drugs that remain in the body for longer periods of time (*cannabis*) to using drugs that are cleared from the body much more quickly but which are more harmful (*heroin*). There are concerns that drug testing programmes may have the unwanted effect that young people are encouraged to learn how to get round the drug test and further conceal their drug use. Finally there are concerns as to whether it is appropriate for a school or other educational institution to be seeking to monitor the behaviour of young people that may be occurring outside of the school environment.

Whereas the momentum behind drug testing within the educational sector has reduced over the last few years, drug testing within the workplace has expanded massively. Whilst workplace drug testing is now big business, the ethical issues associated with such testing are similar to those that have been discussed in relation to student drug testing: Should an employer have the right to test all employees even where their drug use may have no impact on their work? What should an employer be allowed to do where an individual declines to be tested? What should an employer be allowed to do when an individual tests positive for illegal drugs? What impact do such testing programmes have on the individual's right to privacy? How long can an employer hold information relating to an individual's drug testing results? and who can this information be passed on to? These are only some of the questions that workplace drug testing gives rise to. These are issues that to an extent remain unresolved even in the face of the growing number of employers who have developed programmes of workplace drug testing.

Drug testing individuals participating within drug *treatment* has been a long-standing component for assessing the effectiveness of those programmes and for making clinical judgements about individual's treatment. It is commonplace within the United States for individuals participating in *methadone* programmes to undergo regular drug testing. Such testing is a means by which clinicians can assure themselves that the individual is consuming their prescribed medication (as opposed to selling it on the black market), as well as determining whether the individual's use of street drugs is diminishing in the light of the medication that is being prescribed.

Although the use of drug testing within the context of drug dependency treatment has become less widespread within the United Kingdom, over recent years there is evidence that the outcomes of treatment are substantially improved where drug testing form an integral part of the treatment programme. Within the United States, addictions researchers Professors Tom McLellan, Robert Du-Pont, and Keith Humphreys found that where drug testing was seen to be part of the treatment programme, and where the results of providing a positive drug test were certain, rapid, and proportionate, the outcomes from treatment were considerably enhanced (Du-Pont and Humphreys, 2011; Humphreys and McLellan, 2011).

The controversy surrounding drug testing within schools, within *employment*, and within drug treatment facilities, is nothing when compared to the controversy which has surrounded drug testing within the sporting arena. Within the sporting arena the use of performance enhancing drugs, the contested results of elite athletes' positive drug tests, the admissions of actual drug use on the part of some of the most well-known athletes on the planet even in the face of persistent negative drug tests, have been a source of constant *media* scrutiny and debate over at least the last ten years. Following criminal investigations some of the most high profile names in elite sports have been given custodial sentences and lengthy bans from competing following the discovery or their admission of having used performance enhancing drugs.

The controversy surrounding the use of performance enhancing drugs and the importance that is now given to drug testing within the sporting arena arises in part as a result of the belief that sporting events provide an opportunity for the individual to aspire to the highest level of his or her accomplishment. The use of performance enhancing drugs, however, raise the very real uncertainty as to whether the performance one is watching and admiring has been achieved on the basis of the individual's own efforts or with the assistance of pharmacological boosting of some kind. There is a sense too of the fundamental unfairness in a situation where some athletes are competing without the use of performance enhancing drugs whilst others are being assisted as a result of their drug use. Yet, despite the controversy around drug testing, it seems impossible now to entirely remove drugs from elite sports and it is arguable whether we can ever now watch an elite sporting event without at least wondering whether the amazing performances on display are a mix of effort, commitment, natural talent and pharmacology. Within such an environment it may be argued that we should accept the inevitability of performance enhancing drugs and seek to openly distinguish between those events that involve athletes that have made explicit use of such drugs and those events that are drug free, appraising the performance of athletes under both regimes (drug assisted and non-drug assisted) rather than chasing what may now be the unachievable goal of a world of non-drug assisted sporting performance.

KEY TEXTS

- Dunn, M. *et al.* (2010) 'Drug Testing in Sport: The Attitudes and Experiences of Elite Athletes', *International Journal of Drug Policy*, 21 (4): pp. 330–332
- Du-Pont *et al.* (2012) 'Random Student Drug Testing as a School-Based Drug Prevention Strategy', *Addiction*, 20 August, doi: 10.1111/j.1360–0443.2012.03978.x
- Hawken, A. and Kleiman, M. (2009) 'Managing Drug Involved Probations with Swift and Certain Sanctions: Evaluating Hawaii's HOPE', available at www.ncjrs.gov/pdffiles1/nij/grants/229023.pdf
- McKeganey, N. (2005) *Random Drug Testing: A Shot in the Arm or a Shot in the Foot for Drug Prevention* (York: Joseph Rowntree Foundation)
- Morente, J. and Zabala, M. (2013) 'Doping in Sport: A Review of Elite Athletes Attitudes Beliefs and Knowledge Sports Medicine', doi 10.1007/s40279–013–0037-x

therapeutic communities

SEE ALSO **recovery; relapse; residential rehabilitation; twelve-step programmes**

Therapeutic communities have had a long-standing position within the world of addictions *treatment* and the treatment of psychiatric and psychological problems more broadly. Interest in the idea of the 'community as treatment' arose in relation to the work of Drs Tom Main and Maxwell Jones caring for patients affected by the trauma of the second world war. In his work Maxwell Jones had noticed that the large group meetings of patients that he had chosen to convene initially as a way of feeding back information to patients were actually becoming events at which patients would share their experiences and thus seek to help and support each other (Jones, 1968a,b). The meetings themselves, initially purely administrative, took on a therapeutic role and in doing so gave expression to the idea that the hospital could itself become a therapeutic community in which patients were largely empowered to help themselves and each other in a form of peer support.

The idea that a community of patients could be therapeutic in their own right resonated with the challenges of conventional psychiatry that were to come some years later from R.D. Laing and others. Within the context of profound doubts that were being expressed in the 1960s about the nature and content of conventional psychiatric care (including the criticisms directed at the use of Electro Convulsive Therapy) the notion of patients taking responsibility for increasing aspects of their own care, and running the therapeutic environment themselves, gained considerable momentum. As a result therapeutic communities of different kinds were developed in a number of psychiatric hospitals within the United Kingdom, with a small number of examples being developed within the *prison* environment (Barlinie Special Unit, HMP Grendon). Whilst the programmes within the different therapeutic communities differed in many ways, the common element in all of the communities consisted in the notion that sick people, living together and taking responsibility for their care and treatment could create a positive therapeutic force in its own right.

Within some of the US-based therapeutic communities, set up and run by ex addicts, the culture is very much one of recovering addicts being confronted, sometimes aggressively so by others within the community. One such community set up in the United States in the 1960s by the recovering alcoholic Charles Dederich (Synanon) expanded widely becoming a major movement in its own right and claiming tax-exempt status as a church (Yablonsky, 1965). The movement was disbanded in 1991 amid a series of criminal investigations covering allegations of violence directed at current and former members and tax related problems. Despite its colourful history Synanon influenced the development of addict self-help communities in many different countries.

Throughout the 1970s and 1980s there was considerable interest in therapeutic communities within the United Kingdom, many of which provided *residential rehabilitation* services for recovering drink and drug users. With political support for the policy of community care many of the psychiatric hospital based therapeutic communities that had developed in the 1980s closed and interest in the therapeutic community idea began to wane. However spectacular examples of the success of the therapeutic communities remain, one of which is the San Patrignano community for recovering addicts based in the hills above Rimini in Italy.

The community was set up in 1978 by Vincenzo Muccioli who had noticed increasing numbers of addicts congregating in the town near his *family* home. Concerned, Muccioli tried to do something to help those he saw in a desperate need, and invited the addicts to live with his family on the condition that they did not use drugs within his home. From that small beginning the community now provides communal living for over 1000 individuals in various states of drug dependency and *recovery*. The ethic underpinning the community is one of peer support aligned to a programme of work and *education*. Whilst the community hosts a hospital, this is not for the dispensary of substitute medication but rather to meet the residents' other health related needs. Within San Patrignano dependency and recovery are seen in educational rather than medical or therapeutic terms with the drug users being provided with the opportunity to learn new skills and thereby to develop a sense of their own self-worth.

Individuals joining the community live in a small group of similarly circumstanced recovering addicts, all of whom are required to work within the community – within the extensive vineyards, furniture workshops, *media* facilities, dog and horse training school, restaurant and so on. San Patrignano charges no fees of its residents who travel to the community from across Italy and in some cases from even further afield. Nor does the community receive funding from the Italian government. Rather, the aim is for San Patrignano to be self-funding and to convey to the addicts that they do not have to rely for their survival on the charity of others. This is a community where recovery occurs not through intensive counselling or substitute medication but through peer support and daily work.

As an illustration of what the residents within San Patrignano are able to achieve, the community hosted the European show-jumping championship in 2004, attracting riders and horses from around the world. The event has now become a regular part of the San Patrignano calendar and is recognized worldwide as one of the premier outdoor show-jumping events. The community also hosts an annual international food expo and a 'Drugs Off Day' celebrating drug *prevention*. Importantly San Patrignano survives and flourishes because of the quality of the products that it produces. For example, San Patrignano wine is sought after throughout Italy, as are many of the products produced within the community. The aim here is to encourage addicts to aspire to be the best they can be and for their recovery and *rehabilitation* to come about through each individual realizing that aspiration.

Despite the inspirational success of centres such as the San Patrignano community, there is a definite sense that the therapeutic community movement itself has failed to use the power of *evidence* and science to carve out a sustained role for itself in mental health provision in many countries. George De-Leon, one of the world's leading researchers on the therapeutic community method, has summarized the achievements of the available *research* whilst simultaneously acknowledging the failure of that research base to persuade the sceptic of the value of the therapeutic community approach:

> Decades of therapeutic community research have been extremely productive but not necessarily persuasive in furthering the acceptance of the therapeutic community among some scientific critics and policy makers … Moreover, while not proof, the evidence consistently confirms the hypothesis that the therapeutic community is an effective and cost-effective treatment for certain subgroups of substance abusers. (De-Leon, 2010, p. 125)

KEY TEXTS

- De-Leon, G. (2010) 'Is the Therapeutic Community an Evidence Based Treatment? What the Evidence Says', *International Journal of Therapeutic Communities*, 31 (2): pp. 104–128
- Jones, M. (1968a) *Beyond the Therapeutic Community: Social Learning and Social Psychiatry* (New Haven, CT: Yale University Press)
- Jones, M. (1968b) *Social Psychiatry in Practice: The Idea of the Therapeutic Community* (England: Penguin)
- McKeganey, N. (2007) 'Riding High', *Drink and Drug News*, pp. 6–7
- Yablonsky, L. (1965) *The Tunnel Back: Synanon* (Basingstoke: Palgrave Macmillan)

tobacco

SEE ALSO addiction; harm reduction; recovery; stigma

Since the twentieth century, smoking has been described as a global killer responsible according to the World Health Organization for around 5 million deaths a year. Within the United Kingdom it is thought that cigarette smoking is estimated to kill around 120,000 people each year – in Scotland it is thought that approximately 30 people die each day from smoking related disease (Callum, 1998). It is believed that one in five of all deaths in the United Kingdom is attributed to smoking and that regular smokers on average die some 16 years sooner than they would had they not smoked (Peto *et al.*, 1994).

In view of the well-known harms associated with smoking, it may be a wonder to some that why individuals start smoking or that those that do persist. Nicotine, however, is an extraordinarily powerful drug with the capacity to reinforce its repeated use. Withdrawal symptoms associated with nicotine dependence can appear within six to twelve hours and persist for many weeks and months with it having been reported that ex-smokers still craving the drug a year after having quit (Hughes, 1992). *Research* has shown that the adverse effects of nicotine withdrawal are rapidly reduced with the resumption of cigarette smoking making smoking an extraordinarily difficult behaviour to change.

Treatment for smoking has encompassed a wide range of psychological (e.g. cognitive behavioural therapy) and physiological approaches (e.g. nicotine replacement therapy). Treatments for tobacco which aim to address either the psychological basis of the dependency or the dependency on particular substances (nicotine) are both based on the presumption that individuals are driven to continue smoking rather than that they choose to continue to smoke despite the obvious harms to their health. The notion of being driven by some external force (nicotine dependence) to continue smoking has, however, been disputed by those researchers who have stressed the volitional element in individuals continuing to smoke (Russell and Davies, 2009).

The most widely available treatment for smoking cessation is the use of 'Nicotine Replacement Therapy' that has been evaluated in multiple, large-scale studies and has resulted in widespread approval for nicotine replacement therapy. This treatment involves the controlled delivery of fixed amounts of nicotine to nicotine receptors in the brain with the effect that the negative symptoms of drug withdrawal that would normally accompany smoking cessation and which would prompt a return to smoking are substantially reduced. An analysis of III nicotine replacement trials involving more than 43,000 smokers found that the use of nicotine replacement therapy was associated with an increased likelihood of remaining cigarette free irrespective of the type of nicotine replacement device that was being used (e.g. nicotine gum, patches, aerosols, tablet) (Stead *et al.*, 2008). Research carried out for the US Public Health Service found that nicotine replacement patches virtually doubled the rate of long-term abstinence (Fiore *et al.*, 2008).

KEY TEXTS
- McNeill, A. and Munafo, M. (2013) 'Reducing Harm from Tobacco Use', *Journal of Psychopharmacology*, 27 (1): pp. 13–18
- Niaura, R. and Abrams, D.B. (2002) 'Smoking Cessation: Progress, Priorities, and Prospectus', *Journal of Consulting and Clinical Psychology*, 70: pp. 494–509
- Peto, R. *et al.* (1994) *Mortality from Smoking in Developing Countries, 1950–2000* (Oxford: Oxford University Press)
- Royal College of Physicians (2000) *Nicotine Addiction in Britain: A report of the Tobacco Advisory Group of the Royal College of Physicians* (London: Royal College of Physicians)
- Russell, C., Davies, J.B. and Hunter, S.C. (2011) 'Predictors of Addiction Treatment Providers' Beliefs in the Disease and Choice Models of Addiction', *Journal of Substance Abuse Treatment*, 40: pp. 150–164
- Zakhari, R. (2013) 'Smoking Harm Reduction versus Abstinence', *Journal of the American Academy of Nurse Practitioners*, 25 (1): pp. 1–2

treatment

SEE ALSO **contingency management; harm reduction; maturing out; methadone; motivational interviewing; prescribing**

If there is one mantra that sums up the approach to drug dependency treatment over the last 15 years it is that 'Treatment Works' – precisely how treatment works, for whom, for how long and in what ways and with what goals has been a source of near constant debate amongst treatment providers, politicians, drug users and many others.

There has been heated debate as to the appropriate balance in government expenditure between treatment and *enforcement*. The Global Commission on Drugs is one organization which has repeatedly called for drug use/abuse to be seen as a health/medical problem rather than a law enforcement issue, and for health services, rather than criminal justice agencies, to have the lead responsibility in responding to drug use and drug users (Global Commission on Drugs Policy, 2011). There has been debate as to whether *prescribing* substitute opiate drugs to individuals who have become dependent upon *heroin* constitutes treatment in the normal sense of the word (National Treatment Agency, 2012). There has been debate as to whether drug treatment services should prescribe heroin to those who have become dependent upon the drug or whether this is simply a route for continuing individual's drug dependency (Strang *et al.*, 2010). There has been debate as to the appropriate balance between abstinence and *harm reduction* services in providing treatment for dependent drug users (McKeganey *et al.*, 2004; Neale, 2011), and there has been debate and sometimes bitter disagreement as to the role of the doctor in treating those with a drug dependency problem (Mars, 2013). There has been debate as to the relative contribution of professional drug workers and peer educators in facilitating individual's *recovery* from drug dependency (White, 2012), and there has been debate as to the most appropriate balance between treating drug users in the community and treating them within *residential rehabilitation* facilities (Keen *et al.*, 2001). There has been debate as to how to measure the success or effectiveness of drug dependency treatment (Unell, 2012; O'Connor, 2012), and there has been debate as to the role of politicians in determining drug treatment policy (Ford, 2010)

In many of these debates, there has been a marked lack of sound, empirical data with which to assess the arguments. Unquestionably the debate that is served by the largest body of *evidence* has to do with the effectiveness of *prescribing methadone* to dependent drug users. However most of the studies here have been undertaken in a small number of countries (mainly the US) with the result that it is far from clear how much the results of that *research* apply to other countries.

In the absence of a clear body of evidence as to the relative effectiveness of different treatments for drug dependency most countries operate on the basis that it is desirable to have a mix of services that can meet the diverse needs of drug users. At best this can be described as ensuring that countries provide an appropriate wide range of treatment services for dependent drug users. At worst this approach can be described in such terms as 'if you don't know what works best it is better to have a bit of everything rather than place all of your eggs in one basket'. It is questionable whether in response to a drug problem that in its current form has been around for at least half a decade we should still be floundering to answer such fundamental questions about the nature, goals, and effectiveness of drug treatment services.

KEY TEXTS

- Ford, C. (2010) 'Methadone Works Stop the Interfering', *Guardian*, 26 July.
- Keen, J. *et al.* (2001) 'Residential Rehabilitation for Drug Users: A Review of 13 Months' Intake to a Therapeutic Community', *Family Practice*, 18 (5): pp. 545–548
- O'Connor, R. (2012) 'Getting Better Outcomes for Drug Users', *Druglink*, September: pp. 12–13
- Unell, I. 92012) 'TOP of the Form', *Druglink*, September: pp. 10–11
- White, W. (2012) 'Medication-Assisted Recovery from Opioid Addiction: Historical and Contemporary Perspectives', *Journal of Addictive Diseases*, 31 (3): pp. 199–206

twelve-step programmes

SEE ALSO **addiction; recovery; relapse; residential rehabilitation; spontaneous remission; stages of change**

Twelve step refers to a staged approach to *recovery* from drug and *alcohol* dependency that has its origin over 65 years ago in the formation of Alcoholics Anonymous (AA) as a fellowship of individuals committed to the goal of ceasing drinking and remaining alcohol free. Alcoholics Anonymous receives no government funding and is not associated with any particular political group, *religion* or cultural group – it is literally a worldwide fellowship of individuals who have got into difficulty as a result of their alcohol consumption and who are determined to stop their drinking. The twelve steps referred to begin with Step 1 which involves the admission that the individual is unable to manage his or her alcohol intake and that in effect the drug is managing them. Step 2, which is one of the most controversial, involves the acknowledgement that their restoration to health and sobriety can only come about as a result of the individual's belief in a higher power – a power greater than themselves as individuals. This step has been interpreted by some critics as tantamount to requiring those who might seek the help of Alcoholics Anonymous to believe in some notion of a religious, godlike figure. Step 4 requires the individuals to make an inventory of their nature including the harms they have caused to other people. Step 9 involves a commitment to make amends to all of those people the individual has harmed during the period of their drinking. Finally, Step 12 involves a commitment to apply the principles of the individuals' recovery during their everyday life and to carry the message of recovery and sobriety to others who get into difficulty as a result of their drug or alcohol use.

A key part of the belief system underpinning the twelve-step programmes is the importance of owning up to the fact of one's dependency (including literally standing up before others and announcing the fact of being an addict). In addition the belief system underpinning AA also asserts that there is no possibility of the individual becoming fully recovered from his or her *addiction*. Rather, the individual remains in a state of being in recovery with the need, each and every day of their life, to reaffirm their commitment to the drug or alcohol free lifestyle.

In the period since the first twelve-step programme was outlined, the notion has been implemented in relation to a wide range of addictive behaviours resulting in the development of such groups as Narcotics Anonymous, Cocaine Anonymous, Marijuana Anonymous, Nicotine Anonymous, *Methadone* Anonymous to name but a few. The essential format of these groups is very similar in being built around the same twelve steps of recovery.

Despite the global reach of Alcoholics Anonymous and the variety of 12-step movements that have developed over the years there has been relatively little *research* that has evaluated the effectiveness of the various approaches. One reason for this is the unwillingness of the various 12-step groups to open themselves up for evaluation by outside researchers. However this is not to say that there have been no important studies of the 12-step approach to recovery with the most well-known evaluation being *Project Match* study. Project Match was an eight-year, 27-million dollar study that sought to ascertain whether there was any *evidence* that assigning individuals to different treatments on the basis of certain characteristics resulted in any demonstrable difference in the outcomes of *treatment* for alcoholic patients. The study included 12-step therapy along with two other treatment approaches (Cognitive Behavioural Coping Skills and Motivational Enhancement Therapy). In terms of outcome, each of the treatments (including the 12-step approaches) were equally effective. Although this may be taken as a positive vindication of the value of treatment, a more critical reading of the study would be to say that it does not actually matter that much what treatment one gets for alcohol dependency – the outcome will be largely the same.

KEY TEXTS

- Buxton, M., Smith, D. and Seymour, R. (1987) 'Spirituality and Other Points of Resistance to the 12-Step Recovery Process', *Journal of Psychoactive Drugs*, 19 (3): pp. 275–286
- Florentine, R. (1999) 'After Drug Treatment: Are 12-Step Programs Effective in Maintaining Abstinence?' *American Journal of Drug and Alcohol Abuse*, 25 (1): pp. 93–116
- Hser, Y. and Anglin, D. (2011) 'Addiction Treatment and Recovery Careers', *Current Clinical Psychiatry*, Part 1, 9–29, doi: 10.1007/978–1–60327–960–4–2
- Strang, J. *et al.* (2010) 'Drug Policy and the Public Good: Evidence for Effective Interventions', *Lancet*, 379 (9810), 7–13 January: pp. 71–83

u

UKATT

SEE ALSO project match; recovery; research

The UK Alcohol Treatment Trial (UKATT) was the largest evaluation of *alcohol treatment* ever undertaken within the United Kingdom and is very much the UK equivalent of *Project Match*. The study involved both quantitative and qualitative assessments of the progress of problem drinkers following their random allocation to one of two treatments – social behaviour network therapy or motivational enhancement therapy. Whilst the latter therapy has been extensively studied and positively evaluated, social behaviour network therapy was an approach developed by the UKATT team comprising an amalgam of counselling aimed at encouraging the development of a supportive social and *family* network around the problem drinker. In total 742 clients with alcohol problems were assigned to either treatment; 689 (93.0%) of respondents were assessed at three months and 617 (83.2%) were interviewed at 12 months. As well as assessing the effectiveness of both treatments the UKATT *research* also involved a strong health economic component that sought to assess the cost of the two treatments and the cost saving and costs incurred as a result of individuals being provided with either treatment. Like Project Match the UKATT study did not use a 'no treatment' comparison or control group on the basis that it would have been unethical to withhold treatment. The results of the UKATT research were that both treatments were equally effective and equally cost effective in reducing individual's alcohol consumption (Godfrey *et al.*, 2005; Orford *et al.*, 2005).

In an interesting critical reflection on the design of the UKATT study, and other similar studies, one of the researchers (Professor Jim Orford) set out his assessment of the methodological and theoretical failures of such research, and the need to re-focus research away from treatment outcomes are more on treatment process that is establishing how different treatments work in practice.

According to Orford the shortcomings of the large-scale outcome studies are that they often neglect the therapeutic relationships established within treatment in favour of focusing on treatment as a technical skill; in assessing the outcomes of treatment they often fail to pay due attention to the element of unaided *recovery*, not recognizing that alongside the contribution of any particular treatment individuals are also engaged in the process of trying to get better themselves; they often impose an inappropriate time frame on behaviour change failing to recognize the fact that where a condition such as alcoholism has taken years to develop, treatment research often looks to identify and measure a treatment impact of only a few months; they pay inadequate attention to the fact that therapists working in different treatment modalities will have their own tacit theories of causation and recovery that may well be influencing their work with clients; they fail often to take a social network view and pay inadequate attention to the multitude of ways in which the individual's social and family relationships may be influencing their recovery; finally they often exclude the patient's view (Orford, 2008).

As a remedy to these shortcomings Orford advises that researchers should 'stop studying named techniques and focus instead on studying change processes', look instead at the much wider context within which treatment approaches are delivered and experienced by clients, and finally recognize and use a much wider range of knowledge than limiting themselves to the quantitative randomized control study design – in particular utilizing qualitative approaches to a much greater degree.

The latter advice is very much in accordance with the guidance offered by Sir Michael Rawlins in his Harviean Oration lecture in which he has castigated the view of a hierarchy of knowledge that often places randomized control trials at the top of a knowledge hierarchy with qualitative research and case studies relegated to a much lower position. According to Rawlins:

> The notion that *evidence* can be reliably placed in hierarchies
> is illusory. Hierarchies place RCTs on an undeserved pedestal
> for ... although the technique has advantages it also has

significant disadvantages. Observational studies too have defects but they also have merit. The decision makers need to assess and appraise all the available evidence irrespective as to whether it has been derived from RCTs or observational studies, and the strengths and weaknesses of each need to be understood if reasonable and reliable conclusions are to be drawn. (Rawlins, 2008, p. 2; emphasis added)

On the basis of Orford and Rawlins's advice, researchers seeking to evaluate the impact and effectiveness of treatments within the addictions (and elsewhere) may need to adopt a much more expanded notion of science and understanding than the almost slavish adherence to certain methodological design (of which the randomized control trial study design is perhaps the most exalted example).

KEY TEXTS
- Godfrey, C. (2005) 'Cost Effectiveness of Treatment for Alcohol Problems: Findings of the Randomised UK Alcohol Treatment Trial (UKATT)', *British Medical Journal*, 331 (7516): pp. 544–548
- Orford, J. (2005) 'Effectiveness of Treatment for Alcohol Problems: Findings of the Randomised UK Alcohol Treatment Trial (UKATT)', *British Medical Journal*, 331: p. 541
- Orford, J. (2008) 'Asking the Right Questions in the Right Way: The Need for a Shift in Research on Psychological Treatments for Addiction', *Addiction*, 103 (6): pp. 886–892
- Rawlins, M. (2008) 'On the Evidence for Decisions about the Use of Therapeutic Interventions', *The Harviean Oration* (London: Royal College of Physicians)

user organizations

SEE ALSO identity; politics; strategies; therapeutic communities

There is a tendency within professional and public discourse to conceive of drug users as people who either pose a health risk (*HIV, Hepatitis C*, drug related *overdose, suicide*) or a criminal justice risk (as a result of their recourse to criminality to fund their drug usage). However, there is an entirely different view of drug users which is the view promoted by the drug user rights organizations which see drug users through neither of these negative lenses and promote instead the view of drug users simply as people who use drugs:

> We are people from around the world who use drugs. We are people who have been marginalized and discriminated against; we have been killed, harmed unnecessarily, put in jail, depicted as evil, and stereotyped as dangerous and disposable. Now it is time to raise our voices as citizens, establish our rights and reclaim the right to be our own spokespersons striving for self-representation and self-empowerment. (Statement by the International Activists who Use Drugs Vancouver, 2006)

One of the very first drug user organizations was the Dutch Junkiebonden set up in 1981 by Nico Adriaans. Under Adriaans's leadership the group sought to counteract the negative image of drug users in the *media*, and to advocate for the development of a range of health services. In 1984 the Junkiebonden was responsible for setting up the first government-backed needle and syringe exchange scheme in the Netherlands. Friedman and colleagues have described the crucial role of drug user organizations in response to the threat of HIV:

> We have seen users themselves as the ones with primary agency in *harm reduction*. It is their actions that do or do not transmit infections, do or do not result in overdoses, do or do not create problems for their neighbours. Agencies like syringe exchanges can provide risk reduction supplies, information and counselling, but users themselves – individually and in groups – take the decisive action. (Friedman *et al.*, 2007, pp. 107/108; emphasis added)

Whilst there is considerable *evidence* of drug user groups responding positively to the threat of HIV, in modifying their own risk behaviour and lobbying for the development of appropriate health services, many of the groups have been critical of the focus on *recovery* that has characterized more recent debates within the drugs field. Elliot Ross Albers from the International Network of People Who Use Drugs has written that:

> Whatever one's views on the value of the use of the term 'recovery' (I personally do not find it helpful, as I do not see

habitual drug use as an illness to be recovered from, but rather a behaviour that people engage in), the insistence that the only satisfactory or successful outcome of an engagement with drug dependence services is abstinence is unrealistic and contrary to the well established evidence enshrined in all internationally accepted guidelines, including the UK's own clinical guidelines ... The new recovery agenda – with its marches, boat rides, right-wing Christian overtones, Russell Brands and happy-clappy 'recovery champions' – silences, stigmatises and further marginalises those of us who are either active drug users or are stable on maintenance scripts. It demeans our choices and denigrates our successes, and it does so on the basis of a disregard for the overwhelming body of evidence that recognises the complexity of drug dependence, and demonstrates the vital need for comprehensive harm reduction services. (Ross Albers, 2013, p. 15)

With such a comprehensive rejection of the policy of prioritizing recovery there is a real sense of a possible schism between some of the drug user rights organizations and the predominant societal view that drug use is something that should be prevented, and from which those who have become dependent should be helped to recover.

If one accepts the view that it is the right of the individual to use whatever drugs he or she wishes, rejecting the view of the drug user as someone in need of *treatment*, then it is difficult at the same time to maintain that society should continue to meet the costs of treatment and support for those individuals whose drug use causes them a range of personal difficulties. It is interesting to note that whilst viewing drug use as a lifestyle choice, Ross Albers also maintains that society should continue to bear the responsibility of providing the plethora of harm reduction services, needle and syringe exchange, *safe injecting centres*, and unlimited opiate substitute medication. In this Albers is in agreement with the Charter of Drug User Rights drafted by Dr Russell Newcombe in 2007 which identifies three general rights that should be accorded to all drug users: that is, the right to consume drugs, the right to receive help for drug problems and the right to be subjected to fair drug laws and policies (Newcombe, 2007).

KEY TEXTS

- Bröring, G. and Schatz, E. (2008) *Empowerment and Self – Organisations of Drug Users Experiences and Lessons Learnt* (Amsterdam: Foundation Regenboog AMOC, Correlation Network)
- Charlois, T. (2009) *Drug User Participation and European Cities* (UK: EXASS Net Pompidou Group Council of Europe)
- Chatwin, C. (2010) 'User Involvement in the Illegal Drugs Field: What Can Britain Learn from European Experiences', *Safer Communities*, 9 (4): pp. 51–60
- Friedman, S., de Jong, W. and Des Jarlaise, D. (1988) 'Problems and Dynamics of Organizing Intravenous Drug Users for AIDS Prevention', *Health Education Research*, 3 (1): pp. 49–57

Z

zero tolerance

SEE ALSO decriminalization; international treaties; strategies

The notion of zero tolerance as it applies to the use of illegal drugs is most closely associated with the public statements and polices of the US governments led by Presidents Regan and Bush. Within both administrations there was enthusiastic support of the role of drugs enforcements directed at both drug users and drug traffickers with the aim being to substantially reduce the availability of illegal drugs within the United States. Indeed for both presidents the drugs trade itself was seen to present a major threat to the security and welfare of the United States and was viewed as a major external threat to the country.

However, the adoption of zero tolerance drug policies neither originated in, nor have they found their sole expression within, the United States. In many of the Asian countries, for example, there are extreme penalties for even the possession of small amounts of illegal drugs. Similarly in many of the countries within the Arabian peninsula the *death* penalty is retained (and used) for those found guilty of drugs trafficking.

Within Europe the country most closely associated with zero tolerance drug policies is Sweden. In the 1960s Sweden was pursuing a liberal drug policy that included amongst other things the prescription of *heroin* to addicts that were dependent upon the drug. By the late 1960s the liberal Swedish drug policy was judged to have been a failure as *evidence* began to mount that many of those who were being prescribed heroin, and other drugs, were selling their medication to other drug users. There was also growing evidence of increasing numbers of drug users in Sweden turning to *injecting* as their preferred route of drug use. From the late 1960s the liberal drug policies that Sweden had been following were changed in favour of what has come to be known as a zero tolerance policy.

The individual that was more influential in shaping that change than any other was Nils Bejerot who consistently advised the Swedish government that the only way for the country to avoid an epidemic of illicit drug use (that was beginning to be evident in other European countries) was by adopting a policy of zero tolerance. Berjerot's argument in this respect was based upon *research* he had undertaken within Swedish prisons.

In 1969 the Swedish government announced a ten-point action plan for tackling the problem of illegal drugs. That plan allocated increased funding to tackling illegal drugs, it increased the penalties for drug offences, increased the provision of abstinence based drug treatments, and authorized the use of wire tapping of individuals suspected to be involved in the drugs trade. The thrust of government policy within Sweden at that time consisted of a commitment to the view that the use of illegal drugs could not be tolerated within Swedish society and that action had to be directed towards eradicating drug use from Swedish society. The approach developed within Sweden at that time placed particular emphasis on stressing the shared responsibility for tackling illegal drug use. Policy documents and statements stressed that drug *prevention* was a responsibility for all Swedish citizens and was not something that could or should be left to specialist agencies:

> Everybody who comes in contact with the problem must be engaged, authorities can never relieve individuals from personal responsibility and participation. Efforts by parents *family* and friends are especially important. Also schools and non-governmental organisation are important instruments in the struggle against drugs. (ONDCP, 2007, p. 19; emphasis added)

In 1978, Sweden's drug policies were further tightened with the clear aim being to eliminate drug abuse from Swedish society.

Whilst the possession of certain drugs is illegal in most countries within Sweden evidence of drug use itself is regarded as an offence. In Sweden, when a *police* officer suspects that an individual has been using illegal drugs, he or she can require the individual to provide a blood sample with which to establish whether the individual has been using illegal drugs. Similarly, whereas in many countries drug abuse *treatment* is voluntarily entered into, within Sweden authorities can require the individual to undergo a course of drug treatment once it is established that the individual does indeed have a drug problem. Although the notion of coerced treatment might be regarded as a violation of the individual's human rights in many countries, the notion of court ordered treatment (drug courts) has become an increasingly central component of the world of addictions treatment. Within the drug court, for example, individuals are presented with the choice of engaging with treatment or face receiving a custodial sentence following their having been arrested for a criminal offence.

In the light of the tough stance against illegal drugs within Sweden an obvious question to ask is whether there is any indication that those policies have led to markedly lower levels of drug use than is occurring in other countries within Europe. In fact Sweden has one of the lowest levels of illegal drug use anywhere in Europe and whilst this is not evidence that it was the zero tolerance policy itself that has delivered the low levels of illegal drug use, or that in the absence of that policy Sweden would have seen a level of illegal drug use closer to the European norm, the low level of drug use within Sweden is congruent with the aims of its zero tolerance policy.

KEY TEXTS

- Bejerot, N. (1980) *Addiction to Pleasure: A Biological and Social Psychological Theory of Addiction* (NIDA Monograph 30), pp. 246–255
- Caulkins, J. (1983) 'Zero-Tolerance Policies: Do They Inhibit or Stimulate Illicit Drug Consumption', *Management Science* (39) 4: pp. 458–476
- Drucker, E. (2012) 'Failed Drug Policies in the United States and the Future of AIDS: A Perfect Storm', *Journal of Public Health Policy*, 33: pp. 309–316
- United Nations Office on Drugs and Crime (2007) *Sweden's Successful Drug Policy: A Review of the Evidence* (UNODC)

references

Abdul-Quader, A. *et al.* (2002) 'Preventing HIV in Developing Countries', *AIDS Prevention and Mental Health*, 283–312, doi: 10.1007/0-306-47157-4_13

Abeni, D.D., Brancato, G. and Perucci, C.A. (1994) 'Capture-Recapture to Estimate the Size of the Population with HIV Type 1 Infection', *Epidemiology*, 5 (4): pp. 410–414

Adams, J. and White, M. (2005) 'Why Don't Stage Based Activity Promotion Interventions Work?' *Health Education Research*, 20 (2): pp. 237–243

Advisory Council on the Misuse of Drugs (1988) *AIDS and Drugs Misuse* (London: HMSO)

Advisory Council on the Misuse of Drugs (2003) *Hidden Harm: Responding to the Children of Problem Drug Users* (London: HMSO)

Advisory Council on the Misuse of Drugs (2011) *Consideration of the Novel Psychoactive Substances (Legal Highs)* (London: ACMD)

Alexander, B. (2008) *The Globalisation of Addiction: A Study in the Poverty of the Spirit* (Oxford: Oxford University Press)

Alexander, B. *et al.* (1981) 'Effect of Early and Later Colony Housing on Oral Ingestion of Morphine in Rats', *Pharmacology Biochemistry and Behaviour*, 15: pp. 571–576

Alper, K. *et al.* (1999) 'Treatment of Acute Opioid Withdrawal with Ibogaine', *American Journal on Addictions*, 8: pp. 234–242

Asbridge, M., Hayden, J. and Cartwright, J. (2012) 'Acute Cannabis Consumption and Motor Vehicle Collision Risk: Systematic Review of Observational Studies and Meta-Analysis', *British Medical Journal*, 344: p. e536

Aveyard, P. *et al.* (2012) 'Brief Opportunistic Smoking Cessation Interventions: A Systematic Review and Meta-Analysis to Compare Advice to Quit and Offer of Assistance', *Addiction*, 107 (6): pp. 1066–1073

Backmund, M. *et al.* (2011) 'Factors Associated with Suicide Attempts among Injection Drug Users', *Substance Use and Misuse*, 46 (12): pp. 1553–1559

Balmelli, C., Kupferschmidt, H. and Schneemann, M. (2001) 'Fatal Brain Edema after Ingestion of Ecstasy and Benzylpiperazine', *Deutsche Medizinische Wochenschrift* [German Medical Weekly], 126 (28–29): pp. 809–811

Bancroft, A. *et al.* (2004) *Parental Drug and Alcohol Misuse Resilience and Transition among Young People* (York: Joseph Rowntree Foundation)

Barnard, M. (2003) 'Between a Rock and a Hard Place: The Role of Relatives in Protecting Children from the Effects of Parental Drug Problems', *Child and Family Social Work*, 8: pp. 291–299

Barnard, M. (2007) *Drug Addiction and Families* (London and Philadelphia: Jessica Kingsley)

Barnard, M. and McKeganey, N. (2004) 'The Impact of Parental Problem Drug Use on Children: What Is the Problem and What Can Be Done to Help?' *Addiction*, 99 (5), May: pp. 552–559

Bates, M. and Blakely, T. (1999) 'Role of Cannabis in Motor Vehicle Crashes', *Epidemiologic Reviews*, 21 (2): pp. 222–232

BBC (2002) 'Doctors Oppose More Heroin Prescription', 15 January, available at http://news.bbc.co.uk/1/hi/health/1759719.stm.

BBC (2007) 'Drug Rewards Given to Addicts', available at http://news.bbc.co.uk/1hi/uk/7049934.stm

BBC (2011) 'Vancouver Insite Drug Injection Facility Can Stay Open', 30 September 2011

Beattie, T., Bhattacharjee, P. and Ramesh, B. (2010) 'Violence against Female Sex Workers in Karnataka State, South India: Impact on Health and Reductions in Violence Following an Intervention Programme', *BMC Public Health*, 10: p. 476

Becker, H. (1953) 'Becoming a Marihuana User', *American Journal of Sociology*, 59 (4): pp. 235–242

Becker, H. (1967) 'Whose Side Are We On?' *Social Problems*, 14: pp. 239–247

Benson, P. (1992) 'Religion and Substance Use in Religion and Mental Health', in J. Schumacher (ed), *Religion and Mental Health* (New York: Oxford University Press)

Best, D. and Laudet, A. (2010) The Potential of Recovery Capital. RSA Projects

Best, D. *et al.* (2000) 'Drinking and Smoking As Concurrent Predictors of Illicit Drug Use and Positive Drug Attitudes in Adolescents', *Drug and Alcohol Dependence*, 60: pp. 319–321

Best, D. *et al.* (2008) 'Breaking the Habit: A Retrospective Analysis of Desistance Factors among Formerly Problematic Heroin Users', *Drug and Alcohol Review*, 27 (6): pp. 619–624

Best, D. *et al.* (2012) 'Mapping the Recovery Stories of Drinkers and Drug Users in Glasgow: Quality of Life and Its Associations with Measures of Recovery Capital', *Drug and Alcohol Review*, 31 (3): pp. 334–341

Betty Ford Institute Consensus Panel (2007) 'What Is Recovery? A Working Definition from the Betty Ford Institute', *Journal of Substance Abuse Treatment*, 33: pp. 221–228

Bienacki, P. (1986) *Pathways from Heroin Addiction: Recovery without Treatment* (Philadelphia: Temple University)

Bird, S. and Robertson, R. (2011) 'Toxicology of Scotland's Drugs-Related Deaths in 2000–2007: Presence of Heroin, Methadone, Diazepam and Alcohol by Sex, Age-Group and Era', *Addiction Research and Theory*, (19) 2: pp. 170–178

Blakey, D. (2008) 'Disrupting the Supply of Illicit Drugs into Prisons', A Report for the Director General of National Offender Management Service, available at http://www.drugscope.org.uk/Resources/Drugscope/Documents/PDF/Good%20Practice/blakeyreport.pdf

Blomquist, J. *et al.* (2007) 'Improving Ones Drinking Habits -on Different Patterns of Change and on the Role of Alcohol Treatment', Stockholm University SoRAD Report, 5

Bloor, M. *et al.* (2008) 'Topping Up' Methadone: An Analysis of Patterns of Heroin Use Among a Treatment Sample of Scottish Drug Users', *Public Health*, 122 (10) October: pp. 1013–1019

Botvin, G.J., Eng, A. and Williams, C.L. (1980) 'Preventing the Onset of Cigarette Smoking through Life Skills Training', *Preventive Medicine*, 9: pp. 135–143

Botvin, G.J. *et al.* (1989) 'A Skills Training Approach to Smoking Prevention among Hispanic Youth', *Journal of Behavioral Medicine*, 12: pp. 279–296

Botvin, G.J. *et al.* (1995) 'Effectiveness of Culturally-Focused and Generic Skills Training Approaches to Alcohol and Drug Abuse Prevention among Minority Adolescents: Two-Year Follow-Up Results', *Psychology of Addictive Behaviors*, 9: pp. 183–194

Buhringer, G. and Pfeiffer-Gerschel, T. (2008) 'COMBINE and MATCH: The Final Blow for Large Scale Black Bock Randomized Controlled Trials', *Addiction*, 103 (5) May: pp. 708–710

Burns, J. (2012) 'Can LSD Cure Depression?' *Daily Telegraph*, 25 September, available at http://www.telegraph.co.uk/science/9565026/Can-LSD-cure-depression.html

Callum, C. (1998) *The U.K. Smoking Epidemic: Deaths in 1995* (London: Health Education Authority)

Carnie, J. and Broderick, R, (2011) Prisoner Survey 2011, available at http://www.sps.gov.uk/Publications/Publication-3696.aspx

Catalano, R. *et al.* (1999) 'An Experimental Intervention with Families of Substance Abusers: One Year Follow Up of the Focus on Families Project', *Addiction*, 94 (2): pp. 241–254

Catalano, R. *et al.* (2002) 'Children of Substance Abusing Parents: Current Findings from the Focus on Families Project' in R.J. McMahon and R.D. Peters (eds), *The Effects of Parental Dysfunction on Children* (New York: Kluwer Academic Press)

Caulkins, J. and Reuter, P. (2007) How Drug Enforcement Affects Price, available at: http://faculty.publicpolicy.umd.edu/sites/default/files/reuter/files/Drug%20Enforcement%20and%20Drug%20Price.pdf

Chatwin, C. (2011) *Drug Policy and Harmonization and the European Union* (Basingstoke: Palgrave Macmillan)

Chen, X. *et al.* (2005) 'Sexually Transmitted Infection among Female Sex Workers in Yunnan, China', *AIDS Patient Care and STDs*, 19 (912): pp. 853–860

Chiauzzi, E. and Liljegren, S. (1993) 'Taboo Topics in Addiction Treatment: An Empirical Review of Clinical Folklore', *Journal of Substance Abuse Treatment*, 10: pp. 303–316

Church, S. *et al.* (2001) 'Violence by Clients towards Female Prostitutes in Different Work Settings: Questionnaire Survey', *British Medical Journal*, 322: pp. 524

Clement, T. (2008) 'Canadian Government Hansard Publication', 39: 2 Hansard – 103 (2008/6/2), available at http://www2.parl.gc.ca/house-chamberbusiness/ChamberPublicationIndexSearch.aspx?arpist=s&arpit=vancouver+insite&arpidf=2006/01/01&arpidt=2010/05/31&arpid=True&arpij=False&arpice=False&arpicl=&ps=ParloSeso&arpisb=Publication&arpirpp=100&arpibs=False&Language=E&Mode=1&Parl=39&Ses=1&arpicid=3535078&arpicpd=3537184#Para1130935

Coffin, P. *et al.* (2003) 'Opiates Cocaine and Alcohol Combination in Drug Overdose Deaths in New York City 1990–1998', *Addiction*, 98: pp. 739–747

Cohen, P. (2003) 'The Drug Prohibition Church and the Adventure of Reformation', *International Journal of Drug Policy*, 14 (2): pp. 213–215

Cook, C. (2009) *Substance Misuse in Spirituality and Psychiatry* (London: Royal College of Psychiatrists), pp. 139–168

Cornish, R. *et al.* (2010) 'Risk of Death during and after Opiate Substitution Treatment in Primary Care: Prospective Observational Study in UK General Practice Research Database', *British Medical Journal*, 341: p. c5475

Cunningham, J., Cameron, T. and Koski-Jannes, A. (2005) 'Motivation and Life Events a Perspective Natural History Pilot Study of Problem Drinkers in the Community', *Addictive Behaviours*, 30: pp. 1603–1606

Dalrymple, T. (2006) *Romancing Opiates: Pharmacological Lies and the Addiction Bureaucracy* (Encounter Books: New York)

Darke, S. (2006) 'Poly Drug Use and Overdose: Overthrowing Old Myths', *Addiction*, 98: p. 711

Darke, S., Campbell, G. and Popple, G. (2012) 'Self-Harm and Attempted Suicide among Therapeutic Community Admissions', *Drug and Alcohol Review*, 31 (June): pp. 523–528

Davies, J.B. (1992) *The Myth of Addiction* (Switzerland: Harwood Academic Publishers)

Davies, T. *et al.* (1995) 'HIV in Injecting Drug Users in Edinburgh: Prevalence and Correlates', *Journal of the Acquired Immune Deficiency Syndrome and Human Retrovirology*, 18 (4): pp. 399–405

Dawe, S. *et al.* (2003) 'Improving Family Functioning and Child Outcomes in Methadone Maintained Families: The Parents under Pressure Programme', *Drug and Alcohol Review*, 22 (3): pp. 299–307

Dawson, D. *et al.* (2006) 'Estimating the Effect of Help Seeking on Achieving Recovery from Alcohol Dependence', *Addiction*, 101: pp. 824–834

De Angelis, D., Hickman, M. and Yang, S. (2004) 'Estimating Long Term Trends in the Incidence and Prevalence of Opiate Use/Injecting Drug Use and the Number of Former Users: Back Calculation Methods and Opiate Overdose Deaths', *American Journal of Epidemiology*, 160 (10): pp. 994–1004

Decker, M., McCauley, J. and Phuengsamran, D. (2011) 'Sex Trafficking Sexual Risk Sexually Transmitted Infection and Reproductive Health among Female Sex Workers in Thailand', *Journal of Epidemiology and Community Health*, 65 (4): pp. 334–339

De-Leon, G. (2010) 'Is the Therapeutic Community an Evidence Based Treatment? What the Evidence Says', *International Journal of Therapeutic Communities*, 31 (2): pp. 104–128

Del-Rio, M. *et al.* (2002) 'Alcohol Illicit Drugs and Medicinal Drugs in Fatally Injured Drivers in Spain between 1991 and 2000', *Forensic Science International*, 127: pp. 63–70

Department of Health (2010) Updated Guidance for Prison Based Opioid Maintenance Prescribing

Des Jarlais, D. *et al.* (1989) 'HIV Infection among Intravenous Drug Users in Manhattan, New York from 1977 through 1987', *Journal of the American Medical Association*, 26: pp. 1008–1012

Dole, V. and Nyswander, M. (1965) 'A Medical Treatment for Diacetylmorphine (Heroin) Addiction: A Clinical Trial with Methadone Hydrochloride', *Journal of the American Medical Association*, 193 (8): pp. 646–650

Dole, V. and Nyswander, M. (1967) 'Heroin Addiction – A Metabolic Disease', *New York Archives of Intern Medicine*, 120 (July)

Dolin, B. (2001) 'National Drug Policy: The Netherlands Prepared for the Senate Special Committee On Illegal Drugs', available at http://www.parl.gc.ca/Content/SEN/Committee/371/ille/library/dolin1-e.htm

Domingo-Salvany, A. *et al.* (1995) 'Use of Capture-Recapture to Estimate the Prevalence of Opiate Addiction in Barcelona, Spain, 1989', *American Journal of Epidemiology*, 14 (96): pp. 567–574

Donelly, J. (2011) 'The Need for Ibogaine in Drug and Alcohol Addiction Treatment', *Journal of Legal Medicine*, 32 (1): pp. 93–114

Drugscope (2009) *Drug Treatment at the Crossroads: What's It for, Where It's at and How to Make It Even Better* (London: Drugscope Publications)

Drummer, O. *et al.* (2004) 'The Involvement of Drugs in Drivers of Motor Vehicles Killed in Australian Road Traffic Crashes', *Accident Analysis and Prevention*, 36: pp. 239–248

Du-Pont, R. and Humphreys, K. (2011) 'A New Paradigm for Long-Term Recovery', *Substance Abuse*, 32 (1) January: pp. 1–6.

Dussault, C. *et al.* (2002) 'The Contribution of Alcohol and Other Drugs among Fatally Injured Drivers in Quebec: Some Preliminary Results' in D. Mayhew and C. Dussault (eds), *Proceedings of the 16th International Conference Eon Alcohol Drugs and Traffic Safety* (Québec City, Montreal)

Easow, J., Varghese, S. and Luty, J. (2009) 'Criminally Invalid: The Treatment Outcome Profile Form for Substance Misuse', *The Psychiatrist*, 33: pp. 404–406

Edlin, B. (2004) 'Hepatitis C Prevention and Treatment for Substance Users in the United States Acknowledging the Elephant in the Living Room', *International Journal of Drug Policy*, 15: pp. 81–89

Edwards, G. (1997) 'Alcohol Policy and the Public Good', *Addiction*, 92 (3s1) March: pp. 73–80

Edwards, G. (2002) *Alcohol: The Worlds Favorite Drug* (New York: St Martins Press)

Egger, M. *et al.* (2000) 'Promotion of Condom Use in a High-Risk Setting in Nicaragua: A Randomised Controlled Trial', *Lancet*, 355 (9221): pp. 2101–2105

EMCDDA (1997) *Estimating the Prevalence of Problem Drug Use in Europe.* EMCDDA Monograph No 1 (Lisbon: EMCDDA)

EMCDDA (2008) *Insights Prevention of Substance Abuse No 7* (Lisbon: EMCDDA)

EMCDDA (2011) *New Drugs and Emerging Trends.* Annual Report for 2011 (Lisbon: EMCDDA)

EMCDDA (2011a) *State of the Drug Problem in Europe.* Annual Report 2011 (Lisbon: EMCDDA)

EMCDDA (2011b) *Harm Reduction: Evidence, Impacts and Challenges* (Lisbon: EMCDDA)

Evans, J. *et al.* (2012) 'Mortality among Young Injection Drug Users in San Francisco: A 10 Year Follow Up of the UFO Study', *American Journal of Epidemiology*, 175 (4): pp. 302–308

Ezard, N. *et al.* (2011) 'Six Rapid Assessments of Alcohol and Other Substance Use in Populations Displaced by Conflict', *Conflict and Health*, 5: pp. 1–15

Farrell, M. and Marsden, J. (2007) 'Acute Risk of Drug-Related Death among Newly Released Prisoners in England and Wales', *Addiction*, 103: pp. 251–255

Fiore, M.C. *et al.* (2008) *Treating Tobacco Use and Dependence: 2008 Update. Clinical Practice Guideline* (Rockville, MD: US Department of Health and Human Services. Public Health Service)

Fitch, C. *et al.* (2004) 'Rapid Assessment: An International Review of Diffusion Practice and Outcomes in the Substance Use Field', *Social Science and Medicine*, 59: pp. 1819–1830

Fitzgerald, J. (2005) 'Policing as a Public Health Menace', *International Journal of Drug Policy*, 16: pp. 203–206

Ford, C. (2010) 'Methadone Works Stop the Interfering', *Guardian*, 26 July.

Friedman, S. (2000) 'What Hath RAR Wrought?' *International Journal of Drug Policy*, 11: pp. 37–39

Friedman, S., de Jong, W. and Wodak, A. (1993) 'Community Development as a Response to HIV among Drug Injectors', *AIDS*, 7 (supplement 1): pp. S263–S269

Friedman, S. *et al.* (2007) 'Harm Reduction Theory: Users' Culture Microsocial Indigenous Harm Reduction and the Self-Organisation and Outside-Organisation of Users Groups', *International Journal of Drug Policy*, 18: pp. 107–117

Furst, R.T. *et al.* (1999) 'The Stigmatized Image of the "Crack Head": A Sociocultural Exploration of a Barrier to Cocaine Smoking Among a Cohort of Youth in New York City', *Deviant Behaviour*, 20 (2): pp. 153–181

Gawin, F. (1991) 'Cocaine Addiction: Psychology and Neurophysiology', *Science*, 251 (5001): pp. 1580–1586

Gee, P., Jerram, T. and Bowie, D. (2010) 'Multiorgan Failure from 1-Benzylpiperazine Ingestion – Legal High or Lethal High', *Clinical Toxicology*, 48: pp. 230–233

Giddens, A. (1991) *Modernity and Self Identity: Self and Society in the Late Modern Age* (Cambridge: Polity Press)

Global Commission on Drug Policy (2011) 'War on Drugs: Report of the Global Commission on Drug Policy', Reports, June

Godfrey, C. (2005) 'Cost Effectiveness of Treatment for Alcohol Problems: Findings of the Randomised UK Alcohol Treatment Trial (UKATT)', *British Medical Journal*, 331 (7516): pp. 544–548

Godfrey, C. *et al.* (2002) 'The Economic and Social Costs of Class A Drug Use in England and Wales, 2000', *Home Office Research Study*, 249

Goffman, E. (1963) *Stigma: Notes on the Management of Spoiled Identity* (Englewood Cliffs: Prentice Hall)

Goldacre, B. (2009) 'Bad Science: A Blueprint for How Not to Do Research', *Guardian*, 19 September 2009, available at www.guardian. cp.uk/science/2009/sep/19/bad-science-blueprint-drugs

Gordon, D. *et al.* (2008) 'The 2007 User Satisfaction Survey of Tier 2 and 3 Service Users in England', *National Treatment Agency for Substance Misuse*, May

Gossop, M. *et al.* (1996) 'Frequency of Non Fatal Heroin Overdose Survey of Heroin Users Recruited in Non Clinical Settings', *British Medical Journal*, 313: p. 402

Gossop, M., Marsden, J. and Stewart, D. (2001) *NTORS after Five Years: Changes in Substance Use Health and Criminal Behaviour Five Years after Intake* (London: National Addiction Centre)

Granfield, R. and Cloud, W. (2001) 'Social Context and Natural Recovery: The Role of Social Capital in the Resolution of Drug Associated Problems', *Substance Use and Misuse*, 36: pp. 1543–1570

Greenwald, G. (2009) *Drug Decriminalisation in Portugal: Lessons for Creating Fair and Successful Drug Policies* (Washington DC: Cato Institute)

Gruenewald, P., Ponicki, W. Remer, L., Johnson, F., Waller, L., Zhu, L., Gorman D. (2012) 'Spatial Models of the Growth and Spread of Methamphetamine Abuse in California', in Deeds, B. (ed.) *Crime Space and Place* (New York: Springer)

Guidichini, P. and Pieretti, G. (1995) *San Patrignano between Community and Society: A Research on the Biographic Routes of 711 San Patrignano former Guests* (Italy: San Patrignano)

Gyngell, K. (2009) *The Phoney War on Drugs* (London: Centre for Policy Studies)

Gyngell, K. (2012) 'Frankly They Don't Give a Damn: When Will the Government Commit to a Proper Drugs Prevention Policy', Mail online, 9 January, available at www.sailymail.co.uk/debate/article-2084174/ When-Government-Commit-proper-drugs-prevention-policy.html

Harken, A. and Kleiman, M. (2009) 'Managing Drug Involved Probations with Swift and Certain Sanctions: Evaluating Hawaii's HOPE', available at www.ncjrs.gov/pdffiles1/nij/grants/229023.pdf

Harris, E.C. and Barraclough, B. (1997) 'Suicide as an Outcome for Mental Disorders: A Meta-Analysis', *British Journal of Psychiatry*, 170: pp. 205–228

Hay, G. *et al.* (2009) *Estimating the National and Local Prevalence of Problem Drug Use in Scotland* (Glasgow: University of Glasgow)

Hay, G. *et al.* (2009a) 'Capture Recapture and Anchored Prevalence Estimation of Injecting Drug Users in England: National and Regional Estimates', *Statistical Methods in Medical Research*, 18 (4): pp. 323–339

Hay, G. *et al.* (2010) 'Opiate and Crack Cocaine Use: A New Understanding of Prevalence', *Drugs: Education Prevention and Policy*, 17 (2): pp. 135–147

Health Protection Agency (2011) Shooting Up: Infections among People Who Inject Drugs in the UK 2010 – An Update, November 2011

Heather, N. (2004) 'Brief Interventions: In Treatment and Preventions of Alcohol Problems' in N. Heather and T. Stockwell (eds), *The Essential Handbook of Treatment and Preventions of Alcohol Problems* (England: John Wiley and Sons)

Heather, N. and Stockwell, T. (2004) *The Essential Handbook of Treatment and Prevention of Alcohol Problems* (England: John Wiley and Sons)

Hedrich, D. (2004) *European Report on Drug Consumption Rooms European Monitoring* (Lisbon: Centre for Drugs and Drug Addiction)

Hedrich, D. *et al.* (2012) 'The Effectiveness of Opioid Maintenance Treatment in Prison Settings: A Systematic Review', *Addiction*, 107 (3) March: pp. 501–517

Hickman, M. *et al.* (2004) 'Estimating Prevalence of Problem Drug Use: Multiple Methods in Brighton, Liverpool and London', Home Office Online Report 36/04

Hickman, M. *et al.* (2007) 'London Audit of Dug Related Overdose Deaths: Characteristics and Typology and Implications for Prevention and Monitoring', *Addiction*, 102: pp. 317–323

Hitchens, P. (2012) *The War We Never Fought: The British Establishments Surrender to Drugs* (United Kingdom: Continuum)

HM Government (2010) *Drug Strategy 2010 – Reducing Demand Restricting Supply Building Recovery: Supporting People to Live a Drug Free Life* (London: HMSO)

HM Government (2012) *Punishment and Reform: Effective Community Sentences* (London: HMSO)

Home Office (2008) *Drugs: Protecting Families and Communities* (London: HMSO)

Home Office (2009) *Extending Our Reach: A Comprehensive Approach to Tackling Serious Organised Crime Cabinet Office Strategy Unit* (London: HMSO)

Hughes, C. and Steven, A. (2009) *The Effects of Decriminalisation of Drug Use in Portugal* (Oxford: The Beckley Foundation Drug policy Programme)

Hughes, C. and Stevens, A. (2012) 'A Resounding Success or a Disastrous Failure: Re-Examining the Interpretation of Evidence on the Portuguese Decriminalisation of Illicit Drugs', *Drug and Alcohol Review*, 31: pp. 103–113

Hughes, J.R. (1992) 'Tobacco Withdrawal in Self-Quitters', *Journal of Consulting and Clinical Psychology*, 60: pp. 689–697

Hulse, G. *et al.* (2005) 'Reducing Hospital Presentations for Opioid Over-dose in Patients Treated with Sustained Release Naltrexone Implants', *Drug and Alcohol Dependence*, 79 (1): pp. 351–357

Humphreys, K. and McLellan, A.T. (2011) 'A Policy-Oriented Review of Strategies for Improving the Outcomes of Services for Substance Use Disorder Patients', *Addiction*, 106 (12): 2058–66, December, doi: 10.1111/j.1360–0443.2011.03464.x. Epub 2011 June 1.

INCB (2007) *Annual Report* (Vienna: United Nations)

Independent Enquiry into Drug Testing at Work (2004) Drug Testing in the Workplace: The Report of the Independent Inquiry into Drug Testing at Work. Joseph Rowntree Foundation.

Independent Working Group on Drug Consumption Rooms (2006) Report of the Independent Working Group on Drug Consumption Rooms. Joseph Rowntree Foundation.

International Narcotics Control Board (2004) 'INCB Cautions against Harm Reduction Measures in Drug Control', INCB Press Release, available at http://www.incb.org/pdf/e/press/2004/press_release_2004–03–03_4.pdf

International Narcotics Control Board (2013) 'INCB President Expresses Grave Concern about Inadequately Regulated Medical Cannabis Schemes Which Can Lead to Increased Abuse', INCB Press Release, available at www.incb.org/documents/Publications/PressRelease/PR2013/press_release150313pdf.pdf

Jelsma, M. (2003) 'Drugs in the UN System: The Unwritten History of the 1998 United Nations General Assembly Special Session on Drugs', *International Journal of Drug Policy*, 14: pp. 181–195

Jenkins, S. (2010) 'Our "War on Drugs" Has Been an Abysmal Failure: Just Look at Mexico', *Guardian*, 9 September.

Jones, A. *et al.* (2007) 'Drug Treatment Outcomes Research Study: Baseline Report', Home Office Research Report 3 (London: Home Office)

Jones, M. (1968a) *Beyond the Therapeutic Community: Social Learning and Social Psychiatry* (New Haven, CT: Yale University Press)

Jones, M. (1968b) *Social Psychiatry in Practice: The Idea of the Therapeutic Community* (England: Penguin)

Jowitt, J. (2012) 'Chris Grayling Puts "Punishment Backing into Community Sentencing"', *Guardian*, available at http://www.guardian.co.uk/politics/2012/oct/23/chris-grayling-punishment-community-sentences

Kandel, D. (1975) 'Stages in Adolescent Involvement in Drug Use', *Science*, 190: pp. 912–914

Kandel, D. (1980) 'Developmental Stages in Adolescent Drug Involvement' in D. Lettieri, M. Sayers, H. Pearson (eds), *Theories on Drug Abuse: Selected Contemporary Perspective* (NIDA Research Monograph 30)

Kandel, D. (2003) 'Does Marijuana Use Cause the Use of Other Drugs', *Journal of the American Medical* Association, 289 (4), 22/29 January: pp. 482–483

Kellogg, S. and Tartarsky, A. (2012) 'Re-Envisioning Addiction Treatment a Six Point Plan', *Alcoholism Treatment Quarterly*, 30 (1): pp. 109–126

Kerr, T. *et al.* (2006) 'Impact of a Medically Supervised Safer Injection Facility on Community Drug Use Patters: A before and after Study', *British Medical Journal*, 332: pp. 220–222

Kimber, J. *et al.* (2010) 'Survival and Cessation in Injecting Drug Users: Prospective Observational Study of Outcomes and Effect of Opiate Substitution Treatment', *British Medical Journal*, 341: p. c3172

Klee, H., McLean, I. and Yavorsky, C. (2002) *Employing Drug Users: Individual and Systematic Barriers to Rehabilitation* (York: Joseph Rowntree Foundation)

Klingemann, H. (1991) 'The Motivation for Change from Problem Alcohol and Heroin Use', *Addiction*, 86 (6): pp. 727–744

Koenig, H. (2005) *Faith and Mental Health* (Philadelphia: Templeton Foundation Press)

Korf, D.J., Reijneveld, S.A. and Toet, J. (1994) 'Estimating the Number of Heroin Users: A Review of Methods and Empirical Findings from the Netherlands', *International Journal of Mental Health and Addiction*, 29 (11): pp. 1393–1417

Kroll, B. and Taylor, A. (2008) 'Interventions for Children and Families Where There Is Parental Drug Misuse', Executive Summary (Department of Health Drug Misuse Research Initiative)

Krupitsky, E. *et al.* (2011) 'Injectable Extended Release Naltrexone for Opioid Dependence: A Double Blind Placebo Controlled Multicentre Randomised Trial', *Lancet*, 377 (9776): pp. 1506–1513

Lacey, J. *et al.* (2007) *Pilot Test of New Roadside Survey Methodology for Impaired Driving DOT HS 810 704* (Washington: National Highway Traffic Safety Administration)

Larson, A., Stevens, A. and Wardlaw, G. (1994) 'Indirect Estimates of "Hidden Populations": Capture-Recapture Methods to Estimate the Numbers of Heroin Users in the Australian Capital Territory', *Social Science and Medicine*, 39 (6): pp. 823–831

Leach, D. and Oliver, P. (2011) 'Drug Related Death Following Release from Prison: A Brief Review of the Literature with Recommendations for Practice', *Current Drug Abuse Reviews*, 4 (4): pp. 292–297

Leigh, L., Bowen, S. and Marlatt, A. (2005) 'Spirituality Mindfulness and Substance Abuse', *Addictive Behaviours*, 30: pp. 1335–1341

Levesque, D.A. *et al.* (2009) 'Evaluation of a Stage-Based Computer Tailored Adjunct to Usual Care for Domestic Violence Offenders', *Psychology of Violence*, 2 (4) 1 October: pp. 368–684

Lister, S. *et al.* (2008) *Street Policing of Problem Drug Users* (York: Joseph Rowntree Foundation)

Littell, J. and Girvin, H. (2002) 'Stages of Change: A Critique', *Behaviour Modification*, 26 (2): pp. 223–273

Littell, J. and Girvin, H. (2004) 'Ready or Not: Uses of the Stages of Change Model in Child Welfare', *Child Welfare*, 83 (4): p. 341

Lloyd, C. (2010) *Sinning and Sinned Against: The Stigmatisation of Problem Drug Users* (United Kingdom: Drug Policy Commission)

Lutsky, I. *et al.* (1994) 'Use of Psychoactive Substances in Three Medical Specialities Anesthesiology Medicine and Surgery', *Canadian Journal of Anesthesia*, 41: pp. 561–567

Lyne, J. *et al.* (2011) 'Comorbid Psychiatric Diagnoses among Individuals Presenting to an Addiction Treatment Program for Alcohol Dependence', *Substance Use and Misuse*, 46: pp. 351–158

Lynskey, M. *et al.* (2003) 'Escalation of Drug Use in Early Onset Cannabis Users vs Co-Twin Controls', *Journal of the American Medical Association*, 289: pp. 427–433

MacDonald, R. and Marsh, J. (2002) 'Crossing the Rubicon: Youth Transitions Poverty Drugs and Social Exclusion', *International Journal of Drug Policy*, 13: pp. 27–38

MacDougall, B. (2002) 'Prisons Offering Drugs to Inmates', *Scotsman*, 20 March

MacGregor, S. (2013) 'Barriers to the Influence of Evidence on Policy: Are Politicians the Problem?' *Drugs Education Prevention and Policy*, doi: 10.3109/09687637.2012.754403

Mackintosh, V. and Knight, T. (2012) 'The Notion of Self in the Journey Back from Addiction', *Qualitative Health Research*, 22 (8): pp. 1094–1101

Maddux, F. and Despond, D. (1980) 'New Light on the Maturing out Hypothesis in Opioid Dependency', *Bulletin of Narcotics*, 32: pp. 15–25

Madge, T. (2001) *White Mischief: A Cultural History of Cocaine* (Edinburgh: Mainstream Publishing Company)

Maher, L. and Dixon, D. (1999) 'Policing and Public Health Law Enforcement and Harm Minimisation in a Street Level Drug Market', *British Journal of Criminology*, 39 (4): pp. 488–512

Mangham, C. (2008) 'A Critique of Canada's INSITE Injection Site and Its Parent Philosophy: Implications and Recommendations for Policy Planning', *Journal of Global Drug Policy and Practice, http://www. globaldrugpolicy.org/Issues/Vol%201%20Issue%202/A%20critique%20 of%20Canada's%20INSITE.pdf*

Manning, V. *et al.* (2009) 'New Estimates of the Number of Children Living with Substance Misusing Parents: Results from the UK National Household Surveys', *BMC Public Health*, 9: 377

Mars, S. (2012) *The Politics of Addiction: Medical Conflict and Drug Dependence in England since 1960* (Basingstoke: Palgrave Macmillan)

Mastro, T.D. *et al.* (1994) 'Estimating the Number of HIV-Infected Injection Drug Users in Bangkok: A Capture-Recapture Method', *American Journal of Public Health*, 84 (7): pp. 1094–1110.

Maxwell, S. *et al.* (2006) 'Prescribing Naloxone to Actively Injecting Heroin Users: A Program to Reduce Heroin Overdose Deaths', *Journal of Addictive Diseases*, 25 (3): pp. 89–96

McCambridge, J. and Jenkins, R. (2008) 'Do Brief Interventions Which Target Alcohol Consumption Also Reduce Cigarette Smoking? Systematic Review and Meta-Analysis', *Drug and Alcohol Dependence*, 96 (3): pp. 263–270

McCambridge, J. and Strang, J. (2004) 'The Efficacy of Single Session Motivational Interviewing in Reducing Drug Consumption and Perceptions of Drug Related Risk and Harm among Young People: A Multi-Site Cluster Randomised Trial', *Addiction*, 99: pp. 39–52.

McDermott, P (2010) 'Use Your Head', *Druglink*, pp. 26–27

McIntosh, J. and McKeganey, N. (2000) 'Addicts Narrative of Recovery from Drug Use: Constructing a Non-Addict Identity', *Social Science and Medicine*, 50: pp. 1501–1510

McIntosh, J. and McKeganey, N. (2002) *Beating the Dragon: The Recovery from Dependent Drug Use* (London: Pearson Education)

McIntosh, J. and Saville, E. (2006) 'The Challenges Associated with Drug Treatment in Prison', *Probation Journal*, 52: pp. 230–246

McKeganey, N. (2002) 'Rapid Assessment: Really Useful Knowledge or an Argument for Bad Science', *International Journal of Drug Policy*, 11: pp. 13–18

McKeganey, N (2005) *Random Drug Testing a Shot in the Arm or a Shot in the Foot for Drug Prevention* (York: Joseph Rowntree Foundation)

McKeganey, N. (2006) 'The Lure and the Loss of Harm Reduction in UK Drug Policy and Practice', *Addiction Research and Theory*, 14 (6): pp. 557–588

McKeganey, N. (2008) 'Should Heroin Be Prescribed to Heroin Misusers? No', *British Medical Journal*, 336: p. 71

McKeganey, N. (2009) 'System Error', *Drink and Drug News*, 12 January

McKeganey, N. (2010) 'Bad Stigma...Good Stigma?' *Drink and Drugs News*, 15 February.

McKeganey, N. (2011) *Controversies in Drugs Policy and Practice* (Basingstoke: Palgrave Macmillan)

McKeganey, N. and Barnard, M. (1992) *AIDS Drugs and Sexual Risk: Lives in the Balance* (Buckingham: Open University Press)

McKeganey, N. and Barnard, M. (1996) *Sex Work on the Streets: Prostitutes and Their Clients* (Buckingham: Open University Press)

McKeganey, N., Barnard, M. and Bloor, M. (1990) 'A Comparison of HIV-Related Risk Behaviour and Risk Reduction between Female Street Working Prostitutes and Male Rent Boys in Glasgow', *Sociology of Health & Illness*, 12 (3): pp. 274–292

McKeganey, N., Barnard, M. and McIntosh, J. (2002) 'Paying the Price for Their Parents' Addiction: Meeting the Needs of the Children of Drug-Using Parents', *Drugs Education Prevention and Policy*, 9 (3): pp. 233–246

McKeganey, N., Russell, C. and Cockayne, L. (2012) 'Medically Assisted Recovery from Opiate Dependence within the Context of the UK Drug Strategy: Methadone and Suboxone (Buprenorphine–Naloxone) Patients Compared', *Journal of Substance Abuse Treatment*, 44 (1): pp. 97–102

McKeganey, N. *et al.* (1992) 'Female Streetworking Prostitution and HIV Infection in Glasgow', *British Medical Journal*, 3 (305): pp. 801–804

McKeganey, N. *et al.* (2004) 'What Are Drug Users Looking for When the Contact Drug Services Abstinence or Harm Reduction', *Drugs Education Prevention and Policy*, 11 (5): pp. 423–435

McKeganey, N. *et al.* (2005) *State of Science Review: Sociology, Foresight Brain Science, Drugs and Addictions Project* (Office of Science and Technology)

McKeganey, N. *et al.* (2007) 'Abstinence and Drug Abuse Treatment: Outcomes from the Drug Outcomes Research in Scotland Study', *Drugs Education Prevention and Policy*, 13 (6): pp. 537–550

McKeganey, N. *et al.* (2009) 'Heroin Seizure and Heroin Use in Scotland', *Journal of Substance Use*, 14 (3) June: pp. 252–260

McKinney, J. (2004) 'Study of High Schools with Student Drug Testing Programmes', available at www.studentdrugtesting.org

McLellan, T. *et al.* (2000) 'Drug Dependence, a Chronic Medical Illness: Implications for Treatment Insurance and Outcome Evaluation', *Journal of American Medical Association*, 248 (13): pp. 1689–1695

McLellan, T. *et al.* (2008) 'Five Year Outcomes in a Cohort Study of Physicians Treated for Substance Use Disorders in the United States', *British Medical Journal*, 337: p. a2038

McQueen, J. *et al.* (2009) 'Brief Interventions for Heavy Alcohol Users Admitted to General Hospital Wards', *Cochrane Library*, 4: pp. 1–36

McSweeney, T. and Turnbull, P. (2007) *Exploring User Perceptions of Occasional and Controlled Heroin Use: A Follow Up Study* (York: Joseph Rowntree Foundation)

Measham, F. and Shiner, M. (2009) 'The Legacy of Normalisation: The Role of Classical Contemporary Criminological Theory in Understanding

Young People's Drug Use. International', *Journal of Drug Policy*, 20 (6): pp. 502–508

Measham, F., More, K. and Ostergaard, J. (2011) 'Emerging Drug Trends in the Lancashire Night Time Economy Surveys', Phase 1 Report, Lancaster University

Measham, F., Newcombe, R. and Parker, H. (1994) 'The Normalisation of Recreational Drug Use amongst Young People in Worth West England', *British Journal of Sociology*, 45 (2): pp. 287–312

Measham, F. *et al.* (2011) 'The Rise in Legal Highs: Prevalence and Patterns in the Use of Illegal Drugs and First and Second Generation Legal Highs in South London Gay Dance Clubs', *Journal of Substance Use*, 16 (4): pp. 263–272

Mehta, S. *et al.* (2008) 'Limited Uptake of Hepatitis C Treatment among Injection Drug Users', *Journal of Community Health*, 33: pp. 126–133

Mixmag (2010) Mixmag Drugs Survey, February, 225: pp. 44–53

Mixmag (2011) Mixmag Drugs Survey, March, 238: pp. 49–59

Mocenni, C., Montefrancesco, G. and Tiezzi, S. (2010) 'A Model of Natural Recovery from Addiction', Department of Economics, University of Siena

Moore, K. *et al.* (2011) 'Emerging Drug Trends in Lancashire: Focussing on Young Adults Alcohol and Drug Use', Phase Two Report, Lancaster University

Moore, T. *et al.* (2007) 'Cannabis Use and Risk of Psychotic or Affective Mental Health Outcomes a Systematic Review', *Lancet*, 370: pp. 319–328

Morgan, C. and Curran, V. (2012) 'Ketamine Use: A Review', *Addiction*, 107 (1): pp. 27–38

National Collaborating Centre for Mental Health (2007) 'Psychosocial Interventions', *National Clinical Practice Guidelines No 51*

National Institute for Health and Clinical Excellence (2003) 'Deep Brain Stimulation for Parkinson's Disease', *Interventional Procedure Guidance 19*

National Institute for Health and Clinical Excellence (2006) 'Brief Interventions and Referral for Smoking Cessation in Primary Care and Other Settings', *Public Health Guidance PH1*, March

National Institute for Health and Clinical Excellence (2007a) 'Drug Misuse Psycho-social Interventions', *NICE Clinical Guidelines 51*

National Institute for Health and Clinical Excellence (2007b) 'Methadone and Buprenorphine for the Management of Opioid Dependence', *NICE Technology Appraisal Guidance 114*

National Institute for Health and Clinical Excellence (2011) 'Psychosis with Coexisting Substance Misuse: Assessment and Management in Adults and Young People', *NICE Clinical Guidelines 120.* Developed by the National Collaborating Centre for Mental Health

National Institute on Drug Abuse (2010) *Drugs, Brains, and Behavior – The Science of Addiction*

National Statistics (2011) 'Home Office Statistical Bulletin: Drug Misuse Declared Findings from the 2010/2011 British Crime Survey England and Wales' in K. Smith and J. Flatley (eds), *National Statistics* (London: Home Office)

National Statistics for Scotland (2012) *Drug Related Deaths in Scotland 2011.*

National Treatment Agency (2004) 'Reducing Drug Related Deaths: Guidance for Drug Treatment Providers', National Treatment Agency, London

National Treatment Agency (2008) Annual Report 2007–2008

National Treatment Agency (2010) Business Plan for 2010–2011

National Treatment Agency (2011) 'Statistics from the National Drug Treatment Monitoring System', Vol 1: The Numbers, 1 April 2010 to 31 March 2011

National Treatment Agency (2012) 'Medications in Recovery: Reorienting Drug Dependence Treatment', NTA for Substance Misuse

Neale, J. (2000) 'Suicidal Intent in Non Fatal Illicit Drug Overdose', *Addiction*, 95 (1): pp. 85–93

Neale, J., Nettleton, S. and Pickering, L. (2011a) 'Recovery from Problem Drug Use: What Can We Learn from the Sociologist Erving Goffman?' *Drugs Education Prevention and Policy*, 18 (1): pp. 3–9

Neale, J., Nettleton, S. and Pickering, L. (2011b) 'What Is the Role of Harm Reduction when Drug Users Say They Want Abstinence?' *International Journal of Drug Policy*, 22: pp. 189–193

Neale, J. *et al.* (2000) *Recreational Drug Use and Driving: A Qualitative Study* (Glasgow: Scottish Executive Central Research Unit)

Newcombe, R. (2007) *Drug Users Charter of Rights* (England: Lifeline Manchester)

NICE (2006) 'Brief Interventions and Referral for Smoking Cessation in Primary Care and Other Settings', *Public Health Intervention Guidance No 1*

NICE (2010) 'Alcohol-Use Disorders: Preventing the Development of Hazardous and Harmful Drinking', *NICE Public Health Guidance 24*

Nickerson, J. and Attaran, A. (2012) 'The Inadequate Treatment of Pain: Collateral Damage from the War on Drugs', *PLoS Medicine*, 1: p. e1001153

NIH (1996) 'Project Match Main Findings', *National Institutes of Health News*, December 17 1996 available at http://www.nih.gov/news/pr/dec96/niaaa-17.htm

Nutt, D. (2009) 'Equasy: An Overlooked Addiction with Implication for the Current Debate on Drug Harms', *Journal of Psychopharmacology*, 23 (1): pp. 3–5

Nutt, D. (2012) *Drugs without the Hot Air: Minimising the Harms of Legal and Illegal Drugs* (England: UIT Cambridge)

Nutt, D., King, L. and Philip, L. (2010) 'Drug Harms in the UK a Multicriteria Decision Analysis', *Lancet*, 376: pp. 1558–1565

Nutt, D. *et al.* (2007) 'Development of a Rational Scale to Assess the Harm of Drugs of Potential Misuse', *Lancet*, 369 (9566): pp. 1047–1053

O'Brien, C. and McLellan, A. (1996) 'Myths about the Treatment of Addiction', *Lancet*, 347: 237–240

O'Hara, M. (2009) 'Nice People Take Drugs Ad Pulled from London Buses', *Guardian*, 9 June, available at http://www.guardian.co.uk/media/2009/jun/09/nice-people-drugs-ads-pulled

Orford, J. (2005) 'Effectiveness of Treatment for Alcohol Problems: Findings of the Randomised UK Alcohol Treatment Trial (UKATT)', *British Medical Journal*, 331: p. 541

Orford, J. (2008) 'Asking the Right Questions in the Right Way: The Need for a Shift in Research on Psychological Treatments for Addiction', *Addiction*, 103 (6): pp. 886–892

Ormston, R., Bradshaw, P. and Anderson, S. (2010) *Scottish Social Attitudes Survey 2009: Public Attitudes to Drugs and Drug Use in Scotland* (Edinburgh: Scottish Government Social Research)

Padgett, T. (2012) 'Mexico's Drug Corruption Arrests: Why Soldiers Make Bard Narco Agents Time World', available at world.time.com/2012/05/31/mexicos-drug-corruption-arrests-why-solderis-make-bad-narco-agents

Paintsil, E. *et al.* (2009) 'Hepatitis C Virus Infection among Drug Injectors in St Petersburg, Russia: Social and Molecular Epidemiology of an Endemic Infection', *Addiction*, 104 (11): pp. 1881–1890

Parker, H., Aldridge, J. and Measham, F. (1999) *Illegal Leisure: The Normalization of Adolescent Recreational Drug Use* (London: Routledge)

Parker, H., Williams, L. and Aldridge, J., (2002) 'The Normalization of "Sensible" Recreational Drug Use Further Evidence from the North West England Longitudinal Study', *Sociology*, 36 (4) November: pp. 941–964

Peto, R. *et al.* (1994) *Mortality from Smoking in Developing Countries 1950–2000* (Oxford: Oxford University Press)

Petry, N. (2006) 'Contingency Management Treatments', *British Journal of Psychiatry*, 189: pp. 97–98

Pilkington, H. (2006) 'Beyond Peer Pressure: Rethinking Drug Use and Youth Culture', *International Journal of Drug Policy*, 18 (3): pp. 213–224

Powis, B. *et al.* (1999) 'Self Reported Overdose among Injecting Drug Users in London: Extent and Nature of the Problem', *Addiction*, 94 (4): pp. 471–478

Prendergast, M. *et al.* (2006) 'Contingency Management for Treatment of Substance Use Disorders: A Meta-Analysis', *Addiction*, 101 (11): pp. 1546–1560

Pridemore, W. and Kim, S. (2006) 'Research Note: Patterns of Alcohol Related Mortality in Russia', *Journal of Drug Issues*, 36 (1): pp. 229–247

Prochaska, J., DiClemente, C. and Norcross, J. (1992) 'In Search of How People Change: Applications to Addictive Behaviours', *American Psychologist*, 47 (9): pp. 1102–1114

Project Match Research Group (1998) 'Matching Alcoholism Treatments to Client Heterogeneity: Project MATCH Three Year Drinking Outcomes', *Alcoholism Clinical and Experimental Research*, 22: pp. 1300–1311

Pryce, S. (2012) *Fixing Drugs the Politics of Drugs Prohibition* (Basingstoke: Palgrave Macmillan)

Rawlins, M. (2008) 'On the Evidence for Decisions about the Use of Therapeutic Interventions', *The Harviean Oration* (London: Royal College of Physicians)

Regan, L., Mitchelson, M. and MacDonald, C. (2011) 'Mehedrone Toxicity in a Scottish Emergency Department', *Emergency Medicine*, 28: pp. 1065–1068

Reith, G. and Dobbie, F. (2012) 'Lost in the Game: Narratives of Addiction and Identity in Recovery from Problem Gambling', *Addiction Research and Theory*, 20 (6): pp. 511–521.

Reuter, P. and Stevens, A. (2007) *An Analysis of UK Drug Policy*, A Monograph Prepared for the UK Drug Policy Commission

Riesma, R. *et al.* (2002) 'A Systematic Review of the Effectiveness of Interventions Based on Stages of Change Approach to Promote Individual Behaviour Change', *Health Technology Assessment*, 6 (24): pp. 1–242

Riessman, C. (1994) 'Making Sense of Marital Violence: One Woman's Narratives' in Riessman, C. (ed.) *Qualitative Studies in Social Work Research* (London: Sage Publications)

Robbins, L. (1974) 'A Follow Up Study of Vietnam Veterans Drug Use', *Journal of Drug Issues*, 4: pp. 61–63

Robbins, L. (1993) 'Vietnam Veterans Rapid Recovery from Heroin Addiction: A Fluke or Normal Expectation?' *Addiction*, 88: pp. 1041–1054

Robbins, L., Davis, D. and Nurco, D. (1974) 'How Permanent Was Vietnam Drug Addiction', *American Journal of Public Health*, 64: pp. 38–43

Robbins, L., Helzer, J. and Davis, D. (1975) 'Narcotic Use in Southeast Asia and Afterward: An Interview Study of 898 Vietnam Returnees', *Archives of General Psychiatry*, 32 (8): pp. 955–961

Robbins, L. *et al.* (1980) 'Vietnam Veterans Three Years after Vietnam: How Our Study Changed Our View of Heroin', in L. Brill and C. Winnick (eds), *Yearbook of Substance Use and Abuse* (New York: Human Science Press)

Robertson, J.R. (1987) *Heroin AIDS and Society* (London: Hodder Stoughton)

Robertson, J.R. *et al.* (1986) 'Epidemic of AIDS Related Virus (HTLV-III/LAV) Infection among Intravenous Drug Abusers', *British Medical Journal*, 292: pp. 527–529

Rollnick, S. and Miller, W. (1995) 'What Is Motivational Interviewing?' *Behavioural and Cognitive Psychotherapy*, 23: pp. 325–334

Rollnick, S. *et al.* (2010) 'Motivational Interviewing', *British Medical Journal*, April 1900: p. 340c

Room, R. and Reuter, P. (2012) 'How Well Do International Drug Conventions Protect Public Health', *Lancet*, 379: pp. 84–89

Rosenbaum, M. (1981) *Women on Heroin* (New Brunswick, NJ: Rutgers University Press)

Ross-Albers, E. (2013) 'Road to Ruin', *Drink and Drug News*, 4 February

Royal College of General Practitioners (2002) 'Royal College of GPs against Increasing Heroin Prescribing', Press Release 15/1/02, available at http://www.rcgp.org.uk/pdf.aspx?page=1298

Royal College of Physicians (2000a) *Drugs Dilemmas and Choices* (London: Royal College of Physicians)

Royal College of Physicians (2000b) *Nicotine Addiction in Britain: A report of the Tobacco Advisory Group of the Royal College of Physicians* (London: Royal College of Physicians)

Rubak, S. *et al.* (2005) Motivational Interviewing a Systematic Review and Meta Analysis', *British Journal of General Practice* 55 (April): 305–312

Russell, C. and Davies, J.B. (2009) 'Empirical, Logical, and Philosophical Arguments against Cigarette Smoking as a Pharmacologically Compelled Act', *Current Psychology*, 28 (3): 147–168

Saleh, M. and Crome, I. (2012) 'National Institute for Health and Clinical Excellence Guideline Psychosis with Coexisting Substance Misuse', *Addiction*, 107 (1): pp. 1–3

Sare, J. (2013) 'Drug Driving Limits', *British Medical Journal*, 18 March

Sarkar, K. *et al.* (2005) 'Epidemiology of HIV Infection among Brothel Based Sex Workers in Kolkata, India', *Journal of Health, Population and Nutrition*, 23 (3): pp. 231–235

Satel, S. (2007) 'In Praise of Stigma' in J.E. Henningfield, P.B. Santora, and W.K. Bickel (eds), *Addiction Treatment: Science and Policy for the Twenty-First Century* (Baltimore: John Hopkins University Press)

Science of Addiction, available at http://www.nida.nih.gov/science of addiction/advancing.html

Scottish Government (2008) *The Road to Recovery: A New Approach to Tackling Scotland's Drug Problem* (Edinburgh: Scottish Government)

Shannon, K. *et al.* (2008) 'Drug Sharing with Clients as a Risk Marker for Increased Violence and Sexual and Drug Related Harms Among Survival Sex Workers', *AIDS Care*, 20: pp. 228–234

Shapiro, H. (2011) 'Speaking at Home Affairs Select Committee enquiry into the cocaine trade in the UK', available at http://www.publications.parliament.uk/pa/cm200910/cmselect/cmhaff/74/7409.htm

Shaw, J. (2010) 'Drug Addicts "Spit Out Methadone Substitute to Resell"', available at http://www.bbc.co.uk/news/uk-scotland-11487404

Shaw, R., Whitehead, C. and Giles, D. (2010) 'Crack Down on the Celebrity Junkies': Does Media Coverage of Celebrity Drug Use Pose a Risk to Young People?' *Health, Risk & Society*, 12 (6): pp. 575–589

Shewan, D. and Dalgarno, P. (2005) 'Evidence for Controlled Heroin Use? Low Levels of Negative Health and Social Outcomes Among Non-Treatment Heroin Users in Glasgow, Scotland', *British Journal of Health Psychology*, 10 (1) February: pp. 33–48

Shiner, M. and Newburn, T. (1997) 'Definitely Maybe Not: The Normalisation of Recreational Drug Use amongst Young People', *Sociology*, 31 (3): pp. 511–529

Sinha, J. (2001) 'The History and Development of the Leading Drug Control Conventions: Prepared for the Senate Special Committee on Illegal Drugs', available at http://www.parl.gc.ca/Content/SEN/Committee/371/ille/library/history-e.htm

Sobell, L., Ellingstad, T.P. and Sobell, M. (2000) 'Natural Recovery from Alcohol and Drug Problems: Methodological Review of the Research with Suggestions for Future Directions', *Addiction*, 95 (5): 749–764

Spear, B. and Mott, J. (2002) *Heroin Addiction Care and Control: The British System 1916–1974* (London: Drugscope Publications)

Spencer, J. *et al.* (2008) *Getting Problem Drug Users Back into Employment Part Two* (London: United Kingdom Drug Policy Commission)

Stimson, G. (1990) 'AIDS and HIV Challenge for British Drug Policy', *British Journal of Addiction*, 85: pp. 329–339

Stimson, G. (2010) 'Harm Reduction: The Advocacy of Science and the Science of Advocacy', 1st Alison Chesney and Eddie Killoran Memorial Lecture 17 November, London School of Hygiene and Tropical Medicine

Stimson, G. and Oppenheimer, E. (1982) *Heroin Addiction Treatment and Control in Britain* (London: Tavistock)

Stimson, G., Fitch, C. and Rhodes, T. (1998) *The Rapid Assessment and Response Guide to Injecting Drug Use* (Geneva: World Health Organization)

Stimson, G. *et al.* (1988) 'Injecting Equipment Exchange Schemes: Final Report, The Pilot Syringe-Exchange Project in England and Scotland: a summary of the evaluation London, Goldsmiths' College', *Addiction*, 84 (11): pp. 1283–1284

Stimson, G. *et al.* (2000) *Rapid Assessment and Response Technical Guide* (Geneva: World Health Organization)

Strang, J. and Fortson, R. (2004) 'Supervised Fixing Rooms, Supervised Injectable Maintenance Clinics – Understanding the Difference', *British Medical Journal*, 328 (7431) 10 January: pp. 102–103

Strang, J. *et al.* (1996) 'Heroin Overdose the Case for Take Home Naloxone', *British Medical Journal*, 312: pp. 1435–1436

Strang, J. *et al.* (1997) 'Why Britain's Drug Czar Mustn't Wage War on Drugs', *British Medical Journal*, 315: p. 325

Strang, J. *et al.* (1999) 'Preventing Opiate Overdose Fatalities with Take Home Naloxone', *Addiction*, 94 (2): pp. 199–204

Strang, J. *et al.* (2008) 'Family Carers and the Prevention of Heroin Overdose Deaths: Unmet Training Need and Overlooked Intervention Opportunity of Resuscitation Training and Supply of Nalonone', *Drugs Education Prevention and Policy*, 15 (2): pp. 211–218

Strang, J. *et al.* (2010a) 'Drug Policy and the Public Good: Evidence for Effective Interventions', *Lancet*, 379 (9810) January: pp. 7–13

Strang, J. *et al.* (2010b) 'Supervised Injectable Heroin or Injectable Methadone versus Optimised Oral Methadone as Treatment for Chronic Heroin Addicts in England after Persistent Failure in Orthodox Treatment (RIOTT): A Randomised Trial', *Lancet*, 375 (9729): pp. 1885–1895

Strathdee, A. *et al.* (2012) 'Social and Structural Factors Associated with HIV Infection among Female Sex Workers Who Inject Drugs in the Mexico US Border Region', *PLoS*, 6 (4) April 2011: p. e19048

Street, K. *et al.* (2007) 'Is Adequate Parenting Compatible with Maternal Drug Use: A Five Year Follow-Up', *Child Care Health and Development*, 34 (2): pp. 204–206

Tanner, G. *et al.* (2011) 'Comparing Methadone and Suboxone in Applied Treatment Settings: The Experiences of Maintenance Patients in Lanarkshire', *Journal of Substance Abuse*, 16 (3): pp. 171–178

The National Centre on Addiction and Substance Abuse (2005) 'Family Matters Substance Abuse and the American Family', CASA White Paper, Columbia University

Tolliver, B. (2011) *Journal of Psychiatric Practice*, 17 (2) March: pp. 152–153

Tran, T. *et al.* (2005) 'HIV Infection and Risk Characteristics among Female Sex Workers in Hanoi Vietnam', *Journal of Acquired Immune Deficiency Syndrome*, 39: pp. 581–586

Travis, A. (2012) 'Relaxation of US Cannabis Laws Violates UN Drug Conventions', *Guardian*, 5 March

Treanor, J. (2012) 'HSBC Money Laundering Fine: Key Players', *Guardian*, 14 December

United Kingdom Drug Policy Commission (2008) *The United Kingdom Drug Policy Commission Recovery Consensus Group: A Vision of Recovery* (London: UKDPC)

United Kingdom Drug Policy Commission (2009) *Refocussing Drug Related Law Enforcement to Address Harm* (London: UKDPC)

United Nations Office on Drugs and Crime (2007) 'Sweden's Successful Drug Policy: A Review of the Evidence', available at http://www.unodc.org/pdf/research/Swedish_drug_control.pdf

United Nations Office on Drugs and Crime (2008) *A Century of International Drug Control* (UNODC)

United Nations Office on Drugs and Crime (2011) *Resolution 54/12 Revitalization of the Principle of Common and Shared Responsibility in Countering the World Drug Problem* (UNODC)

United Nations Office on Drugs and Crime (2011a) *World Drugs Report United Nations Office on Drugs and Crime Vienna* (UNODC)

Van den hoek, J. *et al.* (1989) 'HIV Infection and STD in Drug Addicted Prostitutes in Amsterdam: Potential for Heterosexual HIV Transmission', *Genitourinary Medicine*, 65: pp. 146–150

Vlahov, D. *et al.* (2008) 'Mortality Risk among Recent-Onset Injection Drug Users in Five US Cities', *Substance Use and Misuse*, 43 (3–4): pp. 413–428

Volkow, N. (2004) 'Addiction is a Brain Disease: Addiction Disrupts Brain Circuitry', NIDA Release, 30 November

Volkow, N. and Li, T. (2005) 'The Neuroscience of Addiction', *Nature Neuroscience*, 8: pp. 1429–1430

Volkow, N., Fowler, S. and Wang, G. (2003) 'The Addicted Human Brain: Insights from Imaging Studies', *Journal of Clinical Investigation*, 111 (10): pp. 1444–1451

Waldorf, D. (1983) 'Natural Recovery from Opiate Addiction: Some Social Psychological Processes of Untreated Recovery', *Journal of Drug Issues*, 13 (2): pp. 237–280

Warburton, H., Turnbull, P. and Hough, M. (2005) *Occasional and Controlled Heroin Use Not a Problem?* (York: Joseph Rowntree Foundation)

Wardle, I. (2012) 'Five Years of Recovery: December 2005 to December 2010 from Challenge to Orthodoxy', *Drugs: Education, Prevention and Policy*, 19 (4): pp. 294–298

Watt, N. (2012) 'Jobseekers Who Reject Help for Alcohol and Drug Addiction Face Benefits Cut', *Guardian*, 22 May.

West, R. (2008) 'Time for a Change: Putting the Transtheoretical (Stages of Change) Model to Rest', *Addiction*, 100 (8): pp. 1036–1039

White, W. (2012) 'Medication-Assisted Recovery from Opioid Addiction: Historical and Contemporary Perspectives', *Journal of Addictive Diseases*, 31 (3): pp. 199–206

White, W. and Kelly, J. (2011) 'Recovery Management: What If We Really Believed That Addiction Was a Chronic Disease', *Current Clinical Psychiatry*, Part 1, 67–84, doi: 10.1007/978-1-60327-960-4_5

White, W. and Schulstead, M. (2009) 'Relapse Following Prolonged Addiction Recovery: Time for Answers to Critical Questions', *Counselor*, 10 (4): pp. 36–39

Wiebel, W.W. (1979) 'Burning out on the Northwest Side: PCP Use in Chicago' in H. Feldman, M. Agar, and G. Beschner (eds), *Angel Dust: An Ethnographic Study of PCP Users* (Lexington, MA: D.C. Heath)

Wilson, L. and Stevens, A. (2010) 'Understanding Drug Markets and How to Influence Them', Report 14, Beckley Foundation

Winnick, C. (1962) 'Maturing Out of Addiction', *Bulletin of Narcotics*, 14: pp. 1–7

Wintour, P. (2004) 'Alarm at Blair's Drug-Test Plans for Schools', *Guardian*, 23 February.

World Health Organization (2004) 'Rapid Assessment and Response: Adaptation Guide on HIV and Men Who Have Sex with Men', Department of HIV, WHO

Wright, N. and Tomkins, C. (2004) 'Supervised Injecting Centres', *British Medical Journal*, 328 (7431) 10 January: pp. 100–102

Yablonsky, L. (1965) *The Tunell Back: Synanon* (London: Collier-Macmillan)

Yamaguchi, R., Johnston, L. and O'Malley, P. (2003) 'Relationship between Student Illicit Drug Use and School Drug Testing Policies', *Journal of School Health*, 73 (4): pp. 159–164

Zinberg, N. (1986) *Drug Set and Setting the Basis of Controlled Intoxicant Use* (New Haven, CT: Yale University Press)

index

'The *A-Z of Substance Misuse and Drug Addiction* is a clearly presented text that covers a comprehensive range of essential subject areas. I would recommend it highly as a core text for all professionals and students working with addiction.'
– *Kirsten Amis, counselling lecturer and manager of counselling service at Glasgow Clyde College, Scotland*

Professor Neil McKeganey is Director of the Centre for Drug Misuse Research. A sociologist by background, he has been influential in developing a recovery focus in drug treatment policy in the UK and elsewhere. He is author of *Controversies in Drugs Policy and Practice* (Palgrave 2012).

PROFESSIONAL
KEYWORDS

'UNLOCKING
KNOWLEDGE
FOR PRACTICE'